Veronica Martinez

David Martinez

Bones Worth Breaking

David Martinez earned his MFA from the University of California, Riverside–Palm Desert, and previously taught English and creative writing at Glendale Community College in Arizona. His work has appeared in *The Coachella Review*, the *Los Angeles Review of Books*, *Broken Pencil*, and *Automata Review*. He is a dual citizen of the United States and Brazil, and he lives in Glendale, Arizona.

Bones Worth Breaking

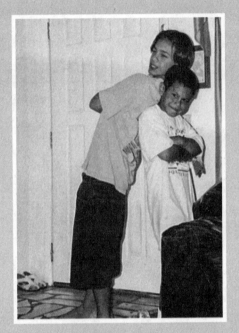

A tale of two brothers

Bones Worth Breaking

A MEMOIR

David Martinez

MCD · Farrar, Straus and Giroux · New York

MCD
Farrar, Straus and Giroux
120 Broadway, New York 10271

Copyright © 2024 by David Martinez
All rights reserved
Printed in the United States of America
First edition, 2024

Library of Congress Cataloging-in-Publication Data
Names: Martinez, David, 1984– author.
Title: Bones worth breaking : a memoir / David Martinez.
Description: First edition. | New York : MCD / Farrar, Straus
  and Giroux, [2024] | Includes bibliographical references.
Identifiers: LCCN 2023041363 | ISBN 9780374610951 (paperback)
Subjects: LCSH: Martinez, David, 1984– | Martinez, Mike,
  1987–2021. | Brothers—Brazil—Biography. | Brothers—
  United States—Biography. | Latter Day Saint missionaries—
  Brazil—Biography. | Drug addicts—Biography. | LCGFT:
  Autobiographies.
Classification: LCC PS3613.A7864235 Z46 2024 | DDC 813/.6
  [B]—dc23/eng/20231204
LC record available at https://lccn.loc.gov/2023041363

Designed by Gretchen Achilles

Our books may be purchased in bulk for promotional, educational,
or business use. Please contact your local bookseller or the Macmillan
Corporate and Premium Sales Department at 1-800-221-7945, extension
5442, or by email at MacmillanSpecialMarkets@macmillan.com.

www.mcdbooks.com • www.fsgbooks.com
Follow us on social media at @mcdbooks and @fsgbooks

1   3   5   7   9   10   8   6   4   2

For Mike. I got you, brother.

Sons, palavras, são navalhas e eu não posso cantar como convém sem querer ferir ninguém.

—BELCHIOR

Contents

Bones Worth Breaking

Just a Flesh Wound

Me with my cast, Idaho

When I was maybe eleven, I walked into the bathroom and burned a piece of skin off the back of my hand on a curling iron. My aunt had left it plugged in for hours—it was hanging off the edge of the sink, waist high, and when I made contact the first layer of skin peeled away, leaving an indent the size and shape of a kidney bean. I thought it was okay at first—at least I don't remember when it started to hurt, if it came with the shock of seeing a piece of my epidermis melted off, or if it was when I'd put it under cold water. I *know* it hurt when I applied the toothpaste—a neighbor had once told me it soothed burns. I had a hard time scrubbing the toothpaste out from the melted flesh. It burned mint-fresh for days. I didn't let anyone see how bad it really was. My parents asked if I was okay. They scolded me on paying more attention and told me not to ever listen to irrational medical advice from stupid neighbors. They asked if I needed to see a doctor. Gripping my hand, careful not to put any weight onto the paste-filled concave, I said no. It was fine. I was fine. I didn't show it to any adults until after it healed over. It seared red and infected around what had become a black scab mixed with fragments of white paste. It lasted days. Weeks. Longer. I hid it under a Band-Aid, and it eventually healed. Now I have a smooth, oblong scar between the bottom knuckle of my right index finger and thumb. But it's okay. I'm okay.

There is nothing on my skin that shows where I was hit by a car, and then abandoned, while walking across a street in Rancho Mirage, California, when I was thirty-three. I have no scar. I wasn't hurt. With no definitive proof of the incident, I'm not sure what to say. How can anything be important if it doesn't leave a mark?

I don't have a mark from when I broke my arm when I was ten. But I know it was my left arm because I was grateful that I could still write. It happened while I was visiting my grandparents for the summer in Genesee—on the sometimes green, sometimes brown and red, or white, rolling hills of the Palouse in northern Idaho and Washington. I broke my arm skating alone with loose, plastic Rollerblades at a school that sat on top of one of the infinite hills. By the time I hit the patch of grass that had been creeping up from the cracked sidewalk I was going so fast that my legs shook from the speed. Luckily, I managed to defy physics and push my body backward.

My arm didn't go crooked or anything. It was just a hairline fracture. It wasn't even immediately apparent it was broken. My great-grandmother—who was raised on a no-nonsense, Depression-era farm—assured me that I was fine. All I needed to do was roll my wrist around and move it as much as I could. "Like this," she said, and twisted her hand in the air. I don't remember how many days it took before we went to the hospital; it was sometime after I tackled my brother Mike, who had deep brown skin and straight black hair and an almost perpetual smile that showcased his crooked teeth. My best friend. We were in the neighbor's slanted yard playing some game we'd made up. My bone was already broken, so falling on top of it with Mike just broke it a little more. The doctor said, "Hey, you want to see what a broken arm looks like?" before pulling up the X-ray. I can't see it now, but I know I *did* see it then. Plus, there were witnesses. It's always better to have witnesses. It doesn't hurt anymore though. It's okay.

I knew the car was coming before I stepped off the sidewalk. It was one of those moments when time slows and the body moves on its own and everything is silent except your thoughts. I knew the car was coming, but I kept walking, no longer in control. The car was low and blue and expensive, the driver oblivious and small—her head not completely visible over the steering wheel. By the time she made contact, I was in the middle of the street. My body reacted like it did in my skateboard days; I jumped without thinking. My body said up, and I went up, landing with both feet on the hood. Everything was so slow that I had time to look at my shoes and consider how the Converse-pattern soles would leave a distinct mark on her car. Already familiar with the rhythm of collisions, I felt velocity beneath me and imagined how much force I would have to transfer to fall onto the windshield if the woman's reaction was too slow and she kept moving. But she stopped, and time resumed, and I fell backward. My right foot hit the asphalt. I crouched as I fell, my left arm behind me, and rolled. I felt the thud on my arm and thought, it's okay if it breaks again. I'll still be able to write.

Mike broke his arm three years later, when he was nine, at about the same age and in the exact spot I did. The difference was he was on a skateboard when he hit the patch of grass, and it was his right arm. *His* fracture left a mark—or at least the eventual surgery resulting from the break

Mike in his cast, Idaho

left a mark. They put him in a detachable metal brace and a soft cast that frayed and had to be changed often. While his body tried to recover, he kept skating and kept falling on his arm and was pushed around in a crowd after being dropped off at Warped Tour '97 when we were twelve and nine, where we tried to find a way to get piercings and tattoos, until I had my wallet stolen while crowd surfing— and then, not only did we not get piercings and tattoos, we didn't eat for the rest of the day. It took Mike forever to heal, and when he did, something was off. It hurt him for years, through our time in Puerto Rico and back to the mainland. It hurt him after he was kicked out of school and I dropped out, through his exile to the annex school after he was expelled, and back to public high school when he was allowed back. It kept hurting seven years after the initial break, even after I moved to São Paulo at nineteen to become a missionary for the Church of Jesus Christ of Latter-Day Saints—where I would hide my wounds more than I ever had before or since—and he stayed behind in Florida. It was around that time Mike was X-rayed, and they found a detached chip of bone floating around the warped ulna (how many years had it floated like that?). They cut him open, removed the floater, inserted a metal rod, and gave him a stack of opiates that would last maybe a day, since by then he already had the hunger for them that we would both know so well.

I put the hole in my leg skateboarding at my high school in Puerto Rico. My board slipped from under me as I grinded a bench. It tumbled, and my right shin slammed against the concrete edge. It hurt less than you might imagine. It went numb. I thought it must have been okay. I mean, it *was* deep. I did see a gape, lined with layers of skin, and at the end of the layers a hole slightly bigger than a sideways pellet, and in the hole, white. The white lasted only a moment before the blood poured out. But I forced it to be okay, forced myself to stop thinking about how that white might have been my bone. I pulled my sock up high enough to cover the mess and took a bus to a friend's house to watch *Welcome to Hell*. I was okay. I kept thinking of bones while we watched the skate video, of how they live inside a person but no one ever sees them. I thought of muscles and organs and all our moving parts. It made me wish that what I had seen really was my bone, so I could say I had seen it. I also wished that it really wasn't. Because maybe then it would be a fantasy, and therefore impossible, and therefore okay. I wished, not wanting to accept what I saw as real, knowing that it was.

The next day my skin had scabbed around the hole. Not over the hole, just the large space around it. I pushed it out of my head. The day after that it started to smell like meat that had been left outside for a while. I was in shorts—wanting someone to notice—eating lunch with friends, when a fly flew into the hole. I jumped and slapped the side of my leg, and it flew out right away. But I had seen it happen.

I spent the rest of the day stomping, so that if anything were to fly in there again, I would scare it out. I could no longer push aside my terror. The stomping hurt. My leg hurt. Fear followed me through classes and the bus ride home. I shook and kicked the whole way, pretending to listen to the fifteen-year-old girl in the seat behind me try to tell me about an affair she had been having with a married man. My fear rode with me in the humid, tropical air that I imagined was riddled with parasites and rot. Everything rotted so fast there. I thought of our trash cans, whose metal interiors crawled in the night.

At home, I rushed to the bottle of hydrogen peroxide. The label warned not to use it on deep or scabbed cuts. I no-

ticed what I didn't want to acknowledge: the area around
the lesion was red and swollen. I took off my shorts, sat on
the edge of the tub with my foot pointed at the drain, and
poured the liquid into the wound. The scab melted and ran
down my shin, leaving the deepest, most infected chasm I
had ever seen up to that point. The cut had bloomed. The
concave was deep and smooth, wet, and the infected and
swollen skin and meat had risen up—my own inflamed
volcano in the middle of my leg. That little pellet hole was
still there, but I couldn't bring myself to look inside this
time. The bone was still there, and I would need serious
medical attention if I saw it. I kept repeating, it's okay.
It's okay. It's okay. It's okay, as I put a Band-Aid over it.
One Band-Aid that covered maybe half the crater. It covered only the middle, deepest part but left two cavities on
the top and bottom of the sideways bandage. I continued
wearing shorts so that someone would see and maybe take
care of my problem. For a week no one did. "It'll pass,"
I thought. "No need to make anyone angry or worried or
scared. I'm okay."

The day I didn't skip gym, the PE teacher noticed. I
didn't often go to his class, but when I did, I would sit in the
top bleachers and read. He was surprised when I showed
up in gym shorts. He gaped at my leg and asked me to
follow him outside for a moment, where he asked if I was
getting beat at home, if that was why I never went to PE.
I said no. He sent me to the nurse. She was excited, jittery
and, grinning, wondering out loud what to do with my leg.

In the end, she tried to close it with butterfly stitches that popped off the second I left her office. She wanted me to ask the doctor if she had done the right thing when I saw him, pled with me to tell her what he said. I was a learning experience. I smiled and said okay because I wanted to be polite. I never did ask.

It took me a couple of more days to get to the doctor. One of my little brothers got sick and I told my mom I was bored and would go with her to take him in. By then the tiny hole had closed—though the swelling was maybe worse. It hurt to walk, and the skin around the crevice seemed to keep puffing up.

After the doctor finished with my brother, I said, "Hey, since I'm here . . . you think you could look at this thing on my leg?" I peeled off the Band-Aid.

"Oh, shit!" He called another man from the hall for a second opinion. This second man, bearded and tall, crouched down and stared at the leg for a long time. They muttered to each other for a couple of minutes before taking me down the hall.

"It's too late to stitch," the family doctor said on the way to the X-ray room. "After so long, and especially with that kind of infection, it's too late to stitch. You should have gone to the emergency room the moment it happened. I don't know why you didn't go to the emergency room."

After the X-ray showed my bone wasn't infected, he calmed down some. "You're about this close to spending the next six weeks hooked up to an IV in the hospital," he said, pinching his thumb and index finger together. "Something like this could cost you your leg."

My mom, terrified of what the doctor was thinking about her, kept repeating, "I had no idea. I swear I had no idea."

Now I have a bald, smooth indent on my right shin, about an inch wide and two inches long—it's shrunk over the last twenty years. But I still have both legs. I'm okay.

I saw the woman who hit me through her windshield before I fell backward. She looked frail. I was afraid she would have a heart attack or stroke because I could feel her sharp breaths in her wide, watery eyes, could feel the entire contents of the inside of her car tremble with her while the car itself stayed solid, heavy. There were two figures in the back seat, but the car rode low and I never saw their faces—chubby children? A senior citizen couple? All too afraid to move.

When Mike, in his late twenties, ragged and worn, was thrown out of his car after falling asleep at the wheel in the wee hours of the morning, he looked down at the blood and his twisted, crooked leg and thought he was going to die. He didn't die then, but he lay in a growing puddle of gasoline as onlookers gathered. No one else was hurt. It was just Mike on the ground. Just Mike who had been in the car. He asked an approaching man for a smoke.

The crowd asked the man if he was crazy. "Look at all that gas!"

"Can't you see he's dying?" the man said. He gave Mike a smoke, lit it for him. The crowd backed away.

Mike smoked his cigarette surrounded by gasoline and spectators—and didn't blow up.

In the hospital though, when the doctors straightened his leg on the table, he knocked over the tiny nurse who had been trying to hold his arms down.

The cops found scars on my arms when I was pulled over in the middle of the night in 2008, three years after I ended my mission, while on my way to buy pills from a one-legged man. I was twenty-four and sick and desperate. My tags were expired and my license was suspended and I was in possession of two used syringes and was infested with strings of track marks following the paths of my veins.

Some wounds pile on and on, frantic, erratic, and I guess the cops had been following my brother and me around for a while, looking for some anxiously made mistake, waiting until we tripped over ourselves. Who knows why. We weren't drug traffickers. We were more stupid than dangerous. All I know is that a year later Mike was arrested, and the cops told him they'd been "on to us" for a while.

The pay phone outside the twenty-four-hour Walgreens prompted them to stop me, thinking I was in the middle of some major deal. I was not. I only had money for three pills, and the one-legged-man ended up not even having any that night. He just yelled at me over the phone because I owed him money.

When I saw the blue and red lights, I couldn't remember if cops were meant to search the person or the car first, if they were allowed to search the car only if they found something on the person, or vice versa. In my confusion I put one rig in my pocket and the other under my seat, screwing myself either way.

"Do you have anything in the car we should know about?" they said. They asked me to get out, put my hands on the hood. They only asked for my license after.

"The syringes are my dad's," I said before they started patting me down. "He's a diabetic."

It was hot out. I was sweating and cold.

The lead cop clicked his flashlight on. "Turn your arms over," he said. "What about those?"

"I'm a lifeguard," I said. "I scratched my arms pulling a kid out of the water." I *was* a lifeguard and was always pulling kids out of the water, almost always because of the parents' neglect. Those were hero-scars. I wanted him to believe they were hero-scars. *I* wanted to believe they were hero-scars, because hero-scars are okay. I wanted my lie to make everything okay, like maybe if the marks were gone, the real reason they were there wouldn't exist.

They didn't arrest me that night. Instead, they gave me a ticket to go to court and followed me around the next few days. I never went to court. I moved to Arizona and spent the next two months working as a bill collector on defaulted student loans and chose to take the non-extraditable bench warrant and become a fugitive.

Who were those motionless figures in the back of the car? I know my reaction. I know the driver's reaction. I know the reaction of the impatient people in the honking cars around us. But what about those people—were they people? I think they were dressed in black, but maybe that's too cliché to be true. Did they really sit as immovable and stoic as in my memory? Were they stunned and clutching one another, too afraid to speak? Were they the ones to whisper to the driver to leave the scene? Twins? A long-married couple who'd taken on the appearance and countenance of one another? They could have been anything. Did the driver plead with them to remain quiet about the incident? Were they all friends, tied together by secrecies stretched over years?

My body is covered in secret scars. They make indents and slight discolorations in my skin; they hide in my bones, behind my eyes. I put most of them there myself. I was born with some.

Some remained hidden, lost for years, until I decided
to disclose them:

> The gash on my back that leaked yellow fat, which
> I wiped off with toilet paper in the bathroom.

> A slit on my finger from when I was thirteen and a
> razor blade slipped while I was making a bong.

> A slice on my wrist from when I fell into a wire
> jutting out from a wall in our rented house when I
> was seven.

> Miles of track marks.

> Aluminum-foil smoke lungs.

> The severe depressions and manias of bipolar
> disorder.

> A chronic expanding hematoma the size of a golf
> ball in the middle of my right thigh.

> My left ankle, which has been rolled so many
> times it shakes in and out of the socket as I walk.

> A cut behind my knee from when I fell down a hill
> during a family reunion when I was seven.

Some that were found:

The cut that resulted in stitches above my right eye from when I fell from a high chair and into a table when I was two.

The cut that resulted in stitches from when my mom accidentally slammed a car door on my head when I was four.

The dent in my forehead from when I face-planted from a couch to the corner of a coffee table while singing a church hymn for my parents when I was four.

The skin burned off my elbows and knees by asphalt while I clutched a rope tied to the back of a pickup when I was twelve.

There are more.

I've spent a lot of time hiding my wounds, showing them only when they become scars, harmless, impotent things unable to instill fear or anger or pain or concern in others or myself.

I'm not the only one. Vovó, my Brazilian grandmother, who was ninety-four when she died, cut the bone out of the top of her own thumb with a pair of clippers when she was younger. Her mutilation started with a boil. She was working as a nurse and midwife in Fortaleza at the time, chain-smoking and drinking vast amounts of coffee between pulling babies out of screaming women. She knew better than to pop the boil. The doctor had told her not to pop the boil.

She popped the boil.

And there it was, the bone, sticking out at her.

Seventy years later, she rocked in her chair—the arthritis-riddled, bowlegged, crooked black woman I loved so much—and laughed loud about it, giving a thumbs-up, displaying the aberration. It looked normal on the bottom but was almost perfectly round and way too large on the top. One side of the preternatural tip had a small, crooked fingernail; the other had an indentation in her skin that folded in on itself: the mark left by her self-surgery.

"You cut it off?" I'd ask. She told the story repeatedly, and I asked repeatedly. It had become a joke.

"I had to do something," she'd say.

I've often thought about those blades sliding against that white bone, thought about how far down she had to go. It made my teeth sore every time.

"It didn't hurt?" I'd say.

"Of course it did," she'd say with a shrug. "But it was already hurting. I just took advantage of the pain."

After the car hit me, I stood up, clutching my arm, knowing that sometimes it takes a while to feel the full extent of an injury, knowing I felt a slight pain, knowing that I'd had slight pains before that grew into miseries.

The driver rolled down her window, confused, and asked if I was okay. The two in the back seat remained motionless sentinels, strange guards.

I said I didn't know—my arm hurt. I said maybe we should exchange information to be safe. She looked around. She looked at the cars behind her who were already starting to get past impatient. She looked at me with a new face, which showed no sign of having registered her accident. All it showed was fear. When she studied me, holding my arm, her expression went hard. "I don't believe I really hit you."

"Of course you hit me, my shoe marks are on the car."

Before I finished my sentence, she had peeled out.

I stood in the meridian a long time, watching the cars honk and whiz past.

My hit-and-run was witnessed. A woman in a yellow sports car rolled down her window and yelled out to me that she had gotten the license plate. Then she drove away, in the opposite direction. I waited for her to come back and give me the number. She never did.

I got on with my night. I had only been in Rancho Mirage for maybe an hour. I had driven in from Arizona to hang out with my MFA friends and go to an alumni party at a resort. I was alone though, as I walked across the street for some food. I had my favorite places to revisit, places I'd come to know while I was earning my degree.

I wasn't about to let a hit-and-run interrupt my dinner plans. But the place had closed down. It was dark inside and under some kind of renovation by the new owners, and I couldn't think of anything else I wanted to eat.

Some wounds run across entire countries, continents, peoples. Sometimes they fester. Symptoms of an underlying sickness emerge, sometimes ignored, but still infected, still shared, as they form a collective scar. Mike's scars and mine ran crisscross between one another like a map of a wild, unplanned city. Each one a partial witness of the other until Mike died. Mike was the one who had jumped in front of me, causing me to fall into the fence that tore into my back. I accidentally broke his finger in a door. He let go of the rope when I didn't, that time I skidded across the parking lot, tied to the back of that truck. He was one of the few I showed the gash on my leg to, knowing he would never tell. We shared and paid one another's debts. We passed our needles back and forth to each other. We stole from one another, stole *for* one another. One was arrested because of the other. Mike's first drugs didn't come from me, but they came from my friends, who he was hanging out with when I wasn't around. He took the opportunity, knowing I kept telling them not to let Mike smoke when I was with them. But once the taboo had been breached and we needed our substances, we made sure the other was taken care of with shit whenever we could.

Some years prior to the hit-and-run, when I still had that warrant out, my upstairs neighbor and her boyfriend got drunk and fired a bullet through my ceiling. The cops said there was nothing they could do since the couple claimed it was their friend, and they didn't know where he'd gone. Instead, the cops lectured me on having an outstanding warrant and told me that even though it was non-extraditable, I still needed to get it taken care of. They had their eyes on me. The upstairs neighbors were white. Is that important? I don't want it to be. Maybe they didn't have any petty, five-year-old outstanding warrants for drug paraphernalia. The warrant was certainly my fault, not theirs. The shot came from right above where I usually studied, it could have caught me in the forehead. But it didn't. It was only a bullet that ricocheted off the floor and landed behind my open computer. It's okay.

The bench warrant caught up with me the day after my graduation ceremony at ASU, during a layover in the Miami airport on my way to Brazil. My marriage to my wife, Veronica, was severely damaged at that point. She is fiercely intelligent and short and brown with pitch-black hair and lovely, and to this day I smile and am happier every time she walks into a room I'm in, but she had had enough of me. Too many relapses. Too many lies. I was positive it was over. We were on our way to Brazil not to mend, but to sever. We were in the middle of talking about how she would go to her parents' house and I would go to mine once we got to Fortaleza when I was taken into custody in front of her.

The arresting officers, customs agents, were nice. They were apologetic in their arrest, asked if the handcuffs were too tight, talked to me about how important it was to have a day in court. They searched my carry-on in front of me and were surprised that all I had were books. They sighed and shrugged. I got it. It was their job. It was fine.

I had been alone in the airport holding cell for a while, frenzied over the loss of Veronica and junk sick, when a tall customs agent opened the door with my Brazilian passport in hand.

"It's illegal for you to have dual citizenship," he said, and grinned. "I should take this right now. I should shred it." He flapped the passport in the air. "Why would you even want this when you have US citizenship? People like you don't know how to appreciate what you have. What, you thought we weren't going to get you? You thought you could come here and think we weren't going to pick you up on the warrant? You're so stupid. People like you never change. You're probably high right now, aren't you? It's in your fucking blood. You'll be a junkie your whole life. You'll always be a pathetic fuckup. Not even a man, running away like that." His voice got louder as he spoke. He leaned into the cell, grinning, daring me to say anything.

Having learned to deal with frothing men when I was a child, I said nothing.

Another bald and muscular customs agent joined him. "Why don't you just drink like normal people do?" he said. "Don't mess with that shit, man. Just get drunk. What's the matter with you?"

They took me into the bald man's office, where they asked me questions and filed my paperwork. "You should just drink like a normal person," he repeated. "You can get drunk every night and not get in trouble. That's what I do." The bald one was calmer, at least. "It's only a few nights in the slammer. It's not that big a deal. Seminole County probably won't even want to come pick you up." I told him it wasn't the idea of being locked up for a few days that scared me. It was that I had just lost my wife, who was already on her way to Brazil. He said that was okay too and changed the topic to his divorce and his new, second wife.

The Dade County cops were cool. They joked and laughed with me. They cuffed me with my hands in front while I rode in the car and pulled over to put them behind me only just before we got to the jail. No one could see that they had done me that small favor.

The Miami-Dade corrections officers were not at all cool. Except for the black female guard. When the other guards were out, she kept telling us how she knew we were good people because we were all not white (except the Cuban, but it didn't count that his skin was white because he was Cuban, so he was also okay). She whispered to me that she would get me another call, but I couldn't tell the others. When she took me to the phones, she yelled at me the whole way, complaining to the other guards about how I wouldn't shut up about calling, how she was just taking me so that I would stay quiet. She had to prove herself to the others. It was fine.

I spent the rest of my time translating for the Cuban. He had a hole in his leg too, only his was a bullet hole. "This is what happens when you don't agree with Fidel," he said, lifting up his pant leg after I told him I was having a bad day. "It could be worse."

The bail bondsman got me out three days later. When I went back to the airport, everyone at the airline already knew what had happened. People I had never met before came up to me and said, in Portuguese or Spanish, "You got to watch out for those gringos, man. They'll throw you in jail for nothing."

I got to Brazil with one plastic bag that contained a dirty shirt, broken sandals, and a cheap, disposable phone. When I got to Brazilian customs, the woman behind the booth said, "Don't worry. You're Brazilian here."

Veronica was waiting for me. We tried again, with only a couple of relapses since. I hired a lawyer I couldn't pay for, and now I no longer have an issue with the state of Florida. So I guess it's okay.

It's not just the dual citizenship. Everything about me is multilayered, and any definition comes with a throng of clarifications. Every detail about me *tem um porém*, has a however or an although. My mother is black *although* she would never describe herself that way. She's indigenous, *although* she doesn't identify with—because she knows nothing about—that culture. This means that I'm part black, *although* I don't look it and have never been treated by people like I was black. It means that I'm part indigenous, *however* I am not a member of an indigenous nation or tribe. I don't know for sure where my indigenous blood comes from, though my best guess would be the Tapebas, who are a conglomerate of the remnants of the Potiguara, Tremembé, Cariri, and Jucá. I also have European blood; *however*, I've never felt comfortable in white culture, nor have I ever been accepted as a part of it. My dad is white, *although* his adoptive father (the grandfather I was close to) was Mexican from Colorado, and his family tree there extends back to when Colorado was Spain—the community he grew up in was Spanish-speaking though they'd been in the US since before the US existed. I grew up in a mix of white and Hispanic culture—*however*, despite my last name being Martinez, I'm technically not Hispanic. I'm Latino, because Brazilians are Latinos, but not Hispanic because my bloodline doesn't come from a Spanish-speaking culture. Could I claim heritage from my adoptive side of the family? Am I allowed? Am I allowed to claim black, indigenous, white? I think about it all the time, every time I have to identify on a form or anywhere else. I thought constantly about it the three days I was in jail. (Mike would have to deal with segregation for the years he was in prison

home so that she could lecture him on his driving abilities.
She got to keep her keys until Mike took her car and to-
taled it after a bender, with me, over Christmas one year.
No one else would let her borrow their vehicle, and most
were secretly grateful her car was gone. She cried upon
losing her freedom. Maybe the woman who hit me is more
shaken up than I am. But for me it was never about the
fall. It was the whip of *her* fear, how her guilt slid into
anger and denial, into hate. She took my victimhood and
made it her own. The thought that keeps coming back to
me, the way flies come to mind anytime I see a scab, is that
she had to throw her panic into what she saw as my weak-
ness: my being unreliable, an other, someone who didn't
belong in her world. I don't want that thought. It's a sign of
severe infection. But I have to have that thought because
I've learned how dangerous neglected infections can be. I
think of my leg and what a contamination of the bone, the
core, might have meant. I think of the swollen heat surrounding the cavity I pretended was never there. I think
of the fly and the stomping, and the fear comes back to me.
Not a fear of what had happened, but a fear of what could
have. I think of the infection of needles and the resurfacing of addictions. I think of my fear of police, even though
I'm a half-white—but definitely not white—college professor with a master's degree. Most of all I think of Mike, who
died alone in prison, sent there because of his wounds.

I walked back to the resort, where my poet and writer
friends and I laughed about how that woman shouted,

"Fake news!" at me, then drove away. We laughed because it was 2017 and "fake news" was being shouted all over, because it was too terrifying to do anything else, because that's what a person has to do sometimes to dispel fear.

My wounds come back to me in cycles. Most are scar tissue at this point. Some still infected. Some keep resurfacing, laughing, asking me if I thought they could ever really be gone. Sometimes I share too many of them with too many people. But everyone has wounds. Everyone has their dead. It's okay.

We're okay.

We're okay.

We're okay.

We're okay.

We're okay.

ghosts like satin

Mike was alive when I began writing this book. It was supposed to be about the two of us: the fucked-up adventures of the Martinez bros. So I asked him about stories, wanting to get down everything he wanted and needed to contribute. It was so important to me to hear from him, what *he* wanted to say.

It was hard for him to write toward the end. While in prison, he had his phone rights taken away after getting in trouble a couple of times. They were all issued tablets, and the one Mike wrote with was low-quality and hard to type on, so I would ask specific questions and see what he was able to answer. When I asked about our late nights in Puerto Rico as children, he wrote:

> . . . And yea dude of course I remember thhatt dude but staying up hanging out always reminds me of the hurricane and everyone being up all night drinking and smokeing! Ya good times!!!! LOL Let me kknow if you are still up dude. LOVE YA MIKE

It was late, but I was still up. For him I would always try to stay up—though that didn't always happen. While we had to pay for each email we sent, it was quicker than letters. He liked when we were able to talk to each other at the same time. "It's like we're texting," he would say, and that would break my heart. I tried to stay awake, but the messages would get blocked by guards sometimes or would just take too long to come. And it was expensive. Our "texting" conversations never lasted long, even if we did send at least one short message a day to one another. I had to take Mike's scant comments and paint the pictures to match his words myself.

The hurricane . . . staying up hanging out . . . Nights in Puerto Rico were warm and salty. We think of them in fragments. Wandering in the dark through the smell of tropical plants and our neighbor's laundry detergent. Nights in the park, surrounded by drunk girls and their boyfriends, our friends and girlfriends, the people we loved. Stumbling through the basketball court and bleachers—the storm had torn the metal roof off those bleachers and sent it bouncing down the street like a crumpled ball of tinfoil.

After the hurricane, the air stopped. We would leave our parents sleeping and sit out in the four a.m. stillness. Saha would rest her back on my folded legs, her spine eating into my knee. Angel did magic tricks, guessing the cards we'd picked each time, while the next-door neighbor stared at him in love. Mike Peña told stories about his old buddies killed off in gang wars. The girls across the street shined flashlights in our faces and giggled if we walked too close to their house.

"I saw a ghost once," Jasmine said. She'd broken up with me, but she still hung around, her hair sometimes orange, sometimes blue. She often brought a girlfriend with her, but never another boyfriend.

Mike gave a half chuckle. He couldn't tell if she was joking. Neither could I. It didn't matter. We were all buzzed and in love with the peaceful isolation of living in the middle of the night with no electricity, at a time and place in which no disaster mattered. We were kids. Jasmine and Saha were fifteen, Mike Peña and I were about fourteen. Mike was eleven, always the youngest among us. Angel was maybe seventeen, the neighbor girl who was in love with him about fifteen. We were in front of Saha's house or in the park with other friends whose names and faces I no longer remember, though I dream of them sometimes.

Jasmine pushed her orange hair out of her face and looked at the dark across the street, serious. "I did," she said. "It hung there in the air for a while. I got a good look. It wasn't like one of those eye-trick things."

Mike and I stared at her, and in this memory he's in more of a shadow than the rest of us. He scratched his head. "Oh."

I followed her gaze into the dark.

"It looked like my grandma," she said. "But like all in white. Like white satin."

And in the dark I thought I saw a wisp of light, blurred, almost real, like this memory is a blurred wisp, like the deepest pull in my chest when I remember Mike, though I can't see him as well as I used to.

There's not a single person in that group I'm still in contact with. For all I know, I'm the only one left with these images in my head, these blips I'm afraid to lose. How much is already lost? The moments in which we sat quiet, listening to the night air, to the coquis, to the sound of card tricks and stories about ghosts. When Mike died, everything he knew that I didn't was lost. And when we're both gone, who will still see us? Believe we existed?

Saudade

Mike and me in front of the pool,
maybe a year or so after the hurricane,
after the pool was refilled with water

I learned to leave behind almost every place and person I
have ever loved, and then I learned to carry their absence
with me. That vacuum they leave, that negative space,
builds and weighs on me. It's a comforter I don't think I
could ever give up. It's in my blood.

My indigenous ancestors migrated up and down the
northeastern coast of Brazil in a crescent shape, always

plans to marry my dad, the man who had baptized her and confirmed her a member of the Church of Jesus Christ of Latter-Day Saints two years prior; my family and I would always seem like an anomaly at church in Idaho and Florida, since with the exception of my dad, we were not white nor were our lives enmeshed in the activities and culture the same way as the other kids, much to the chagrin of my father. The intense religious aspects were expected, like obeying commandments and staying chaste and staying away from drugs (none of which we did), but whether because of race or demeanor or our itinerance, we weren't as involved in the social aspect. Moscow is in the Palouse, on the border with Washington, not two hundred miles from Canada. My dad was attending the University of Idaho there, after growing up in the neighboring town of Genesee. They were in transit, and I guess that rolled over on to me. We drifted between apartments and my paternal grandparents' house. My mother created a daycare in our various homes, and my dad did Domino's pizza delivery and worked as a video-rental clerk while finishing school.

Moscow is green and hilly with humid shadows. I remember the sidewalk in front of my aunt's old house was cracked. She had a garden that seemed huge to me as a child, and what I remember can't be real: flowers towering far over my head and trees that might house creatures from fairy tales. Other than that, all I remember is a dark apartment and a hospital that might not even have been in that town. Moscow is little more than pale imprints to me now. I haven't been there in over twenty-five years, and there's only a faint impression of a connection when I see pictures. I was born a foreigner there because my mother was a foreigner. My mother would never admit to not loving it there, though I never believed she did, the way I never believed she's ever truly felt comfortable anywhere (not even when she went back to Fortaleza for a few years when she was middle-aged) except maybe Florida. Northern Idaho belongs to other people, like my dad's side of the family. Not me. Most places I've spent time in carry that same sentiment: they are a series of spaces that other people are from and that I am only passing through.

Northern Idaho doesn't belong to my dad anymore either. Nowhere does. My parents never carried a sense of locale or lived with any type of permanence, as if the key to a happy home was incessant traveling. They took us on constant road trips. We drove everywhere: to Yellowstone, to Craters of the Moon, through and over mountains when we lived in Rigby. My dad always played music so loud it would drown out the sound of speaking. Whenever we went up north to visit my grandparents, we traveled by way of the long and solitary Lolo Pass, through the mountains between Idaho and Montana. We passed through during a thunderstorm in the middle of the night once, the car vibrating REM, and later Mozart, amid the lightning. What could have been fear of all that blue voltage became part of an adventure, like I would have read about in a book. The electricity fused with a car full of music and motion while I caught brief glimpses of the forest along the road that rushed past us in shadow. The lightning left imprints of light in the dark when I closed my eyes, like negative film. It was magic.

Soon, they'd move us from Idaho to Puerto Rico to Florida and on. Before that though, there was Genesee. Genesee is my grandparents' basement, where I stayed whenever we visited or moved there. It almost felt like home, because unlike my parents, my grandparents seemed so immovable and stable. It's where Mike and I fought and played on the shag carpet. It's the school I never attended, but where I broke my arm and where Mike broke his. It's the new-asphalt smell around the granary where my grandfather worked while Mike and I rode bikes. It's a little girl with big glasses and dark hair whose name I can't remember, and an old woman whose name, I think, was Mary, who used to tell me how much I looked like my father. But that woman is dead. And Mike is dead. And my grandparents moved to Arizona.

One summer, when I was between ten and eleven, my dad got a gig teaching at St. Simons Island in Georgia. We drove there from Rigby, Idaho, passing through states until we reached the coast. We stayed on the island, and I spent all the time I could at the beach. Mike and I walked to the ocean from the condo our family rented, and later from the Embassy Suites attached to a mall where we stayed for almost two months. The family went all over that summer. On the weekends we drove to Disney World and Universal Studios in Orlando. One weekend we went out to Savannah and saw Civil War sites. I was floored by the thick, timeworn air that felt like it was pushing that history through me. Another weekend, we went to Ponce de Leon's Fountain of Youth in St. Augustine, not knowing that we would visit the ruins of de Leon's house in Puerto Rico over a year later, or that we would move to Florida almost four years after that. Seeing de Leon's old places, that Spanish side, mixed with that tropical (or almost tropical) landscape stirred something in what I can only describe now as generational memory. I wanted more. I wanted more of Latin America, of that history that pulled me toward it, that felt so important to me, the history I didn't know. By then I'd only ever been taught the history of the United States and the history of the Church of Jesus Christ of Latter-Day Saints, which to me seemed like the same thing. Even years later in Puerto Rico and Brazil, where there were many black and brown Latter-Day Saints, I was never able to divorce the white, American vibe and gospel the church taught. By the time we got back to Idaho, it was too late for me to be still like my grandparents or the friends I had there. All I wanted to do was move, keep that momentum, wander through remnants of history, find myself somewhere new, somewhere that housed what I inherently knew (without knowing what) I was missing.

Though we lived in Rigby a long time—maybe five years—it's split into two categories for me: the blue house and the brick house. Childhood and early adolescence. Before spending the summer in Georgia and after. Each place has its own palette. Early Rigby is a dim living room, stifling on freezing winter nights. It's the yellow-orange afternoons spent wandering the town barefoot. It's building a raft on green, summer lawns after reading *Huckleberry Finn* and imagining that I would one day float through the brown, local-farm canals, out to the Snake River, down the Colorado, and out to the ocean. It's the devastation when my little raft broke when I threw it into the water.

Adolescent Rigby is where I spent my gray afternoons waiting for the day we would move to Puerto Rico, like my father had been talking about for a long time. It's where I started to resist going to church, to fight with my dad and call him self-righteous, and then lower my head in obedience when I realized I had hurt him. When I saw how much power I had to cause him pain, I started to acquiesce more to his will, or at least pretend. I would hide myself knowing that what he didn't see wouldn't wound him. Adolescent Rigby is riding black asphalt on a yellow or purple skateboard surrounded by my friends and Mike. It's the smell of the glue on the deck and oil in the bearings. Still, Rigby is not home. I was a stranger there too, like in Moscow or Genesee. My skate buddies were always with Mike and me when the cops brought us home after curfew; the ones whose parents also made them go to church (and in Idaho there were a lot of Latter-Day Saints) would sneak out the chapel windows with us when no one was looking to run to the gas station to drink cappuccinos, but we knew that wouldn't last. Our friends went with us to the mini ramp in the old barn, but I knew they would stay and grow up together and we would leave. Mike would be the only friend I could count on. It was preordained, and my knowledge of the preordination caused a gap between my friends and me, the town and me, Idaho and me, the church and me—binding me ever more to Mike. That separation between us and everything else would go on to inform my relationship with church, almost every place I've ever been, and most people too. There was Mike and me in one reality, everyone and everything else in another.

I was still a foreigner when we left for Puerto Rico. Even on the tiny isle, we drove, from the Atlantic to the Caribbean on tropical-mountain roads. From San Juan to Ponce. From El Yunque to Mayagüez. Once around the perimeter of the island just because. We drove everywhere, not speaking, listening, until we never wanted to go home again. I didn't belong in Puerto Rico (I am not Puerto Rican; my Spanish was terrible at the time, and only passable at best after we spent more than three years there), but the Isla del Encanto has become one of my most important homes. It was one of the few places that I wanted to stay when it was time to leave. I felt a primal familiarity there, like maybe the landscape surfaced my Latin side, my tropical side, the side I had been without in the whiteness of Idaho. Maybe it was an antidote for the loneliness of rootlessness I never even knew I needed.

I wandered Old San Juan and read about Caribbean pirates in a book I'd bought in a tourist shop housed in a centuries-old building. I read about Blackbeard with his smoking ears and stared at the topless representations of Anne Bonny and Mary Reed. I was enthralled with a crude drawing of a ship etched into the walls in the jail in El Morro and would later think of the despair of the prisoner in a locked cell, looking at the ocean, only able to scratch (probably with a pebble) the likeness of his freedom. I walked in and out of African shops and art galleries and on roads that slaves built. I watched my feet on the cobblestone and thought of the builders—knowing that my ancestors were also slaves, but in a country I did not yet know. I thought of the Taíno, knowing I had ancestors who were uprooted, murdered, and unnamed, but in that other country I did not yet know. Puerto Rico was almost mine, a reflection of at least a history, if not a homeland.

At a plaza that faced the ancient El Morro fortress and ocean, I'd stare at the Atlantic and think about how old the water was—older than the fortress—and how long before the Spaniards warred and enslaved, the water had been there, always in flux. There's something about the scent of the ocean: it goes way back for me, with origins I can't remember. I just know it conjures immensity and longing and comfort. Even when I'm *in* the ocean I desire it. Its immensity and continuity pull me toward it, evoking adventures that I feel but have never experienced, memories I've never had.

I went to school on an army base with people who were from all over the world and across more than one ocean: the island, Panama, Guam, Japan, New York, California, Germany. We were somewhat united as travelers in passing, all familiar with the membranes that separated us from other people and places. We expected friends to leave. We expected to leave ourselves, making vague promises to keep in touch, then breaking them. I've spent years not speaking to old friends, though I loved them. I've spent years thinking of our adventures rolling around the island in a stained Volkswagen Beetle, listening to Bob Marley. Or the midnight when Brian and Rose and I started a fire next to an abandoned building on the beach and sat there talking until the cops chased us away. Or swimming in the rain at Mar Chiquita with Mike and Evelyn and her family, the droplets bouncing up from the ocean to the sky.

My memories are slippery. I can feel a shade of light that reminds me of being a missionary in São Paulo. Seconds later, that light will feel like LA, only to newly remind me of the rooftop on our old house in Bayamón, Puerto Rico, where Mike and I tried (and failed) to grow some weed. From up there, I watched people I never knew walk out of a lonely Catholic church I never set foot in. The church was not mine, but the drawing I made of it when I was fourteen and stoned is. If I push my finger to one of the charcoal lines and lift it to look at the mark, I am reminded that it was all real. The rooftop, church, and charcoal were real. That place was real, and it's all part of me.

It helps me remember that house existed, that I existed at that time and in that where.

The day I turned sixteen, we left Puerto Rico. We stopped drifting for a while and stayed in Florida, our immobility making us mad—so mad Mike and I buried needles into ourselves with heroin and coke, became both enlightened and destroyed by bipolar disorder, both fell away from and clung tighter to the religious ideas of our father even if neither of us could ever live up to the godly expectations. Something was missing, the way something is always missing when we're stagnant, so we had to fill the void.

The feeling of absence has a word in Portuguese that does not translate into English: *saudade*. A person can feel saudade or can have saudade. It turns the invisible into an entity, and it is only dispelled if it is killed or leaves. If a person reunites with someone whose absence they carry, then they've *mataram a saudade*—killed the absence of. Otherwise, the saudade can be permanent. *Tenho saudade de todos e de tudo que eu já deixei para trás.* I have saudade for everyone and everything that I have left behind. Like the cearense musician, songwriter, and poet Belchior sings, *"Agora eu quero tudo, tudo outra vez."* Now I want everything, everything all over again. And I do. I want the beautiful and the terrible, and more than anything I want

The drawing I did from the roof of my house in
Bayamón when I was fourteen

again every moment I ever spent with Mike. Saudade
is what I gain through my constant moving. It's what's
gained for daring to stay alive. It's the sweet sadness that
comes from knowing there is never a chance of going back.

My earliest memories aren't in Idaho, but in Fortaleza,
where we stayed in the house paid for by the grandfather
I never met. I was three, and it was right before Mike was
born. A love in the shape and sway of ocean emanates from
there. The memories come in flashes: an old woman in a
rocking chair (my great-grandmother) and a parrot in the
window; sleeping in a white hammock in a room full of sun
with my *vovó* (my grandmother); outside baths in a tin ba-
sin; that taste of ocean. My vovó was mythical, one of the

few constants in my mother's rare stories of her childhood. She was the one I wanted to know the most. One who— like Mike—I never learned to leave even after she died.

The space of those early childhood memories is a phantom place I can never get back to, though I've often tried. That place remained a ghost even when I moved into that same house as an adult. It's another home that was never really mine, no matter how badly I wanted it to be. Maybe desperation convinced me there is somewhere I could have come from but do not. After all, I wasn't raised there. I didn't see Fortaleza from the time I was three until I was eighteen. When our family returned after our fifteen-year exile, I sat on the floor with my cousins and we talked through the night until morning. We had been ghosts to each other, only rumors, vague shapes, even if we had pictures together as babies, smiling, laughing. I'd never really met them, but it felt like I had known them all my life. In fact, I had felt their absence all my life, their shadows, the same way they grew up with mine, because when something moves from one place to another, it leaves a space.

I'm doomed to that movement, so I keep wandering, longing, witnessing. I keep leaving to long for and witness something else. I no longer know how to form intimacies with anything. Instead, I'm dependent on the saudade that I know will always be there. Without saudade, there can be nothing new since newness only exists as a foil to oldness and vice versa. Newness cannot come to be without the sacrifice of something old: an experience in exchange for ignorance, enlightenment for a changed worldview, death for life. Saudade only exists because newness does, because experience is too nuanced to always separate or even understand what is good and what is bad. How can I know how to cherish without ever having lost? How can I lose without having cherished? My relationships with people follow this same pattern. Most of my people are tied to the places where they are from and where I have left them. They become fictions, no matter how much I love them. My faint, fictional loves stack up and haunt me, and I want them to haunt me, so I hold them as long as I can, clutching my saudades. I'll forget faces but will find familiar movements in strangers. I'll fill in spaces I've forgotten with what I can remember from others. I have yet to run into most of the friends I had in Idaho or Puerto Rico or São Paulo or Florida, but if I do, they'll be more alien than familiar. Even if they haven't changed, I have, so how could anything stay the same?

Places are no different: the way cities change over time, or maybe cities stay static but people change, making it impossible to see a place for what it used to be. When I went back to Rigby the year I turned thirty, my elementary school had been demolished. The middle school was a weed-filled pasture. The Stop-N-Go where I would drink cappuccinos with my friends and Mike was turned into a Chevron and was more cluttered and crowded than I remembered. But the town itself seemed cleaner, newer. Emptier. I drove around and walked into stores hoping I would run into Dan Carter, Carlos Greenfield, Jon Hansen—those best, early-adolescent friends I had lost. But they weren't there. Rigby became the absence of Rigby.

In Brazil, there was a Fortaleza from when I was a child that's now faded. There was a Fortaleza when I was a teenager, and everything was new and wild and charged. A Fortaleza I lived in at the end of my twenties, which by then had no more magic, just the dim and creeping fear of knowing that it was changed and changing and would never be the same, or safe, again. A Fortaleza the time I fell in love with a girl who I have not learned to leave. That Fortaleza is a frozen setting for the girl, who is now my wife, and everything in that Fortaleza is just a description of us. The city has deteriorated, become more dangerous, more dilapidated now. The last time Veronica and I lived there, we spent days mourning its decline. I will spend my life going back, yearning for what was, and watching the new Fortalezas emerge, knowing they will, and hoping each one will be better than the last.

It would be easy to claim that roaming has made me alone, turned me into someone who draws churchgoers from my rooftop and wanders the world in agony, but that isn't the truth. For all the foreignness I've felt I've also acquired familiarities—solidarities. I haven't been back to Puerto Rico since the day I turned sixteen. Two years before we moved to Florida, Hurricane Georges changed the island. We didn't have running water for a couple of weeks or electricity for a month. So many trees were blown down that the expressway a mile from our house became visible. The neighborhood kids and Mike and I would stay out all night in the dark, talking about ghosts while drinking whatever we'd managed to steal from their parents' home bars. No one had been untouched. We'd all sat in that shared anxiety of the stillness before the storm, and then in the quiet pleading after the destruction, desperate for a breeze to push away the muggy air. We cleaned and rebuilt, shared water and resources, generators and boxed milk. We all shared the phrases "After the hurricane . . ." or "Before the hurricane . . ." When I saw the news of what Maria had done in 2017, I cried at images of trees I'd once skated under that were now uprooted and destroyed, of the familiar faces of worn people after a tempest. My impotent love went out to them. I wanted to be there, to help where I once had a home, but I've never been back.

I can't even stay still from one second to the next. I can't sleep until I've twisted my body around the bed for a while. I can't sit without shaking my leg. I try to shift that itinerancy into something productive. I work in movement— I like to see the words travel across the page. I like to feel the rhythm of speech and the tap of the keyboard. I pace around the class when teaching, the living room or bookstore between paragraphs, muttering to myself and waving my hands. I drive somewhere I don't really need to go just to travel, to hear the music so loud I can do nothing but sing along with my saudades.

I'm never satisfied with where I am because I keep feel-

ing the lack of where I'm not. There is always something
else. There are always more people. And yet there is never
enough to fill the space of everything left behind: Warped
Tour in the northwest with Carlos and Dan; wandering
through suburban Floridian streets at night with E and
Aldo, our long conversations filling the silence around us;
Ricky and Mike and me recording songs on our 4-track in
my room, banging on garbage because we had no drums;
all my Palm Desert people with whom I shared the chaos
of writing; Marília and Natália and Vovó and Titia, the sis-
ters and grandmother and aunt I knew so well yet hardly
knew; sitting with my mother-in-law and Evandro, strum-
ming his guitar around a fire in front of their house under
the expansive starry sky in the *serra* in Baturité; living
with Daniel and Sandra and Sarinha, who at five years old
would ask me to play Tom Waits or David Bowie when I
drove her to school; listening to my grandfather talk about
his feeling at peace at the end of his life, about his childhood in Utah and Colorado, those long days I sat with him
as he lay dying of cancer in his living room, waiting for
him to turn into a saudade.

I go to the next place, knowing I will probably never
find that sensation of home, and that's okay. The initial
shock of the new locale only drowns out the saudade for
a moment. Then that vacuum builds up again and I start
winding up for another move, another shot at another adventure. That's the way it has to be. Saudade is the force
that moves the object at rest. It's the impossible physics of

perpetual motion. It's the prize gained for the sacrifice of leaving, the thing that gives the movement meaning. It's the blood that has to be spilled. And I have to love what I'm leaving. It doesn't work if I don't hurt.

I know I'll never find what I'm looking for because it's always behind me. Since I can't go backward, I can never be at rest. The saudade for my lost brother, of the adventures we thought could never end, is a hurt I will carry forever, and I love the pain. Like the charcoal from my drawing, I can touch it and prove that I was there, that there was something that happened somewhere with someone. Proof there even after that something has left. I tell myself it doesn't matter because at some point everything becomes saudade. And because of that, even the moments with Mike in the now-empty gas stations and old houses and apartments and bus stops scattered across Phoenix where Mike used to wander and live, and where I used to fight every day to see him, to *matar a saudade*, will never die. And having that saudade is a relief because it proves he was alive. It proves I'm right to rush forward with all the movement I can, that all new moments and experiences eventually turn to old moments and experiences, and building those saudades—even the ones that hurt most—is okay as long as I keep moving.

a QT somewhere

"No, dude," I said as we walked into a QT gas station somewhere in Phoenix. "I told you I got this shit!"

"The fuck you do," Mike said, walking over to the Freezoni wall. "I'mma get this shit." Mike was still holding up his sagging pants as he walked, the way we both did when we were teenagers. I was approaching twenty-nine and was about to finish my bachelor's degree, no longer wearing my pants like that, or keeping a cigarette tucked behind my ear, like Mike. He was twenty-six, a pocket full of cash from slinging black tar, but as energetic as he was at fifteen. Sagging pants, sure, but wore a clean button-up shirt, silver necklace, a stainless-steel ring with a gold band in the middle, and tried as best he could to mask the cigarette smell with cologne.

"No, motherfucker," I said. "I told you I'm buying." We were loud and high and smiling, knowing we were making people stare. We loved to put on a show when we were together, see how many people we could make laugh.

Mike started pouring a little of each flavor of ice into

the extra-large cup he picked up, standing wide-legged so his pants wouldn't fall down.

"That looks gross as fuck," I said as I watched him stir the slush between each addition.

"No, dude. It's actually pretty good. I promise. Here. Try it." He pushed the cup, almost full, toward me.

"Nah. That does not look good," I said. My pants were kind of tight. Not on purpose. I had put on weight and the pants were old. I always wore my hair (black when shorter) combed back, and a button-up shirt, not unlike Mike's, to attempt to disguise my daily drug use.

"I promise, bro," Mike said. "Look, I'm not going to take no for an answer. Just, like, taste it."

I sucked some of the concoction through the straw.

"Not bad," I said. I walked over to the Freezoni wall and filled my cup with the Coke flavor.

"You should have mixed all the flavors, man!" Mike said. "You said it was good."

"Yeah, good for at first," I said. "Three sips in I'd be tired of that shit."

We filled our arms with snacks, arguing about which were best, and while I was making my case for cheese-filled hot dogs, but only if they were the right flavor, Mike jumped in front of me in line, dumped his armload on the counter, and, while tipping his head back in my direction, said to the woman in her early twenties working the register, "Don't listen to whatever he says, I'm paying for all this, and his stuff too."

"Damnit, Mike." I unloaded my stuff on the counter next to his. I pulled my card out of my wallet and smiled at the laughing cashier.

"Sorry," Mike told me as he pushed my card away. He looked at the cashier and said, "Here," pulling a wad of cash from his pocket and laying it next to our stuff.

"You don't even know how much it is yet," I said.

"Doesn't matter," Mike said. "She already took the money. It's on the counter. She already has the money."

She started ringing up the items. I had lost. I put my card back in my wallet.

"You guys brothers?" she said, lifting her eyes up from the products she was scanning, still smiling.

"Fuck yeah," Mike said. "How did you know? Do we look alike?"

"Not really. But you argue like it."

"Oh shit!" Mike said. He looked over at me then back at the cashier. "Which one do you think is older?"

She sized us up. She was short, Latin, like us, with straight black hair and intelligent eyes. The kind of woman Mike had to talk to. "He is," she said, pointing at me.

I grinned at Mike.

"What?" he said. "I'm the one with gray hair!" And he was—with a small patch that sprang up after bouts in jail, long years on drugs, an infection in his leg from a dirty syringe that landed him in the hospital for a month a few years prior. He pulled at it to show her.

"So, you're the older one?" she said, taking Mike's money.

"No," Mike said. "He is. But how did you know?"

"He just seems like it," she said.

"Fuck," Mike said, his grin never leaving his face. "Yeah, this is my big brother."

We continued arguing as we left. We argued in the car. We argued, laughing, until I dropped him off at his apartment.

"You know," he said, getting out of the car, "if you weren't married you and I would pick up so many women, all the women."

"Mike. You have a girlfriend."

"That's what I said, dude. If *we* were single."

"No," I said, reaching into the back to make sure he didn't forget his bags on the seat. "You said if *I* wasn't married."

"Don't put words in my mouth," Mike said. We still hadn't stopped laughing.

"I'm not putting words in your mouth, man," I said. "I'm just providing details that you omitted."

"You know what I meant," he said, hanging on the door.

And I did.

Papo with Mike I

Me and newborn Mike

I was three when I was ushered into the hospital to meet the brother who came into the world eyes wide open. He drank in every sight and movement in the delivery room, not crying, just watching. All the adults had been nervous for his arrival. I was the first child, grandchild, great-grandchild. They were worried I'd be jealous.

"Why don't you come say hello to Michael, your baby brother?"

I walked up to my mom, who was holding Mike in a tan chair by the window. I was embarrassed when they had me kiss his cheek. I was always embarrassed when adults had me kiss anybody, especially boys. I looked down

at the new kid with his flat, black hair, sleeping. He didn't
do anything, but I couldn't deny his presence. The family's worries that I'd be jealous were unfounded. We were
never enemies, even when we fought. Soon, they would be
worried about the trouble we got into because we were so
close.

When our small, half-black, half-indigenous mother
was pregnant with me, she had a miscarriage. My twin
was old enough that I didn't absorb him. She was aston-
ished when one fetus left her body and was told a couple
of weeks later that she was still pregnant. It was a belly
both dead and alive. More than once, while speed-talking,
Mike told me he was that twin, that god had decided last
minute that sending us both at the same time would be
disastrous, so he held him back for a few more years. I
didn't know about that, but every time Mike was in danger, every time he was arrested, I knew somehow. We had
a soul connection. It's hard to imagine it could have been
stronger with my miscarried twin. Maybe the shared time
in the belly isn't the only thing that causes that connection. Maybe brotherhood alone is enough. Maybe that
twin connection I would have felt if my brother had not
died in the womb rolled over onto Mike, latched onto him
instead.

I have a recording of a conversation between Mike and
me. It's a few years old now and our voices are interrupted

and surrounded by the sounds of clicking lighters, coughs, sucking the alternating smoke of black-tar heroin and meth through cut straws, the crinkling of tinfoil squares, and bursts of laughter. It's an hour of us talking over one another in a hotel in Palm Springs about being kids, jail, our parents, regret, lack of regret. It's a revolving conversation—riotous, melancholic—the same one we'd had for years, cut up and garbled and unintelligible to anyone but us:

Someone sparks a lighter.

ME: I know you've seen me get that kind of bad.
MIKE: Yeah, but you know you've seen me there too.

Mike's voice is a little louder than mine, more urgent, though the timbre and accents and way we say words is the same. It's obvious we're brothers.

ME: Right.

I pull in smoke and cough. Black tar is hard on the lungs, hard on the throat. Tastes like dirty chemicals and vinegar infused with what I've always thought of as toxic cotton candy—probably because it was usually cut with brown sugar.

ME: We both have that hard-core sadness that—
MIKE: That's the best way, you know, to describe it. Honestly, I think that it was probably the best rea-

I felt sad all the time. Now I know it was more complicated than simply feeling sad. It was a web of the intricate
melancholy we felt at home, our developing mental health
issues and bipolar disorder, the intense religious tension,
and the traumas we tried to hold at bay. It would turn into
a nightmare, but back then it just felt like feeling good.

When we lived in Puerto Rico, our mom and one of
my friends' mothers from church would take turns driving us to the weekly seminary class in a woman's dark
living room that we were forced to attend with the other
church kids. By that time, I had read the Book of Mormon
and much of the Bible. They were part of my understanding of the world, and my life was caught between their
teachings, the church people teachings, and the growing
desperation stemming from sexual tension, drug abuse,
and heavy family depression. I was confused because I felt
good reading scriptures about the tenderness of god, but I
hated the vengeful and strict parts. I was told I wouldn't be
able to feel god if I was sinful, but one of the most intense
spiritual moments I'd ever had was while I was on acid
and felt an overwhelming love from god and for god and
for all people. One day, I made all of us late for seminary.
Mike—who was too young for seminary but happened to
be hanging out with me before—and I were waiting on a
guy we called Hawaii to come through with some shit. He
was late. I knew I had to get home, that Mom would be
waiting, but we needed to get high, at least find some pills
or weed, something. Anything. Hawaii wasn't at his house

up the hill from where we lived, but his girlfriend told us to wait. By the time he showed up and we smoked in a wooded area off the side of the road, I was more than late getting home for seminary. Mom was quiet-angry. I ran past her, straight upstairs, to wash off the smell. I opened a bottle of Mike's cologne and spilled it all over myself in a paranoid haze before getting in the car. I said I'd lost track of the time. She didn't question me or the smell. She just cried while I sat in the back seat. She didn't want to know what was going on with me, and I couldn't say.

It was like she wanted to distract herself from her own life. She, like us, would tell the same stories in cycles, move through some of the same saudades: the time we broke the windshield wiper while trying to rush into a gate behind another car; the time our dad had gone on a work trip and she drove up the wrong ramp to the freeway while we all screamed that we were going to die; the time she had to babysit the kid next door who let the dog out, and when we asked him who opened the gate he kept saying, "The gog did it, the gog did it." She'd get us to tell the story as loud as we could about that dilapidated minivan we drove with the driver's-side door wired shut with a metal hanger after it was almost blown off by a semi while my dad was changing a tire, and the cloth drooping from the roof, and the busted tape deck that wouldn't eject tapes. We had two that got stuck, two different times. One was Queen: *Bohemian Rhapsody* on side A, *Sheer Heart Attack* on side B. The other was an album of monk chants my dad picked up on a whim to teach us music history. Because of the broken door, there was that constant dinging noise that told us it wasn't closed, and the light blinked on and off incessantly. If the music wasn't loud enough, we would go crazy over the dinging, so whatever was in the tape deck had to be loud. The air-conditioning also didn't work, and the windows were stuck open, so the van could be heard from a block away. Once, my parents packed up the whole family and drove around San Juan doling out food to the homeless at night. A lot of them looked at the blinking, screaming van and walked away as fast as they could, uninterested in the food we offered through the open window. We laughed about it even then: Mike and I and our siblings trying to sing along as loud as we could with "The Prophet's Song," the dinging in the background, the flashing light, and our mother and aunt howling with laughter. It gave my dad a migraine, and we had to go home with bags of food still in the car. It gave my mom another story to retell.

In Puerto Rico, we used to sit around the table, laughing all night after my two youngest brothers went to bed. My mother, my little sister, my aunt, Mike, and I would get drunk on our own fatigue after my dad had stomped upstairs because of the noise. While he could handle loud music, he never could seem to handle loud chaos, the sound of a family. It seemed he could never find humor in the scars we turned to jokes. It looked to us like his method of avoiding scars was forgetting or pretending not to notice (the latter being my mother's method when she couldn't laugh). It seemed like he felt excluded, and that made him furious and sad.

"Mah-mah," my mom would call to Mike. "Tell the story again!"

Mike would tell whatever story again, about how he had shimmied up the beam to the upper patio to break into the condo we were staying at in Georgia when he was eight, because we were locked out. Or, when he rolled under his broken bed one night and woke up screaming, thinking he was in a box.

"Tell it again, Mah-mah," she would say, wiping tears from her eyes, her legs crossed. "But wait! Wait! I have to pee! I have to pee!"

Those stories were told until they were pointless, scars proudly displayed after the wound had healed (no matter how badly). They were told and retold in attempts to assuage guilt and build saudades out of the broken pieces we had. To laugh was to minimize, and that's how my mother took care of the guilt of apparently not wanting to see. My parents' seeming desire not to see expanded as we got older. The more trouble we gathered around us, the more my mother laughed, the more my father seemed to forget what little about us he knew.

There are things my mother did not laugh about, never talked about, couldn't say out loud. There are stories she didn't retell, even if Mike and I did. She never laughed while watching us and whatever friends we had at the time crowd into my room downstairs in Florida in those years after my mission, between my dropping out of college and moving to Arizona. We thought she knew what we were up to. Three, four full-grown men jammed into my cluttered room and locking the door. It was a ritual. She would watch the door, alone—my dad either locked in his room or at work—her eyes growing slowly red, that immense and terrible silence building. She had to know that Mike and I and whoever else was in the room were shoving needles into our veins, stumbling to the door a few minutes later to kiss her cheek and walk out into the night. Of course she knew, we thought. Someone *had* to know. But I think they thought it was better not to. Better to stay quiet. Easier not to see, like if it's never talked about then it doesn't exist, like if the addictions didn't exist then the tension in the house, how it was clear we were unhappy and damaged, wouldn't exist either.

That's how I moved: unseen by youth leaders at church because I was quiet and, having read the scriptures, capably answered any questions they had for me about the gospel; unseen at school because though I never did any work I was polite; and most of all because my parents didn't want to see and brushed aside any comments at parent-teacher night and told church leaders that we were fine. We were all fine. So the stories they didn't want to know were the hidden stories Mike and I told one another the most because being secret they seemed the most important, the most sacred.

~~

Sometimes, the stories told became legend, and like all legends, there was the version told and the real events, and only the people involved ever know what truly happened. There is the version our parents know about when Mike and I were caught smoking for the first time, and there is the version Mike and I told. When Mike was eight and I was eleven and we planned to steal the smokes, I was leaning against a table we had in our basement, excited at the prospect of an accomplice. It felt like a grand heist at the time, though the story is more valuable than the loot. We were still talking about it all those years later.

There's a knock at the door.

ME: Oh shit!

MIKE: Yo, I think someone—

The recording cuts out for a moment. It's room service. Though it's not recorded, after I tell the woman at the door she didn't need to clean the room that day, we laugh at how freaked out I got while pulling the foil and little baggies of dope from the backpack Mike had brought with him. All we hear on the tape is a click.

MIKE: So, we were talking about that whole cigarette thing.

ME: Yeah.

Someone moves the phone that's recording the conversation. Probably me.

MIKE: Haha! It was really, I mean, it was really a kind
    of an asinine plan.
ME: Hey, come on. It was pretty good.
MIKE: I mean, yeah. It was *pretty* good, for, you know,
    two dumb-ass kids.
ME: It was my plan.

*It's not recorded, but I know, I remember: Mike looks
at me like the younger brother he is looking at the
older brother I am, a hint of that old worship I always hated because I didn't deserve it.*

MIKE: I know. Fucking mastermind over here.

My plan was we would grab this old fanny pack my
dad had in the closet, I would put it on, and we would ride
our bikes to the local grocery store, which at the time kept
their cigarettes up front by the register together with the
gum and candies. We were going to buy something and
take it to the line, where I would open the *National En-
quirer* to cover Mike while he grabbed a couple of packs of
Marlboro Reds and stuffed them into the fanny pack.

MIKE: And that was the funniest shit. We like got all
    scared at the last second and yelled, "Hey, I'll meet

you outside," so everyone could hear us and then
walked out the doors at the same time to just meet
up right in front of the store.

ME: And no one paid any attention!

*I'm laughing. Or Mike's laughing. At this point in
the recording it's hard to tell which. By this point
we're both loud. We're both traveling through our stories with a velocity that binds through sheer force.*

MIKE: No, man! No one saw shit. We thought like everyone would be watching us and the cameras would
be on us but no one was ever going to pay attention
to these, like, two random kids.

When I Made Jesus Cry

In Post Falls, Idaho, when I was four or five, the little girl my age from the upstairs apartment and I used to go behind the neighbor's exercise equipment in our shared basement and laundry room area of the complex and play doctor. We played in the shadows on the floor between the tangled white metal bars as the sunlight came through a small window overhead. It was the first sexual experience I can remember vividly, the first one with a narrative. I never forgot the melancholy that enveloped that girl, and I wonder if I absorbed that melancholy, if she inadvertently passed it on to me: a shared secret attempt to alleviate something she didn't understand, so it could be something we didn't understand together. I don't remember when the games started—though I'm positive they didn't start in that basement—only that they were played multiple times and that I liked to play and that it was intense. I don't remember her name. Now I can only see her shape and her mother's and brother's and the baby's.

Strangers filtered in and out of the little girl's home. Everything I know about those people and that time is dis-

tilled through a confused child's point of view. My mother
was never sure who lived with them, but there were thun-
derous and violent brawls in that apartment. We heard
the screams and thuds and crying through the ceiling at
night. Later my mom told me that those neighbors were
always getting high. The girl's mother always asked my
mother if she could watch her baby while she disappeared,
telling my mom she had to run off to work unexpectedly.
My mom didn't trust her. The girl and her older brother
were often alone while their mother went out with whatever boyfriend she was with at the time. Mike (who was a
toddler) and I weren't allowed to go inside that upstairs
apartment. But I did. I disobeyed and felt awful for it because I was taught to. I was learning to feel awful and
ashamed about a lot of things. The problem was I didn't
know what I did wrong until my dad yelled at me or my
teacher lectured me.

I knew the games in the basement weren't good because
they were a secret we had to hide—but I didn't know they
were bad either, or at least why they were bad. I only
learned that after we got caught, and we were caught by
multiple people who told my mother. I'm not sure how
many people saw us, only that it got back to my parents
eventually. Once, a woman came down to do laundry and
saw me in the middle of a game, prostrate on a weight-lifting
bench with an erection. She started to cry before silently

turning around and going back upstairs. The girl suggested we stop. I told her I didn't want to stop, even though seeing the woman cry gave me a stomachache. I can't imagine how confusing it must have been for my mother, how horrifying. It must not have made sense. Her religion told her that children are pure and cannot sin. I can still see the shock and disgust on her face every time we were caught, as if from both inside and outside my body at the same time—but for years I wondered if it was all a dream. If it was real, why didn't the woman pull me away? Why did she just walk back upstairs with the dirty laundry in her hands?

Each time I was caught in that basement (the only place I ever was caught, perhaps the reason I remember it so vividly), I lied. Swooning from the tension in the room, I'd only give as much truth as necessary. I never revealed it all. It was always my father who spoke to me about it when he came home from work at sundown. He never saw for himself how the girl and I had played. My mother, knowing more, maybe sensing even more than she'd seen, tried not to let me see her face when he spoke. I have no idea what she told him, if he took whatever she said seriously, if he convinced her that whatever was happening was an exaggeration that didn't need to be addressed, if they both thought it might have been serious but convinced themselves otherwise. Fear ruled our household. Fear of mistakes, fear of anger, fear of god. Fear of damnation. Fear of letting others down.

"Your belt is crooked," my dad said one of the last times I was caught. "Have you been playing games you shouldn't with that girl again?"

"No."

"Don't lie." He was stern and scary and so big in my memory as he crouched to my eye level. I think now that he was probably terrified of everything even then. I wanted to say what people wanted to hear, to confirm what they wanted to believe, to cause no problems. "I know you were," he said. My mother was in the kitchen looking away. "Look at your mom. Look. It makes your mommy very sad. Look. She's crying. It makes Heavenly Father sad too. It makes Jesus sad when you play with those parts of your body. Those parts aren't secret. They're sacred, which is different than secret, *more* important. We shouldn't be playing with what's sacred." He spoke those words quietly, like he was trying to teach a gentle lesson, but there was aggression there. Every lesson from my dad came with a threat, a godly punishment if not an earthly, physical one. It was a mindset and point of view passed down to him by generations of Christian forebears. It was what his Latter-Day Saint family and community had taught him. It was in the books he read written by prominent church members and leaders, like *Mormon Doctrine* and *The Miracle of Forgiveness*, the Bible, the Book of Mormon, and Christian sermons stretching back more than two thousand years.

Lengthy discourses on guilt and god's punishment are as old as organized religion. Love and fear and shame are intermingled and even taught as being the same. Scriptures like Proverbs 13:24 say, "He that spareth his rod hateth his son: but he that loveth him chasteneth him betimes." In *The Miracle of Forgiveness,* by Spencer W. Kimball, is a quote from Heber J. Grant, a late president of the Church of Jesus Christ of Latter-Day Saints, where he says, "There is no true Latter-Day Saint who would not rather bury a son or a daughter than to have him or her lose his or her chastity." Love and violence, love and shame, love and punishment taught as one and the same.

I had known about Jesus and Heavenly Father my entire life. I knew about the Plan of Salvation—the plan god had for all people to return to him in glory and be like him—before I could read. My dad had taught me using the pamphlets and pictures and materials he used on his mission. I was taught in church with cartoons and sheets from church coloring books. I knew that when we died we spent some time as spirits before the resurrection, when we would be judged and placed into one of three kingdoms of glory, or heavens, but it was only in the highest heaven that we would live with Jesus and Heavenly Father, and if we sinned and didn't repent, that's not where we would go. I knew—though I didn't understand how it made sense—that Jesus had to die for that plan to work, that he was perfect and loved me and was so kind, and that making him cry was the worst thing I could imagine. I loved him.

I loved the kindness I felt from the stories about him and couldn't imagine him hurting or destroying anyone. The Jesus in the Bible never scared me, but the people who taught me about him horrified me. I was terrified of not being able to live with Heavenly Father and Jesus again for being bad, because I knew I was bad all the time. I couldn't seem to stop being bad.

After the incidents with the girl stopped, my parents never mentioned them again, as if they never happened. For years, I wanted to bury the encounters. I didn't want them to be important, but the fact that I remembered and was hurt by the memories, and my feelings toward them, told me they were.

When he was younger, our dad read to us, and I loved to listen. I used to run to the door when he came home, excited to see him when I was little. Though that excitement was later mixed with fear and later still shame at myself after those games started and trouble I'd get into later, there was a happiness that remained. He wasn't always aggressive, and he could be fun. Until I was a teenager, he had thick blond hair parted on the side and always wore a mustache—the last vestige of his rebellion from younger days. He was interested in history, especially Civil War history. Books and music. Modern literature and contemporary writers like Stephen King. He played the Beatles and Jimi Hendrix and Simon and Garfunkel and Led Zep-

pelin and Jethro Tull and Yes LPs on the record player he
had. He took me to his room and opened the cover for his
copy of Pink Floyd's *Animals*. He wanted to show me the
words as they sang, to help me better understand them,
but not long after told me he never listened to lyrics. He
only focused on the music because it was safer than the
words. He switched back and forth like that, an unending war between his religiosity and his passion for the
music and books considered worldly by religious leaders.
He'd go on and on about how much of a sinner he was
for corrupting us but would become visibly gleeful when
talking about the bands he loved and the trouble he got
into as a teenager. He was compelled to tell us about what
he'd loved as a kid, but he didn't want us to repeat his
actions, telling us that while it might be fun to misbehave
in the moment, real happiness came from obeying god's
commandments. Too much focus on the world would be a
sin on our parts, and he'd be responsible for introducing us
to wickedness, which to us meant if we weren't good, we
could condemn him as well. Mike and I both learned that
church demanded a sacrifice. For our dad, it seemed that
sacrifice left a profound sadness and a smothering sense of
missed opportunity. Sometimes, when he noticed he was
getting too sentimental about what he was missing out on,
he would turn to us and say that we were the best thing to
ever happen to him, that he was so happy to have a family
and kids. Even as a kid, I couldn't believe that was true.
Even as a kid, I was sad for him.

When I was seven, we watched *Misery* as a family (I'll never forget Kathy Bates's sledgehammer), but a few days later, my dad declared that we weren't going to watch R-rated movies anymore. We all ignored him and did it anyway. He ignored his own rule as well, though he would complain when we did. Sometime prior to this, a church leader preached that R-rated movies were too worldly and shouldn't be watched. I think the result might have been my dad's version of following the letter of a law he didn't really believe in. When it came to books, I could read whatever I wanted, and did. I think he felt reading was learning, and therefore safe, and sometimes I wondered if the books that were left about were crumbs for us to find, worldly pieces we could pick up and read that he didn't directly give us. I couldn't watch *Misery*, but I could read it and did, along with the rest of my dad's Stephen King books and his Hemingway and science fiction anthologies. It only left me more unsure of what was right and what I should do to make my parents and god happy. I wanted to make god happy. I wanted to make my parents happy, and I believed full-heartedly what they taught me about god, about love, fear, and punishments. That's why when I was told that playing those games with that girl was bad, I felt horrible, and when I kept doing it anyway, I felt worse.

My dad seemed to oscillate between fantasizing about being a rock star and trying to squelch anything that didn't have to do with church, going so far as to burn part of his record collection before I was born after hearing a church leader proclaim that rock and roll was of the devil. From what I understand, the church leader had claimed that the repetitive rhythms had tribal African roots that Satan used to hypnotize its listeners. A week or so later, my dad changed his mind and tried to buy his records back but lost a few collectibles for good. Every time I heard the story, my confused heart broke for him. I don't know if he realized his books and movies and LPs gave me the tools I needed to survive and find peace, while the church people and beliefs are what hurt me the most.

By the time I was a teenager, I saw a huge difference between church people and their teachings, church teachings, and spirituality. As someone condemned by church rules and church people, I didn't know whether to pay more attention to those I was told were teachers sent by Christ or to how I felt when I read about Christ. It was confusing. I felt connected to some of what I read and repulsed by so much else. A lot of what church people said didn't feel spiritual to me. It felt like fear. Spirituality to me was something much more calming and loving, something I could find in *some* official church teachings, like how we are literal children of heavenly parents and that we are meant to progress and learn and grow throughout this life and after death throughout all time and eternity, but usually spirituality was something I would find most when I was alone and reading literature and history and listening to the music I connected with—and especially when listening to silence.

My dad came from a long line of staunch believers, Latter-Day Saints who crossed the plains as pioneers in covered wagons, or Puritans in Massachusetts before that, and when he was a missionary in Fortaleza, Brazil, he baptized our mother. We grew up with a three-inch-thick hardcover book of our father's genealogy on the bottom of our shelf at home. It was compiled by our great-grandmother (his mother's mother) and her brother, and a copy was made for each of her children and grandchildren. In it were dates and pictures and, most importantly, first-person accounts of righteous deeds from early church members. There was even a genealogical list that claimed to follow the bloodline to Adam. We grew up with stories from the book: the guy who married his teenage stepdaughter after his wife died so that she could continue to raise her siblings and bring up more children to the lord, the guy who was a bodyguard for Joseph Smith (founder of the Church of Jesus Christ of Latter-Day Saints), names of babies and wives and husbands who died crossing the plains and in other service to their faith. There are stories of missions and conversions, miracles and visions and story after story of ancestors who gave their all to god with their grim, pioneer, black-and-white photos under their names. Names of bishops and apostles and other church leaders were reverenced. It wasn't all church related. There were long lists of European royalty as well. And it wasn't all morose. My great-grandmother's writing is packed with her wit when she tells about the chickens she traded for supplies during the Great Depression or the work she did on the farm as a child. The beautiful parts of the book are the lives, the names, realizing that each individual lived and was a real person. The sad part is the terror of god and anxious and fearful obsession with sin.

My dad tried to break away when he was younger, but the gravity of family history eventually pulled him back in. He used to talk about the time that he'd left the church as a teenager and into his early twenties, about the darkness that it brought to his life. He never really told us why he felt the way he did, just that he had been bad and wicked and rebellious. For him, the important part of the story was going back to the fold and following the legacy of his mother's side. (His Hispanic father was really his stepfather—the grandpa I was close to—hence the last name Martinez. My dad never seemed to feel connected to his Hispanic side.) When he mentioned the darkness of being away from the church, it came with a mixed look of vague fear, despair, and longing. I had a hard time imagining what greater terror he found out in the new world that made him run back to his old one. But whatever he'd gone through, it was real, at least to him.

He tried the best he could, in his broken way, as he

sat us kids down to read the stories from the book. He taught us the commandments we were expected to keep out of a genuine concern for our well-being. The Word of Wisdom taught us not to use drugs and alcohol or smoke cigarettes or drink coffee; the Law of the Fast told us to go without food or water for twenty-four hours—though we were never clear as to why; the Law of Chastity taught us that any sex not between a husband and wife (specifically man and woman) was dirty—and even some sex between husband and wife was dirty, though it was never specified more than that. And touching ourselves was dirty, except to use the bathroom or bathe. We were taught that sexual sin was almost as bad as murder, which I later discovered came from a chapter in *The Miracle of Forgiveness* called "The Sin Next to Murder" and a scripture in the Book of Mormon that taught that sexual sin was "most abominable above all sins save it be the shedding of innocent blood or denying the Holy Ghost." Our dad pleaded with us to keep these commandments, and others, sometimes through tears. He was earnest, and we didn't want to disappoint. He used to read the Book of Mormon to us each individually with that pleading voice, expounding every few verses, desperate that we would have a spiritual experience.

Around the time I was caught with the girl, my dad and I finished the Book of Mormon together. It taught that anyone could know the truth of the book if they prayed after reading. *That* was the moment my dad was trying to get to, the moment he wanted to have. We were at his par-

been so long maybe I did, though now I couldn't claim to feel anything in that moment more than the desire to do something else.

He smiled. "That's the Holy Spirit testifying to you that the Book of Mormon is true."

I just wanted to get out of that room, away from that weight of expectation, and go play with Mike, or be by myself for a while, or even hang out with my dad if he wanted to do something not churchy. Still, I would use that experience for years as a confirmation that the book was true because that's what my dad told me. Later, when I would feel inspiration from other places—literature, music, documentaries—that weren't scripture, I would become confused again. Was the Spirit the pressure in the room and at church, or was it what I felt when I read and listened to worldly things and when I was alone? Where I differed most from my father on this point was that I never even considered giving up my art and music and books. They gave me the comfort I needed and much more solace and peace than the Book of Mormon did.

Sometimes I think of my uncle's dirty room. I think of my mother crying in the living room and my dad crouching, telling me I was making Jesus cry. I think of all the intimidation he must have felt from his own long line of adults, before he passed it all down to us. For a long time, I never doubted what my parents told me about god, myself, and the world. It was only through the pain of growing older and living more that the intensity of their beliefs lost sway in my mind, and I began to decide for myself how to be and how to act rather than let myself be led.

I developed stomachaches as a child. Bad ones. They would stop me mid-conversation with my mother and bring me to my knees in the kitchen. They would make me cry mid-sentence and derail anything I was doing. When I felt them coming on, I learned to crouch with my arms crossed over my abdomen to prepare. The doctor said it was nerves, that it was common, that many four- and five- and six-year-olds got them, it was no big deal. To me it was. They came with the growing feeling that whatever I did I would end up being a disappointment, the unease that deep down I was bad and there was nothing I could do about it. I was always suspecting that I'd done something wrong, though never quite sure what. The stomachaches were another secret weighing on me. They grew until my soul was impossible to unburden, until it was sagging and threatening to crack.

A study from the University of North Carolina School of Medicine on abdominal pain in children suffering abuse reports that "among children in the study, sexual abuse preceded or coincided with abdominal pain in 91 percent of cases. In addition, in children who said they recalled ever being abused physically, psychologically or sexually, there was a statistically significant association between abuse and both abdominal pain and nausea/vomiting." Maybe my stomachaches were a sign of my own abuse. Maybe I hurt myself by making Jesus cry. Maybe it was nothing at all. According to the adults around me at the time, sometimes a stomachache was just a stomachache.

These days, my dad has the sunken, green eyes of someone who is perpetually tired and in pain. I used to believe this was a symbol of his devotion to his family, of his fight to be what he needed to be. The eyes I see now belong to a man who struggles without reason, without remembering what he struggles for. I see the fear that's been there all along. I see a man who lost a son he never really knew or understood and therefore could never really appreciate. There has to be an awful pain in that, in losing a child whom you know by natural and moral and godly laws you're supposed to love but whom you mostly ever seem to feel disdain for and anger at and distance toward. There's brokenness there that's tragic and complicated. I wouldn't wish it on him or anybody.

Our home was rife with that fear—so much so that I didn't learn to recognize it until after I had moved away and stopped using drugs and decided to try to clean the terrors out of my own life. The memories of those incidents with that girl and in that apartment and those neighbors haunted me. I was wracked with more shame and guilt than I had ever allowed myself to acknowledge before. I wanted to know more about those people, more about what my parents didn't say to me back then. I assumed my parents were embarrassed—I was embarrassed—and knew my dad wouldn't handle my inquiries well. He would become angry or sick, so I spoke to my mother first. She didn't wear her pain like he did, and despite her own difficulties, she was stronger than him in many ways.

I read in an article by Beverly Engel in *Psychology Today* that it takes most people an average of twenty-four years to disclose traumas. It took me over thirty to talk to my parents. That delay might stem from faulty thinking and misunderstanding, but I think sometimes it's because we know exactly what to expect if we disclose: more trauma. Almost a year into the pandemic, months with no job, I lay on the living room floor of my apartment complex, stared up at the ceiling, and thought. I was no longer on drugs and was unemployed and stuck in my apartment, nowhere to go. My memories took advantage of this and flooded my head. I spent hours poring over articles online to try to understand. That *Psychology Today* article listed reasons why adult victims of child abuse don't disclose: confusion, denial, fear, shame, self-blame, and a need to protect the perpetrator. The same reasons appeared in almost every article I could find.

I walked out to the third-floor balcony of my tiny apartment in the desert heat with my phone, sat on the dusty rug, breathed deeply, and FaceTimed my mother. She smiled at me from the screen. This would be the last time

I'd feel she was genuinely pleased to hear from me. We spoke about inane topics for a while. As I looked at the small woman I was about to disturb—after she'd lived for so long with her own life's worth of secrets—I almost lost my nerve.

She froze when I finally brought up the incidents with the girl. "Look, I wanted to come to you because I know Dad can't handle these types of things," I said into the phone. No jokes now. This was something she would only ever get angry at me about. Or sad.

"Oh, no," she said in a still, almost toneless voice. "Your father would never be able to talk about anything like this. But I'm sorry. I can't help you. My memory is so bad . . ."

"But you do remember the upstairs neighbors?" I asked.

She fidgeted and squirmed. "Yes. I remember the little girl and boy and the baby."

"And you remember I kept getting in trouble for playing sexually explicit games with that girl?"

"I think I remember something like that." She shook her head. "But, sweetie, it was a long time ago, and I remember almost nothing."

"I remember I was caught." It was over a hundred degrees out on the balcony. Dry. The kind of heat that burns the eyes. I was sweating in the open air, but it was better than being enclosed inside. "I remember you crying about it. I remember you crying when Dad lectured me about it after."

"I only cried because I could just never imagine children ever playing games like that," she said. "*If* I did cry. I don't remember."

"You do remember crying or you don't? I just want to know more about the neighbors, what kind of people they were. If you think they were the types that would mess with a kid."

"Not really," she said quickly. "I mean, I watched those kids all the time because their mother and her crazy boyfriend or boyfriends would fight and it was loud and probably scary for those kids up there. But I don't think they would do anything that was like child abuse. Sometimes kids just get curious and explore. It was probably nothing. It was probably not a big deal. That's all it was. I can't help you, sweetie. I'm sorry."

Confusion was my mother's most used tool. I've heard "Are you sure that really happened?" all my life. Or "I don't remember it the way you do." I don't know how many times she's said, "I doubt you remember your grandpa's mother," even though I was twelve when she died. Or, "I'm sure you don't remember our neighbors in Puerto Rico," even though I would have been fifteen.

Beverly Engel writes that many people question whether they experienced abuse because of their memories. "They may have only vague memories or no memories at all, just a strong suspicion . . . Some people will even doubt the memories they do have, fearing that 'I'm just imagining' or 'I'm making this up.'" My mother wanted nothing more than for me to be imagining, making it up. She did what she could to shut down what she didn't want to know. I'd wanted to believe it would be different, but I knew it wouldn't be. I'd gone out on a limb after decades of feeling shame and fear, and for what?

I hung up and walked inside to the air-conditioning. I got back on the floor and watched images form from the popcorn texture in the ceiling, as if some new, important detail, some epiphany, would appear there, as if I had the capacity to project my own ghosts there to examine them. If I stare at any pattern long enough, shapes and faces appear. Back in Post Falls, I used to have what I thought were fever hallucinations whenever I had a temperature— which was often. They would start as static. A growing sense of dread would approach me from my left and right, descending on me from the ceiling. Sometimes I'd feel my hair being pulled as the static formed into two ever-shifting faces—a man and a woman who'd rage at me. I could not hide. Those screaming faces followed me even with my eyes closed. Their noise tumbled through me, shaking the room. I'd cower, unable to move, except to tuck into myself and try not to cry for fear it would stoke the figures' wrath. If I could manage to get up, I'd go to my parents' room, but I usually didn't want them to know. I'd just lie there praying it would pass. *That's* what I remembered, not those brawls from the upstairs neighbors. When I learned about the fighting, those fever visions of the screaming couple made sense. It wasn't all in my head.

Whether she had intended to or not, my mother confirmed that there were fights she could hear above us, that
there was a little girl, that there were games, that my
mother did cry because of them. It wasn't a dream, which
meant maybe the other memories also weren't dreams. I
was afraid I'd invented the whole thing—but I never forgot
how a couple of days after the last time we were caught,
when that little girl came to see if I wanted to play, I yelled
at her and told her my parents didn't want me playing
with her anymore. I cried when I heard her wailing behind
the door after I slammed it. I never wanted to make anybody sad, ever. But I made Jesus cry the way I made that
little girl cry on the other side of the door, the way I made
my mother cry as I straightened my belt in the hot living
room at that time of day when the sun goes down.

I was caught with a boy once too, in Post Falls, though I
knew I couldn't talk to my mom about that. With him it
was only once. The game, this time, had been my idea—
I was the one who'd already been taught and wanted to
teach someone else. I was the one mesmerized even then
by sex, without knowing what sex was or why touching
felt the way it did. The boy's father was a painter, maybe a
construction worker. Their house was littered with empty
beer cans. Dog shit leaked into the carpet. We were caught
under his bed next to a pile of shit. His younger sister
caught us (her face was scarred because she'd supposedly

fallen out of her father's truck while they were driving alone on a gravel road one night).

Their father told me what we had been doing was wrong. I stood straight, trying not to show emotion. "You afraid of me?" he yelled.

I nodded my head yes.

"Why? I'm your father's friend. Why are you afraid of me?"

I could only think of my father asking me that same question when I wouldn't tell him what I was doing in the basement, or anytime he got angry with me for whatever I might have done: broken a door or a cup, called someone a name, stolen a toy, fought with Mike. It was the question asked anytime I lowered my head or got too silent, the question that came up when he felt bad about showing his anger. If I told the truth about why I was afraid of him, my dad would tell me how sad that made him or how silly I was. If I said I wasn't scared, I'd be asked why I wouldn't speak. I was learning that sometimes it was easier to stay silent. So that was what I did.

I was terrified of my friend's dad and sobbed after he told my parents. In front of his friend, my father explained once more the difference between secret and sacred, which to me seemed almost the same except that the sacred seemed more important, which meant I was dirtier somehow. It would be a long time until the word "sacred" would have a positive connotation in my mind, but by then it meant something far different than the church meaning.

It came to mean real, human experience and connection to me. The days and nights I hung out with Mike and our friends in Idaho and Puerto Rico and Florida were sacred. The memory of the three days I spent on the floor in the packed Miami-Dade jail with rats skittering around our legs and in the corners was sacred—horrible, but sacred because it meant something and because it changed me. The walks Veronica and I take together are sacred. My meditation is sacred. Learning is sacred. Rules and lectures on chastity have always been fear. On the ride home in the dark, I looked out at the passing lights of the other cars as we drove through the forest. I imagined shapes like stories between the trees. On his better days or evenings, my dad had read *The Hobbit* to me, and I imagined the woods full of hobbit holes in the shadows. Could I run away and find my way there? If I looked hard enough into the night, I could transport myself to a place and time in which I wouldn't feel so filthy, a place that separated me from what others referred to as reality.

We were raised by denial, our home bathed in it, infecting everything we did. Of course when I tried to talk to my parents about Post Falls, denial would still reign. "Like dissociation," Engel says, "denial is a defense mechanism . . . But denial can also prevent us from facing the truth and can continue way past the time when it served a positive function."

The next time I heard from my mother after our conversation on the balcony was during a family Zoom meeting. She acted as if I hadn't called her the week before. The square on my computer showing where my parents lived with one of my younger brothers, his wife, and their daughter was dark. Their apartment was dim and cramped, windows closed. I knew it was stuffy, the same as any of the houses or apartments we lived in growing up. Everyone moved like shadows on the screen. My youngest brother joined the call from New Jersey, his black hair down to his shoulders, laughing when my dad complained that none of his sons looked like good respectable church members. My sister called in from her bed, her children running around and jumping in front of her from time to time. My brother spoke about politics and movies and history. My sister talked about her kids. Mike wasn't there. Mike was in prison. My mother nodded to whatever my sister said, and my dad sat back in his chair making puns.

My brother was walking around outside, and behind him the trees and apartments seemed to walk with him.

"Hey, those apartments look like where we used to live in Post Falls," I said, smiling.

My mom's silhouette froze. The sudden stillness seemed to seep through our collective devices. Everyone was on edge as if a wire had been tripped.

"It's crazy," I continued. "I've actually just been thinking of that place." My mother was visibly terrified. "Dad, do you remember our neighbors?"

"My memory is so bad, son." He sounded scared too, though I couldn't see him. I was certain my mother hadn't told him about the conversation we'd had. I was certain she had been too scared for him.

"Do you remember the landlady?" I said. "The one with the baby who died?"

"Vaguely," he said from the dark.

"We lived in number one," I said, trying to make him remember. "The neighbors who had baby twins and who were always smoking weed lived across the hall and a little up the stairs in number two, and the little girl and her brothers and their mom lived right above us in number three."

"I don't know how you can remember all that," he said, still not visible. "You were so little."

"You were so little, honey," my mom said, repeating her husband as she so often did.

I listed everything I could to prove I did remember, so they would believe me when I brought up the details that counted. "We had a wood fence outside the building where the neighbor's blackberries and raspberries would creep through. I got splinters on that fence and was told not to play next to it, but I did anyway. My friend Scotty and I used to wander the field behind the building and break windows on the old school bus with rocks until we got in trouble and had to be checked for the lice that were abundant out there. Mike and I once stayed a few hours at the neighbors' apartment in number two, and they smoked so much weed that their apartment was full of smoke, and Scotty and I crawled on the ground and pretended we were in a fire while Mike played with the twins. Mike remembers that too."

"Ugh, I remember Scotty," my mom said, unable to control her disdain for the kid she felt was always getting me into trouble.

"Joia!" my dad said. "There is no way they can remember any of that! Michael was a baby, for Pete's sake!"

"Dad," I said. "We left there when I was seven and Mike was four. I can remember some things from when I was four. In fact, my first memories are from Brazil when I was three. I'm sure there are things from Post Falls he remembers."

"Well," he said. "I don't even know why you need to bring it up and remember those things."

My other siblings didn't chime in. Post Falls had been before any of them. The only ones who had been alive, the only ones who were old enough, were Mike, me, and our parents.

"You know, sweetie," my mom's silhouette said, "I don't think any of your problems came from you kids playing in Post Falls. Your problems came from school because your teachers didn't understand you and because you were bullied."

My siblings squinted and raised their eyebrows.

"Mom," I sighed, "I've never been bullied in my life. At least not by other children my age."

"Well, you and Michael had problems because of school and bad influences," she said.

One of my nephews put his face in the camera and said, "Hi, Grandma!"

"Oh, he's so cute," my mom said.

The conversation shifted. I never attended another family Zoom meeting.

Shortly before he died, Mike told me that one of his first memories took place in Post Falls. He followed me up a tin-roofed toolshed in the back of the complex. The shed was hot, and it was summer, and our group of friends took turns jumping off it into the grass below. I remember it too. It hurt my feet, and I learned that it hurt less if I rolled when I hit the ground. I don't remember Mike jumping, but I'm positive he did, with a four-year-old's grin plastered on his face. He'd chipped his front tooth somewhere in Post Falls, running up another neighbor's stairs. The neighbors whose apartment was full of smoke were eventually kicked out by the landlords, who lived across the street, for using drugs. The landlord's family consisted of a tall—everyone seemed tall then—thin, anxious mother with dark circles under her eyes, a father I don't remember ever seeing, a little blond boy my age, a little blond girl younger than me, and a baby who was sick all her short life and died one day. After that, the anxious mother started looking dead herself. When the weed-smoking couple and their twins were evicted, they called Mike over to them and gave him a dime to tell the bereaved landlady to go fuck herself.

"Fuck yeah, I did," Mike said over the prison phone. "It was a dime, man, and I was like four. I didn't even know why I got in trouble for that, and I didn't care. I had a fucking dime."

Mike never knew about the other, older boy in the shared apartment garage, because I never told him about it. He would have been way too young to understand, as was I, and I never told anybody. But I know it happened. I don't remember who the boy was, but I know that unlike the construction worker's son, this one wasn't a friend. I was five or so, and I think he was nine and somehow connected to the older brother of the little girl I played those games with. She was terrified of him. I was too. He'd heard about our games—or maybe witnessed them. I don't know how he got me into the storage space. Probably with the promise of a toy. I remember dust everywhere and the swinging, yellow lightbulb when the door closed as he said, "Take off your pants."

By that time, I'd learned the games were bad. I'd yelled at the girl through the door and told her we weren't going to play them anymore. I'd gotten in trouble for playing with the construction worker's son. But now I said nothing. Or I don't remember speaking.

"I want to try something," the older boy said.

The boxes dug into my back as I lay against them with my pants down, the boy rubbed against me, there was a mixture of fear, excitement, disgust, and shame. I was bad. I knew better than to talk. I never told anyone.

Their family left the storage space open one day not long after that. I found a few plastic *Ghostbusters* stencils in there and took them. When my parents saw me playing with them at church, they asked where I'd gotten them. I was scolded for stealing. My parents asked how I would feel if they were my toys that someone else had stolen, and though I didn't want to, I returned them. I slid them in the storage through the space between the door and the concrete.

At some point, my friend Scotty and I were playing with a broom by that unit door, slipped, and pierced the door with the handle. It popped through the wood with a satisfying crunch. We grinned at one another and took turns pretending the broom was a spear and the door a dragon or some kind of enemy we could slay if we plunged holes in it. I kept ramming, knowing I would get in trouble later, not caring.

"Many people think of childhood sexual abuse as being an adult molesting a child," Engel writes. "But childhood sexual abuse also includes an older child molesting a younger child."

I didn't know what was happening to me in that storage unit, but I knew it didn't feel right. For years I told myself it was just kids playing, feeling like I had done something wrong, like I was perverted and weird. Between two kids, who is the abuser? "Add to this the shame associated with being involved with something that the child knows is taboo. Sometimes a child also feels shame when her body 'betrays' her by responding to the touch of the perpetrator." My body had responded, so I had always figured I was bad. I never forgot, and for years as a kid when I remembered how my body reacted to that event and the others with the girl and with the other boy under the bed, I felt wrong. My thoughts made me bad. My reactions made me bad, and I couldn't stop them. Shame has always been a tool for the devout. "The feeling of shame can be one of the most powerful deterrents to a victim disclosing having been abused." There were only ever two options for me: expose my shame and almost inevitably have more shame piled on, along with ridicule and punishment, or bottle it up.

When I was nine, in another city, I shut myself in the living room closet in the cool dark, sat cross-legged on top of jackets and shoes and coat hangers. I tried to stop the flood in my head. I became frantic because I couldn't distinguish between what god wanted me to do and what Satan wanted. It wasn't the cartoon-demon-and-angel-on-my-shoulders trope. It was polarizing, garbled thoughts

brawling and thrashing against one another. Each decision I made was confused. No matter what I did, I couldn't
stop feeling bad all the time. Worst of all, I was still making Jesus cry.

I was a chronic masturbator and had been since at least
that time in which I played those games with that girl,
a shame and sin born of shameful and sinful thoughts. I
would never admit it to anyone. Ever. The first time I came,
I thought I'd broken myself and was sick and shocked and
became convinced the mess I'd made was my punishment.
I wondered if I had to tell anybody about what had come
out of me, if I would have to go to the hospital, but in the
end I kept quiet. By the time I was in that closet, I no
longer knew which thoughts were mine and which had
come from god. Or the devil. I had been taught that sinners didn't get to hear god. Maybe god was trying to reach
me, but I couldn't hear under all my filth. Maybe I'd never
heard god's voice to begin with.

I thought-screamed at the confusion in the dark, "I'm
not listening to you anymore! Any of you! Shut up!" My
thoughts didn't cease, but I was determined to stop giving them credence. "You're being ridiculous," came one in-
trusive thought. "Get off the floor. If anyone ever saw you
there, they'd think you were a lunatic." "So, I won't tell
anyone," I said. "Plus, everyone already thinks I'm weird.
I bet they wouldn't say anything." "Listen to me," came
another thought. "I am god." "I don't care," I said. "You're
confusing. Stop."

At youth groups they kept repeating how sexual sin was the worst sin next to murder until it almost became a refrain anytime they wanted to talk to us about chastity. It needed to be confessed to and dealt with immediately, and if it wasn't, we would grow to regret it. But I knew confession wouldn't take care of the urges and needs. I would still be expected to face and temper them in a way I knew I couldn't. Doing so would only lead to me lying again. Why tell the truth in the first place and risk perpetual suspicion thereafter? Drugs were bad and alcohol was bad, but touching ourselves and others was worse. Boys were disrespecting and dirtying girls' bodies if they sought any kind of sexual encounter—even if their sexual encounter was the girl's idea or something she also enjoyed. Us boys were tasked with protecting women so that they could retain their cleanliness and worthiness and honor as unsullied servants of god. David O. McKay, one of the presidents of the church, taught, "Your virtue is worth more than your life . . . Conduct yourselves seemly and with due regard, particularly you young boys, to the sanctity of womanhood. Do not pollute it." Girls touching girls was bad and boys touching boys was even worse, so much worse that there's another chapter in *The Miracle of Forgiveness* that's dedicated to homosexuality called "Crime Against Nature," in which Kimball states, "Homosexuality is an ugly sin, repugnant to those who find no temptation in it." Those behaviors would damn us. Church people taught us that the unworthy and the condemned included gay people; drug addicts; those unable to control their carnal thoughts or impulses; fornicators; Muslims (who we were taught were terrorists—period); the ancient Jews, who lost their way and killed Christ (but were still blessed); people who spoke out against the church or their families in any way; and attention-seeking liberals. Most of the messages, and the way they were taught, weren't official church doctrine. Local leaders were just members, ordinary people who were unpaid. They often, and especially in Idaho, were constitutionalists and survivalists and at the very least far-right conservatives, and they taught scripture alongside their political views.

After a while in that closet, I quit reacting to the answers my mind threw at itself, trying to roll the words away as they hit me instead of focusing on them. I focused instead on not paying attention, only concentrating on the dark, hearing the nothing and stillness coming from the space around me until I didn't hear the words in my head and only felt them crashing and rolling into one another as if above me, until I was alone with the quiet underneath the confusion. "I don't care what they say," I thought to the quiet dark, "even if one of those voices is god." Inside the space was still, as if to say, "Okay." As if to say, "Do what you have to do." I cried like the child I was. The stillness loved me, because it didn't expect anything I couldn't give. When I finally opened the door and walked out, the brightness spilling from the windows was warm and fuzzy.

I think people have an innate need for what some call spirituality, others call inspiration, others call humanity. Spirituality for me is about accessing that quiet I found, which I reached through what I came to learn was meditation. All I know is that when I feel it, I come to the realization that we are all connected through life, death, and time, and what I find there always tends to be love and a drive to keep trying. I've only ever reached that quiet by searching inward. I've only ever reached it by accepting truths for what they are, like knowing that Mike's dead, that I will be one day too, that nothing lasts, and that's okay because I am not the center of the universe but am still a part of it. I can't reach that stillness when I have a crowded and nervous mind obsessing over whether I've obeyed the right rules or not, or when I've been strung out and out of control on drugs. I've never been denied my concept of spirituality because I did or did not jack off. It's never been less because I had premarital sex. If anything, that quiet has been one of my only true constants. That said, it has been a journey and I still can't feel it all the time, only when I'm able to concentrate, and that was the same when I was a kid in that closet. I quit obsessing like I was over the rules, but that didn't mean the expectations others had for me didn't have any sway. It didn't mean I was no longer confused. It just meant that I had found some respite for when everything got worse.

For years I tried to pretend I was okay. It was the least I could do, I thought. I didn't want anyone to be sad or scared. I knew the dangers of showing an open wound. I understood that my family didn't know how to function if their lives didn't have a simple formula that worked it all out for them. I thought it was my responsibility to stay quiet because I knew how intense my problems would be for church leaders and my parents if they knew. I first read parts of *The Miracle of Forgiveness* when I was maybe fourteen, and like many traumatizing moments, I remember exactly where I was. I was in Puerto Rico, the upstairs of the house a mix between family room with the TV, laundry room, and computer room, where I would spend hours looking at pornography terrified that someone would spot me, and there were books on a shelf against the wall. I was shirtless and brown because I spent most of my time in the sun on my skateboard or smoking on the streets with Mike and our friends. I was looking for something to read and came across the book my father had raved about as being one of the best and most spiritual books he'd ever read. Despite my drug use and what I considered to be abnormal sexual appetites that meant I was weak, I was always after spiritual experiences, so I thought I'd give it a try. Being the adolescent I was, I looked at the index and went

Grievous sin or virtue. There was no in-between, no nuance, no room for anything but the rules. Because of that,
I knew there was something wrong with me. I was positive I felt the spirit just like my dad said I would when I
read scriptures and prayed and meditated alone, though
almost never at church—the semiannual General Conferences usually left me either bored when I was younger, a
mix between spiritual high and terror at my sins when I
was a teenager, peace for a short while as a young adult,
which eventually led to a mixture of hopeful longing and
sadness. At a church camp I went to when I was fifteen
and lived in Puerto Rico, the couple giving a lecture on
chastity gave each of us a sucker. They had us unwrap
them and put them in our mouths but ordered us not to
chew them while they spoke on cleanliness. When they
told us to take the suckers out of our mouths, give them
to the person sitting to our right, and suck on them, I took
my purple-haired friend's, and I did as I was told. She and
I had shared joints and pipes and food, but I really did it
to see the look on the leaders' faces. A couple of other confused kids followed suit, but most looked down in disgust.

"You weren't supposed to do it! It's to illustrate what
it's like when you sin, how sins can change you, take something away that you may never get back." It was a lesson
on the importance of staying sexually pure until marriage.
Otherwise, your spouse will get a used sucker. Kimball
wrote about chastity, that "once given or taken or stolen
it can never be regained. Even in a forced contact such as

rape or incest, the injured one is greatly outraged . . . It is better to die in defending one's virtue than to live having lost it without a struggle." The peace I had found in that closet had never said anything remotely similar to that, but I didn't know if I could trust it because I knew this was what I was supposed to believe. That quiet had told me that I was in god's hands, or the universe's, and that I was okay. How could god have me in his hands if I was infected with sexual thoughts, memories, desires, and I habitually and compulsively participated in onanism and what was turning into serious drug use? I knew god couldn't abide any unclean thing. I didn't know whether to believe the memories I had regarding those sexual games. I didn't know if they counted. What I did know is that while at that time I hadn't yet had sex, I would the moment I had the chance, and I wouldn't wait until I was married either. By the time I did finally have sex, no matter how I tried, I felt no remorse at all despite not being married—and as it turns out I didn't feel like I was polluting the one I was with either.

"Well, fuck," I thought as that couple at camp spoke. "I'm no better than a sucked sucker, and I don't even have the privilege of sharing my sin with anyone."

What Kimball had written seemed brutal to me. I knew I was supposed to believe it was right, but instead I decided not to think about it at all. Instead, I decided to dedicate the rest of my time at the camp to finding someone who had some weed. No one did.

I've sat in church-leader offices being interviewed about my worthiness more times than I can count. I've lied more times than I can count. When old men I hardly knew asked me with gravity and importance if I was keeping morally clean in both actions and thoughts, if I had ever touched a girl or boy inappropriately, if I ever touched myself inappropriately, I would look him in the eye and say, "No." It hurt to lie. They told me I was betraying god if I did. I would feel ill, and the room would spin. I would get dizzy. But I never broke eye contact, always matching the solemnity in front of me, conscious of my face and movements until I was sure nothing was giving me away, and they would move on to the next question.

I would spend nights wondering if they knew, if god told them, told my parents. With each interview it became easier to lie. By the time I was deep into drugs I could lie without even realizing I was doing it. What became most important was that no one ever knew the secret me, the sacred me. No one could know because no one could understand. They would try to fix what they couldn't, and then become frustrated. It was better for me to be silent. I learned to adjust my reactions and expressions with the same fixation I had to learn to adjust my pants as a child.

My dreams are filled with sexual infidelities followed by whatever partner I'm with in the dream, woman or man, reminding me of how we'd fucked before, long ago, and though I'm not supposed to remember, I do in those moments. They tell me, or I tell me, we need to keep what we'd done secret—not the present but the past—that I'd better not let it out.

I have a notebook from when I was a teenager filled with similar dreams. I had two, until my mother read one and confronted me about what she considered filth written in it. I knew it had to be particularly bad since it was so rare that she confronted me about most things. I burned it because it had been defiled by someone who didn't understand. The notebook I kept houses scrawled dreams of abused girls my age who I tried to help. I told them I was taking care of my abuse with drugs and that they should too. It was better than suffering.

Veronica often told me that I moaned and cried in my sleep. Those feelings discharge themselves in real life too, even now, halfway through my thirties. One day, after someone I love confided in me about a traumatic experience she'd had as a child, I had an episode. Veronica and I were getting ready to go for a walk, and I'd just texted my mother about something mundane when it started: a sorrow creeping in. Powerful, nameless, bad. A physical pressure weighed on me as I tried to put my shoes on. I was going to shatter unless I said something out loud. I turned to my wife and said, "Nothing matters. It just feels like nothing matters. Everything is off." She looked concerned and confused but not surprised. A few minutes before, I'd been consoling *her* over something. I chalked up my sudden intense mood shift to our financial situation, to her not feeling well, to job uncertainty, to anything I could think of. But I knew that old untamable despondency had managed to break through.

We left the apartment and walked through the parking lot as the desert sun started to set. It was that deep-red time of day, and it was cool spring out. The dirt on the asphalt was orange. We passed a yellow lighter on the ground with a thumbtack stuck in the bottom; I remembered that abandoned school bus in the empty field behind my Post Falls apartment where Scotty and I used to play after kindergarten, breaking the windows with rocks, messing with lighters we'd find on the ground as we walked over orange dirt under deep-red light. That time of day can leave me sick for hours after it's gone. On our walk, my angst was building. The people outside their apartments seemed sad and pointless. We walked by a bent-over old woman holding on to three leashed dogs with her right hand while smoking a cigarette with her left. "She's in such bad health," I thought as we passed. "She's in such bad health and the smoking will make her deteriorate faster and she lives in this shitty apartment and I bet all she has are those dogs and she'll die and it won't have mattered. Her whole life, like mine or anybody's, won't have mattered." I remembered the box of pornographic magazines Scotty and I found in his mother's closet and how embarrassed his mother was when she told my parents that she had caught us going through them. I remembered the acrid smell of spilled beer and those old stomachaches.

There was no way my parents were going to believe me if I tried to say something again. I'd always known that. I knew it as it was happening. I knew it when I was ten and walked the beaches with Mike in Georgia on a family trip, tempted to take the cigarettes and booze unattended on scattered tables. I knew it at twelve as I tried to look over my shoulder while watching porn on the family computer, using a dial-up modem and floppy disk to save images. I knew it when I was fifteen and getting high and drunk in the park until three in the morning with Mike. I knew it when I was in my twenties, through my years with Mike on dope. I knew it when I was thirty-six and a few years off drugs.

My worsening nightmares and sudden depressions and anxieties were getting to my wife. "We have to do something," she said. We didn't have insurance or money to see a therapist, so she suggested a letter to my parents. I wasn't sure about the idea, but after days of discussion and long talks, we decided to write a letter. Veronica insisted on trying it herself, knowing my family wouldn't take me seriously. We wrote three drafts together, detailing what I remembered and the difficulties it was causing our marriage.

I imagined my family clamming up as they read it. Engel writes about the abusee's need to protect the abuser, because sometimes the abuser is someone they love. This isn't my case, but that doesn't mean I never had to protect anyone. I had to protect my family from my memories, from every reality they never wanted to see. I had to protect them from themselves.

I told Veronica I doubted the letter would work. She did too. "But maybe they'll surprise you," she added. "The only thing to do is try. But they probably won't listen to either one of us."

We sat at our small kitchen table, contemplating how to deliver what we'd written. I could talk to them directly, but I was sure they wouldn't listen. I could give them the letter and wait, but they might never get back to me. In the end, we gave the letter to another family member we figured my parents would listen to and respect more. That way they had someone to be accountable to, someone who could verify the letter had been given and read, let them process the information, and then talk to me after.

I don't know what exactly happened when they read the letter because I wasn't there—and I regret that. What I understand is that my dad walked out before my family member was done speaking, and my mother told her she was crazy for listening to me.

My mom texted me the day after reading the letter to ask if I wanted to set up a time to talk to them a week later. Just me and them—without my wife. By then I had no hope left, and I was so angry not only that Veronica wasn't included but that she was specifically not invited, as if it would be easier to discard me, convince me nothing was wrong, if I was alone. They didn't want her around, as if she didn't matter, as if she hadn't reached out to them as well. I'm not sure if it was a tactic to make it easier for them to dismiss my experiences and what I'd said, but it felt that way.

"Sure," I texted back.

That night, as I was getting into bed, my phone rang. It was my mother. I got up and walked into the living room in the dark. It took her fifteen minutes of banal pleasantries before she asked me to call my dad, who was out driving. He was just having such a hard time, she said. He had no idea that I could ever have any of those types of problems my family member told them about. It was just so hard on him. She was so worried about him. "It's just that he loves his children so much," she said, "that sometimes it makes him sick."

I paced as she spoke, wanting to hate them, wanting them to understand the damage their emotional coercion had on me, how it held me hostage. What she said roused an anger I had kept suppressed for years. Still, I couldn't hate them. In that moment, and in every memory I have of them, now and in perpetuity, they look, sound, and act like children—more scared than I was—and I became acutely aware of the generations of parental manipulation that had been piled on the both of them, and I felt sorry for them. Responsibility came down on me again, like when I was asked to watch my siblings, or when I knew I had to hide from my parents what they didn't want to see.

"It's just that you understand your daddy so well," my

mom said, after spending half an hour talking about how upset he was. "Could you call him and tell him that you're okay and see how he's doing?" she asked again.

"Yeah." I wanted more than anything for her to get off the phone. "Fine, Mom," I said. "Let me hang up so I can call Dad. Okay?

"But you know what?" I said before hanging up. "I want you to know, this is why I've never told you anything that's ever happened with me. You've always said I was so secretive and always lied to you guys. This is why. I've always known that in most cases, and with most anything even remotely serious, Dad would overreact and stomp off and you would ignore it. Just, before I call Dad, I wanted you to know this is why."

She was silent for a moment. "Mmmm," she said, the way she did when I was a kid and she didn't want to hear what I was saying, so she'd change the subject with a non sequitur. "You know," she said, "I know you're okay and that nothing happened to you as a kid, because the Holy Ghost would have told me. One time, when you were a baby, I broke a glass cup. I thought I cleaned it all, and in those days, you used to crawl all over the place and follow me everywhere. I knew. I could feel that I had to check in your mouth. I checked, and there was a huge piece of glass in your mouth. The Holy Ghost told me to look. And your daddy too. When you got in trouble that one time in Florida, you know—"

"When I was arrested," I said, and smiled despite the

fresh rage bubbling up. She couldn't even say it, like she was eight and trying to describe a curse word without pronouncing it, as if not saying a word would mean it wasn't real, as if denial could obliterate anything.

"Yes," she said. I could envision her on the other end of the phone closing her eyes. "When that *thing* happened. Your daddy knew there was a problem. He said, 'Joia, something went wrong with David.' So, I know nothing could have ever happened to you because the Holy Ghost would have told us."

There was no point in arguing. I don't know if she even had the ability to hear me at that point. But I still wanted to be next to her. I wanted to pull my shirtsleeve up to expose the three-inch gash in the back of my shoulder and ask her when the Holy Ghost told her about that. When did she discover that I had fallen into that fence in Dorado, Puerto Rico, while skateboarding when I was thirteen and needed stitches that I never got? It was after it was healed, no longer a danger, and *I* showed it to her. The Holy Ghost didn't tell her about that hole in my leg. I did, almost two weeks later, when the infection was unbearable. What did the Holy Ghost say when I came home reeking of weed and booze, when track marks began to grow on my arms? And when I was caught with that little girl and my dad lectured me on being morally clean in that living room in Post Falls while my mother wept, did the Holy Ghost whisper to her then? And if the Holy Ghost did, what did she do about it?

I hung up and called my dad. I sat at my small kitchen

table, eyes closed, my head in my hands, and asked how
he was.

"Perfectly fine. Everybody's healthy at home. I'm just
fine."

"Are you really?"

"Of course," he said. He was out driving alone, and
my voice was coming to him on his car speakers. I could
hear the car running and almost see the streetlights in the
dark. "I just never think about the past, keep my head in
the now, and so I'm always calm and fine."

"I've never known you to ever be calm and fine in your
life," I said. "You're usually nervous and angry."

"Well, that's your perception."

"You know," I said, "I was talking to Mike earlier. We
were talking about our journeys to get and stay off drugs
and what it's meant to us. We were talking about how important it's become to us to fully understand why we feel
the way we do, act the way we do, and we were talking
about the acceptance that comes from a deeper understanding of things. It's like the yoga and exercises I've
been doing. It can be really hard to get through the practice or workout, but after I'm done, I usually feel better
and more able to get through the day, and it's helped me
feel more capable. But I have to go through the hard stuff
first. Just because it's difficult doesn't mean it's not worth
it." I felt saudade for Mike while we'd had that conversation earlier, even then, even before he died. It was like his
absence had been building for a long time, partially be-

cause he was in prison, but also because at that time he'd started to sound tired. It was so unlike him. It was as if he knew he wouldn't be around long, and I loved him so much then and do now, and I knew and know that he always loved me unconditionally, more than I felt my parents did, and certainly more than the church did. Just talking about him gave me peace.

"That's nice that you and Mike were able to talk and have that conversation," my dad said. "But I'm not on heroin, recovering from heroin, or in prison. And I'm fine. Never been better." I could see him with that look he gets, his head high, eyebrows up, haughty and immovable.

"I'm glad you're feeling so good," I said.

And that was that.

I used to feel guilty about Mike's drug problems before he died. I didn't introduce him to drugs. We didn't use together until we'd done it alone first. But I still have survivor's guilt. Why Mike and not me? Why prison and homelessness and death for him, a college education and professional opportunities for me? It was ridiculous to even imagine I was a victim—Mike didn't think of himself that way—and anyone in my family who knew anything about me felt the same way. But reading has taught me I'm not the only one. Engel writes, "'Victim' has become a dirty word in our culture, where victims are often blamed and even shamed . . . Cultural influences like this serve to blame victims rather than encourage a self-compassionate acknowledgment of suffering." I've spent years in drug circles, hearing tweaked-out, drunk, and high people tell me stories about their abuses in tears. Almost all of them were sure to say, "But I'm not a victim." That was Mike's mentality too. Whenever he talked about how horrible and terrifying prison was, he would make sure to say he deserved it. Five years on a four yard for drugs, and he said he deserved it.

But when I told him what was going down between our parents and me, what Mom had said to me over the phone, he said, "Look, man, anything you say I believe. Of course I do. I got your back, brother. Always."

The dream that's soaked with the most dread and panic hit me when I was maybe sixteen. It's not sexual at all. It starts with a girl my age taking me by the hand into her apartment—which looked and felt like the upstairs apartment I knew as a child. I meet and talk with the girl's mother, who offers us a large mason jar of weed. We take it into the girl's dark, crooked room, with wooden beams in triangle shapes like that of a cabin. Her older brother comes in with heroin. We all shoot up. The dark in the room invades my chest, casting a green-gray feel over everything. Somehow Mike is there, as a baby in diapers, as if he had always been with me and I hadn't noticed. The girl's brother shoots him up too. I try to stop him, but I can't. It's so much dope, and Mike is sick. The girl's brother wants to kill Mike so no one will know what he's done. I pick my brother up and run down the stairs, out of the apartment, over broken buildings, until I come to a brick wall that looks blue in the night. Mike is limp and a greenish blue, and I'm sobbing. Our father shows up in a helicopter with a bullhorn asking me what I've done to my brother, what I've done to his boy. While his presence is pure fear, the true terror, the true devastation, was holding my dead brother.

Sometimes silence feels inevitable because the secrets are so far down they forget themselves. Those are the ones that should worry us the most. The things that we abandon, unexamined, have a tendency to decay, have a tendency to spur in us extreme defense mechanisms, like sepsis— a fatal and painful disease in which chemicals in the blood cause inflammation in the organs until a person reaches septic shock and lungs, kidneys, liver fail. The disease that ultimately killed Mike.

I can't say why Mike ever acted as he did or got high or had his long list of toxic relationships. I don't know all of that story, and I never will. What I know is that he told me once about the older neighbor boy in Idaho who told him he wanted to have sex with Mike to see what it felt like, when he was about nine and the boy was twelve. Mike had shaken his head when he told me and laughed it off, making fun of the neighbor and telling me how fucked up it was and how he had run away. What I know is that when my ex-girlfriend, who I had unquestionably fooled around with and therefore sinned with, in Puerto Rico came to hang out at the basketball court with us while we skated, she said as loud as she could that everyone masturbated. And Mike looked up at me with that little brother look and asked if that was true, and it was obvious he needed it to be; I shushed him, waved my hands as if to say I didn't want to talk about it, because I wasn't sure myself. What I know is that Mike hated going to church and quit going despite my father's rage when Mike refused. What I know is that we were both diagnosed with bipolar disorder at different parts of our lives. What I know is that Mike was loving and kind and funny and wild and uncontrollable but also haunted, also stuck, doing whatever he had to do to survive, battling that old hard-core sadness, that empty space within himself that he longed for and never found, until infection took him.

It took me a long time to admit that my sexual experiences were the true source of my shame that reached back as far as childhood and therefore the true source of my drug addiction and self-destructive tendencies. It took me even longer to admit that the shame I felt wasn't my fault. It took me even longer than that to understand that church was one of my biggest and most dangerous triggers. It took me so long because I thought I had to believe that either what the leaders had taught me was right and

I was the only one to blame for my shame, or they were wrong and the child and adolescent me, and the adult I would become, was okay. I would have to accept that my parents were as broken as I was, as traumatized by life as I was, and they didn't have a clue what they were doing. I didn't want that to be true, but it was.

the preacher

There was a preacher who would stand close to the Arizona State University library. He was neatly dressed, tall, always in aviators, and from morning to night he and his followers handed out pamphlets and sermonized nonstop under a tall, yellow sign that read: "Fornicators, Adulterers, Masturbators, Homosexuals, Murderers: Hell." He would preach hellfire into his microphone, voice emanating from the small amplifier at his side, while a crowd gathered around him to argue and watch the spectacle. The preacher never yelled. He was loud. He was offensive. He liked to egg people on, liked making the students who gathered around him angry, making them engage with him. But he never yelled, opting instead to keep a smug, serene, holy smile on his face.

I never interacted with the guy and always made a wide path around his disciples to avoid being inundated with flyers and cards and advertisements for church that I would have had to dodge.

I was a junior, and while I had a 3.8 GPA, I was still getting fired from most jobs, was back on drugs, and feeling out of place as a student. My previous university experience was working landscaping and irrigation at the University of Central Florida, where the Mexican workers and I would make fun of the rich kids in Spanish as we saw them in their fancy cars while we did lines of coke and drank beer on our lunch break, caked in dirt and sweat.

By the time I had moved away from Florida and was attending ASU, Mike was living on the other side of Phoenix but had taken the light rail to go see some concert and stopped by the ASU campus to hang out with me for a few hours. It was on the way, and he had time to kill. I skipped my classes and walked around with him, laughing and talking nonstop like we always did. We were retelling some story about ourselves to each other as we came out of the library. That was when Mike saw the preacher and his sign.

He stopped mid-sentence, looked up at the pastor who was standing on a bench arguing with irate passersby, raised his hands to his mouth, and yelled as loud as he could over the pastor's amplified voice, "Woot, woot, masturbators!"

We continued casually away as the crowd stopped arguing and started laughing.

That was the only time I ever saw that preacher falter.

Bones Worth Breaking

Mike doing a kickflip in Puerto Rico

Despite bruises and dislocations and broken bones and deep gashes that needed stitches, skateboarding saved my life. I knew it as I was skating as a kid. I know it now. It was something Mike and I did together, and Mike—often my only friend through all our family's moves, my only confidant even into adulthood—saved my life too, in ways I wouldn't understand for a long time.

Skateboarding was about outrunning. Outrunning our parents' unhappy lives—our frustrated dad, who followed church rules he didn't seem to want to follow and worked a job he seemed to hate dealing with taxes and financial fraud, and our mother, who lived seemingly bored and away from her familiar culture and homeland most of her adult life. Outrunning whatever misery made them lock themselves away in their rooms when they were home. Outrunning ourselves, our flunking-out of school or being expelled, our mistrust and unease at church and being around church people and hearing them lecture us and our guilt every time we were interviewed about our worthiness. Outrunning the church kids who were nice but whose experiences were so vastly different than ours that we often didn't know how to interact with them, and sometimes they seemed afraid of us and our sins. Outrunning the sadness that was building inside, as wide and unstoppable as the ocean I stared at from the park we skated in Puerto Rico. It was about being desperate and accepting it, thriving within that desperation by deciding which bones were worth breaking for the thrill of some sense of progress. Skateboarding was falling until we didn't.

I learned to ollie—jumping with the skateboard, one of the first-learned and most essential tricks in modern skateboarding—in our low-ceilinged basement in an Idaho winter in 1996, when I was twelve and Mike was nine. We learned on a shared, ten-inch-wide, outdated, heavy board from the eighties, rolling around the wide downstairs area that no longer had carpet because it had flooded the year before when our family had been away for three months in

Georgia on a work trip with our dad. We took turns dodging, or accidentally rolling over and breaking, our sister's toys. I may have cracked a piece of tile. Mike may have cracked another piece. We fell. We hurt ourselves. We got yelled at. We failed for days, but by the time the snow melted and we could skate outside, we could both ollie.

Our skating started in Idaho and Puerto Rico (where we'd move seven months later) and ended in Florida. We never lived in the same place long, but we brought skateboarding with us. I can't remember how we convinced our parents to get us new boards, but we did. We bought them at the only place around at the time, in the shop we went to in Idaho Falls, twenty minutes from the small town where we lived. My first real board was a Hook Ups Nabiki Demon Killer deck with a brown-haired anime girl in a ripped skirt and holding a long sword on a yellow background. I had Grind King trucks, Bones Swiss bearings, and Spitfire wheels. Mike's was a World Industries deck with a devil flame winning a fight against a drop of holy water, Independent trucks, and the same Spitfire wheels as me. With new equipment, not only could we skate, we could do so with ease. I became known as the fearless kid who could clear a garbage can on its side and jump off monuments in church parking lots. Mike became known as the equally fearless little kid who could ollie and was always wherever the older ones were.

There was nothing like sticking a trick after failing a hundred times in a row, nothing like understanding a micromovement until it became second nature. Nothing like the excitement of sticking a kickflip or 360 flip, knowing it was my own feet that made the board spin the way it did, knowing that at least in that setting, I had mastery over something. Mike and I learned to get back on a board the day after setting a crooked arm in a cast, learned from studying skate videos for hours, learned to fall all day for one trick. Those are transferrable skills. Those are skills that, through heroin addiction and job losses and arrests and restarts and mental health collapses, made it possible for us to keep moving.

Our home held a tense current that hung in the air. The chemistry had to be just right for my father *not* to throw a tantrum. He occasionally wanted to play guitar with Mike and me or talk about movies and books, but it seemed that most of the time his desire for connection was overrun by his anger or tiredness or sadness, often set off by Mike but not always—it could have been work or something that happened at a store or a pothole he hit driving home or just that he wasn't feeling well. He could talk to me but almost never to Mike. Sometimes he wasn't angry. Sometimes he seemed more depressed and distant, locking himself in his room when he came home from work to avoid the noise and chaos of having a family. It depended on his mood. Sometimes in the afternoons, when his religious zeal flared up, he'd step into the downstairs living room and yell to everyone in the house as loud as he could that it was prayer and scripture time. Every good Latter-

Day Saint home was supposed to have at least weekly Family Home Evenings that revolved around some type of spiritual activity or discussion. When my dad was on his spiritual highs, he often tried for daily scripture study—which never lasted more than two or three days, and often not even one, before we'd go days or weeks without. With a smile, he would sit on the love seat next to the bookshelf full of the books he collected from the Folio Society, the large-print scriptures open on his lap.

If my mother, sister, three brothers, and I didn't immediately drop what we were doing to run to him, he would call again, "Come on, guys!" The longer we ignored him, the more stressed he would become and the bigger the resulting explosion. If most but not all of the family trudged in with a sigh, we would sit on the couch or love seat while he yelled at the absent—usually Mike, though not always. Anything that didn't result in everyone's immediate compliance would end with my dad throwing something nearby, his scriptures at the wall or to the floor, a steel-toe boot thrown at the chest if we were talking. He'd shout, "Fine! Do whatever you guys want, then!" as he stomped upstairs to his room, shaking the house when he slammed the door, which he broke more than once. The rest of us would roll our eyes and scatter.

I used to get mad at Mike for it, not because he didn't indulge it but because I was the one who was left to console my dad and try to make sure he wouldn't yell and throw things. I wasn't afraid *of* my dad by the time I was a teenager. I was afraid *for* him, afraid he would hurt himself. Mike didn't seem to care about that. He'd only heed the random calls to scripture if I went up to his room. I had to beg him: "Come on, man, are you seriously going to leave me to deal with this shit again? Please help me out?"

My mother shut herself in her closet to read romance books or stood and watched TV while holding our youngest brother on her hip. She nodded with a disinterested yes to whatever we had to say—we had no need to avoid her. She seemed to live in a perpetual state of dissociation, wanting to be gone but with nowhere to go. My dad laughed at her Brazilian accent and ridiculed her ideas. She in turn would make fun of him when he threw his tantrums. Sometimes they would laugh and play when I was younger. But the older they got, the more she seemed to become his emotional caretaker, especially after Mike died, and the less I saw laughter.

She seemed to always be looking for peace and wanted us kids out of the house. She sent our four-year-old brother, John, with Mike and me as we wandered Bayamón and Old San Juan after moving to Puerto Rico. Mike and I took turns watching John while the other hid behind a building or bleachers with a foot-long bamboo pipe I'd made.

Our parents' unhappiness inspired in us a dangerous need for attention. Mike and I were each other's testaments of the collected neglect and hurt we tried to hide from ourselves and everyone else. We needed to be seen, so I kickflipped off baseball dugouts in front of crowds of teenagers into the grass below, or I hardflipped the seven set of stairs during lunch at school, only to get the board taken by a teacher after sticking the landing. Both Mike and I broke our boards heelflipping off bleachers, tumbled down handrails, slammed into mini-ramp edges made of wood. It was all worth it to us for the prize of being noticed. Mike continued to skate in his cast after breaking his right arm. He seemed to wear it for months because he kept breaking the bone over and over. Still in that cast, he once climbed up on a foot-and-a-half-wide, eight-foot-tall brick wall to skate along the top and ollie off.

"Mike, man," I said while walking with my group of friends on the sidewalk below. "That's a bad idea. You're going to fuck up your arm."

"No, brother," he said as he pumped his board forward above me. "I got this shit. Don't worry. Watch."

I watched him, with his straight, coal-black, indigenous hair and brown skin, shorts so baggy the bottoms hung to his ankles, and shoes two sizes too big because he wanted to wear the same size as me. He didn't have the momentum needed when he hit the floor and fell forward onto the arm, still in a cast, but he never let on that it'd hurt.

The best part of skating was that we did it together. Skateboarding became shorthand for a shared childhood and adolescence marked by a unique and unconditional love that we'd never found anywhere else.

John skating and me and Mike standing on top
of a mini ramp in Puerto Rico

But Mike and I weren't satisfied being alone. We also needed the attention we gained from other skaters and kids by hitting up handrails and gaps no one else would try. We spent our evenings, and often entire days, commiserating with the other broken children, with a blunt or a bottle or later pills and needles, gathering anyone who wanted to be around us. Mike and I were magnets who attracted the damaged.

We needed skateboarding in a way we thought was our own. Our group considered ourselves serious skateboarders, a different breed, distinct from those we considered casual skaters. We never saw them hit up the handrails or learn to 180-flip an upright garbage can. We judged them, thought they only skated on the side because it was a fad, and they would quit whenever football or basketball or baseball season started, or their parents told them to, for fear of injuries. We were not like those who only played sports sanctioned by parents and school and church and teachers and coaches. We distrusted adults. They were never on our side.

Now the judgment seems silly, but at the time, skating was our religion. We had our own versions of sanctity, to which we remained devout through the years. We respected people like Carlos, one of our best friends from our neighborhood in Puerto Rico, not because of his skill but because of his tenacity. One day, Carlos, Mike, and I dragged the wooden box I'd made in shop a few blocks out to the basketball court, like we did almost every day. There were two outdoor courts and an indoor one. One of the outdoor courts was slightly higher than the other one, and between it and the sidewalk, behind one of the hoops, was an eight-foot gap of grass that descended slightly until it met the pavement. I had ripped my ankle out of the socket on that gap maybe a year before and had to hobble around on crutches for a month.

We set the box up on the decline, leaving a healthy gap between it and the basketball court, and skated it, flipping the board into slides and grinds down the metal rails I'd put on the sides. We kept pushing the box out farther and farther, testing ourselves and what we could do. Carlos wasn't nearly as experienced as Mike and me, but we egged him on. Mike told him all he had to do was pump faster and not be afraid. Carlos pumped, sped up to the box, ollied up, but not high enough. He caught the back of the board on the edge, fell over the top of the wood, and landed on his right arm, which he'd stretched in front of his face. Mike and I flinched as we calmly walked over to Carlos, who was screaming when he came up. His arm bent into an L two inches below the wrist where the bone was pushed against his dark skin. Some of our group helped him home, while he cried and yelled at us that we shouldn't have told him to try.

"Fuck," Mike said. We lugged the box back home in silence. Mike and I knew how to carry a silence, carry one another's secrets so the other wouldn't have to be always alone, like all the times we stole our dad's pills, or when I told him about my acid trips before he had any himself. When we got home, we didn't say a word, and since no one asked, we didn't need to.

The next day, Carlos was back at our house, arm in a cast, and, ready to get back out and skate, did a kickflip in our driveway. We revered him for that. He didn't have to or want to be home. He chose to hang out with us, to break himself with us, and we loved one another for it. None of us had a better place to be. The strongest bonds I made were with those who didn't have something better to do than to just hang out.

Sometimes, when we were still kids or young adults, after
Mike got in trouble or arrested, our mom would glare at me
and, with all the venom of a soft, angry voice, say, "I never
thought Mike would've ever done any drugs or alcohol or
anything, because he was always with his older brother. I
always thought you were watching him. I never imagined
you boys were ever getting into so much trouble." Her outward anger never lasted long before she went back to her
shows, back to the closet with her romance books, back
to wanting us out of the house. I think she really wanted
me to be responsible, so much that for years she made me
think that I was, made me forget I had been a child too.
Forgetting was what our parents had always done best.

We would hang out in the cool air with my high school
friends 'til three in the morning some nights, drinking Bacardi 151 and smoking weed until we couldn't remember being disappointments to our mother and father and church
and teachers and school, until we could barely stand or
our parents, noticing our absence in the early hours, would
come hunting us down. We could barely stand, but we could
still skate, and we did, in the dark, laughing and dodging
the crack vials on the sides of the concrete. We were broken but magic, because then everything was magic. Everything was before us. We felt we could be broken and
maimed but not killed.

Magic, like everything else, like every sin and every act
of righteousness, had to be paid for. The more complex the

trick, the more impressive, the higher the risk, the greater the price. We paid in time, which bought us skill and comfort on the board. Skill and comfort equaled learning to fall, which diminished the severity of injuries—though they could never be avoided completely. They meant that new ledges and banks and stairs and rails and gaps became attainable. They gave us a love of progression and taught us to cultivate a focus in a way no institution or family setting was ever able to. They meant evolution on our own terms when we couldn't change anything else in service of our survival. We weren't evolving toward anything the rest of the world considered productive because we didn't have the structure for it. Skateboarding provided a structure, a scaffolding, though we didn't know for what.

We often walked some miles, through horrific neighborhoods, to a skate spot in downtown Bayamón. It was a park with a few stairs and a couple of skateable benches where a homeless woman lived. It was the first time I had seen someone in such a miserable state up close like that. She paced barefoot, murmuring to herself in urine-wet sweatpants. I watched her and wondered how she got there, how easy it would be for me or anyone else to end up like that. I feared, though I never let that fear linger long, that the addictions and the sadness that led to the addictions would do something like that to us, cause or bring out insanities that were lingering, hidden in our minds. I wondered how dangerous it was for that woman in the

I want to say I landed this. I probably didn't. Rigby, Idaho

I stopped skating after dropping out of school at sixteen, not because of friends or a girlfriend or a new car—I didn't have any of that. I had slowed down in Puerto Rico as I started driving around with my friends in their cars, smoking more weed, taking more acid and pills, doing more coke, instead of spending as much time on the board, and when we'd moved to Florida, I felt there was something so wrong with me that I just couldn't dedicate myself to it anymore, and it faded from me. My skateboarding was replaced with saudade. Mike stopped soon after, after falling and launching my last skateboard—a Toy Machine Monster deck—down a sewer grating. He avoided telling me for days, and by the time he did, my sadness had grown so much and so far into my substance abuse that I'd already stopped caring.

The last time I skated was half a decade later in Florida, after our little brothers had gotten a couple of boards and a kicker ramp for Christmas. I was coming home from the landscaping job I had after having met up with Mike and our friend K, another former skater, the three of us on methadone. I decided to show our little brothers, nine and eleven, how it was done. I asked to borrow one of their boards, terrified I would end up breaking it and causing them pain but needing to try anyway, still needing to be seen; aimed toward the opposite side of the kicker ramp; and pumped as fast as I could. I was going to kickflip down it—something I would have done with ease five years prior and not floating on methadone—but, like Carlos years before, I caught the back of the board on the ramp, hovered horizontally about five feet in the air for a moment, and came crashing down on my left shoulder with an audible tearing sound. I lay in the middle of the cul-de-sac asphalt, gasping. K and Mike, dirty from work, ran to me and asked if I was okay.

"No," I said, and pulled for air. "I'm not."

I lay there for a long time, and when I went inside the house, my mother asked if I was all right. I told her I was fine, grabbed some ice, and went to sleep.

The next morning, as the methadone was waning, I woke up and ran to the bathroom to puke in the toilet, my body feeling off and twisted from my injury, only going to the doctor when I had to. I had no insurance, so the doctor decided to do nothing about the disconnected clavicle. It became another badly healed wound, worth it in the end, if only for the retelling.

Of course, skateboarding couldn't save us from everything. It couldn't even save us from most things. It didn't save Mike from developing septic shock in prison in Tucson after weeks of having been sick during the time of COVID when he was thirty-three. I didn't pick up the phone when an unknown number—which I knew was Mike, unknown numbers were always Mike—called me at three a.m. I'd had problems sleeping that week, had been nervous and anxious, staring at the dark ceiling, feeling hot even though it was cold out. I knew something was off. We'd been talking about our skating days not too long before—even in our thirties, we talked about when we wandered as unsupervised children and how insane it seemed to us looking back.

It could have been the prison that had called. I was his emergency contact and beneficiary, a role I'd always played when he was alive, same as when we were kids and he followed me everywhere. The prison called my dad a few hours later, after not being able to get a hold of me, to say that Mike was unconscious, that he might not wake up. When I found out, I was already exhausted, not having slept the night before, but prepared for work teaching college classes from home in my button-up shirt and pajama pants. My dad wasn't the one who called me. It was our younger brother John, whom we had taught to skate before he was out of diapers. My dad was at least halfway from Phoenix to Tucson by the time John knew, by the time I was called and told that my oldest and best friend was about to die.

What Mike had left me as his beneficiary, all his belongings, was a small box of papers, old shoes, and a cup caked with dried coffee. But in those papers was an envelope with a letter I'd written him, one of two letters he had—the other was a letter to my parents that had been returned to him. Under the flap of the envelope was written over and over in the proud hand of a perpetual little brother, *professor*, my occupation at the time. What Mike had left me was the gift of being seen.

That time when we spent all day on the street skateboarding, laughing, smoking, just walking down busy sidewalks and back alleys, will never come back. Mike is gone. Our friends are gone, many also dead or in prison, and I've lost contact with most of the survivors. We had that childlike hope for a future that would never exist, a future that was always impossible because it would have required a sturdy past. What we had in those days was one another, and I loved Mike more than anyone. And he loved me, and we saw one another, noticed one another. I was lucky to have him. At that age, there was a salvation in that skating obsession, something so ethereal and particular to a kid who doesn't yet understand how much they will lose, how much the obsession can maintain for a while but in the end will never be enough. We were never meant to live perpetually in wonder at the world, frozen in a time capsule like a desired purgatory. What we'd been building all that time were moments we didn't realize were pure until they were over and would never repeat. Things will never be the same, and though bittersweet, maybe it's for the best. Maybe an end is required for something to become immortal.

After I was hit by a car as an adult, I flinched every time I had to cross a street or parking lot, every time I had to drive through a crosswalk, until I started watching skate videos again. I stopped flinching as I began to remember what it was like to know I might break myself somehow but decide to throw myself onto a ledge or over a bank anyway. I forced myself to watch, to remember what it was to defy pain and gravity for the thrill of catching the board under my feet, midair, after flipping it and hovering for a moment until meeting the pavement with enough velocity to roll away with style.

There was one terrifying spot in particular at a neighboring school in Puerto Rico—an unnaturally long and high twelve-set of stairs. We all had to squeeze through a bent part of a gate to get in. It was good, smooth concrete, soft, as far as concrete goes, but slanted at a crooked downward angle at the bottom of the stairs, and it scared the shit out of me. I rode up to it and stopped at the top, tense, many times before actually ollieing the set. As much as I loved hitting up the benches and ramps and ledges and lips, doing tricks over parking cones and small gaps, I did not like hurling myself down dangerous stairs or onto large handrails. But I did it. I had to prove that I could to whoever was around. I did it, trembling. I rolled away after sticking the landing, feeling accomplished and lucky that I hadn't broken my leg. I didn't want to try the stairs again, but I knew I would. My friends were cheering me on. The only other person in our group to ever attempt those stairs was Mike. Everyone else had more sense.

When he was in prison, I sent him a piece I'd written about those stairs.

"It's good, brother," he said through the prison phone. "But you have to put in there that I only ever tried those stairs to impress you. You were my fucking idol, man. I was always trying to impress you, and I mean, if you write about it, it doesn't mean shit unless you say that. That's like the most important part."

He was right. It was the most important part. I wanted Mike with me everywhere I went, all the time, and he often seemed like the only person who wanted to be there with me. Even after our lives slowly drifted apart, that remained true. We made plans to write his book together after he got out of prison and could tell me all the fucked-up shit he couldn't say over the phone where the guards listened. I was going to somehow make money to help him for when he got out, so it would be different than the last time, when he left the halfway house. It was all going to get better. It was all going to be okay. We were going to be old men sitting on a porch together, laughing through the aches we'd accumulated, finally free of what we were trying to outrun on our skateboards, or with our drugs, with every mistake we'd ever made.

Mike skating away

he was black but he was white

I can see Mike sitting up against his girlfriend's garage door in Florida at three in the morning, smoking a cigarette while he hums and stares across the street. The house opposite has its garage door open. Clinking and clanging echo as the man in there works on his motorcycle. Mike told me this story over the phone right after I'd gotten married and moved to Phoenix, and he stayed behind, before he later moved there too.

MIKE: So, anyway, the neighbor across the street was working on his motorcycle. He was like this black dude I would talk to sometimes but like never really knew him all that well. And I could see him moving around in there, and there were all these barrels of shit. You know those like blue barrels? I mean, they were like those. But like all over the garage, and I'm thinking, you know, it's kind of fucking weird, right? But then I'm like, whatever, I mean, I'm up and smoking at this random time of the night. Whatever. I can't judge the guy. But then he starts running his hands over the barrels, and he starts pushing them over and I guess there was gas in there or something because a few seconds later there was this explosion, like boom! You know? And there was this flash of light and shit, and I was like, "Oh fuck! Dude just blew himself up!"

So I run up to his garage and pull this dude away. He was all looking around and shit like he was all surprised, and he was all like, "Did I do that?"

And you know how like when you get burned if you're like dark it can turn all white, like it burns the pigment out of the skin or something? Well, dude's arm was like all burnt and shit, and you know because he was black it was like this big contrast, right? And I'm like freaking out, and this dude's saying, "Holy shit. Holy shit. Holy shit," over and over. And then he starts laughing. And it's freaking me out even more, so I like try to calm the guy down.

It was all fucked up. But that's not even the crazy part. So, I was obviously the first one on the scene, right? So I was the one who told the firemen what happened and all, but then this news crew shows up. I shit you not. It was a fucking news crew, and they ask me what's happening, and it's like four in the morning at this point and I'm tired as fuck and all freaked out by all this shit, and the news crew actually comes over and asks me what happened. I explained the whole thing, right? Except I'm tired as fuck and I was, you know, trying to describe the burns and shit, and I was all like, "Yeah, there was this black dude, but he was white!" And like I sounded like a fucking idiot, and I'm on some news channel sounding like some crazy asshole going, "There was a black guy, but he was white!"

Oh, and get this. That's not all. Turns out, the whole burning-his-house-down thing wasn't an accident. I guess the bank was going to like take his house or some shit, and he tried to burn it down for insurance money. When the cops came, they found a bunch of shit crammed into his car, like documents and family photos and shit. Oh, and there was a dog. The dog had like jumped their eight-foot fence in the backyard. And get this. Apparently there was no insurance money anyway. Besides getting caught, the dude was too late. The house already legally belonged to the bank or some shit.

I swear. I don't even know how I always get into these situations.

Education

Me and Mike all smart in our suits

At his sentencing, Mike stood in his orange jumpsuit, head shaved, and, in his energetic, hyperactive voice, explained to the judge that there had been a mistake. According to what was written in the case file, Mike actually had a couple of hundred *more* days of time served than what his lawyer had said. From the pulpit, the judge shuffled through documents, eyes angled behind bifocals, muttering to himself. He put the papers down and in awe said, "You're right." Mike's lawyer scowled.

The judge, a seemingly kindly grandfather, a white man in a distinguished robe, lectured Mike from his high seat. At thirty-one, he said, Mike was a young man with his whole life in front of him. The judge talked about the evils of drugs, how it's never too late to change a life, how it was a shame Mike had to go to prison because of mandatory sentencing laws.

In prison, Mike studied law books for fun and he liked that he understood them. "None of this will help me with my case," he once told me over the phone. "As far as the law is concerned, I'm fucked. But I think I would have made a good lawyer." Mike, who dropped out of high school, earned his GED in jail, never went to college, and spent more than half his adult life incarcerated, *would* have made a good lawyer. But the judge was wrong about Mike having so much time ahead of him. The extra days of time served would never matter in the end. Mike would be dead, after a horrific sickness, by the time he was thirty-three. As a cop guided him out of the courtroom in his chains, Mike turned to where I was sitting with the rest of the family members of the condemned. He grinned, looking as always for that approval from me. I smiled and nodded my head. The entire time I pleaded again to the universe, to a god, to anything or anyone that might listen that it wouldn't be the last time I saw him. But it was.

We grasped at intelligence and clung to it. It was something we wanted to claim to prove we were more than what our grades or criminal records said about us. We repeatedly bragged to one another about it, with no shame.

"Neither one of us is particularly stupid," he would say over the prison phone. "I mean, like, we got away with a lot of shit," he'd start.

"No," I would say. "And you're like one of the smartest motherfuckers I know."

"Right?" He laughed.

"Then why the fuck are we so dysfunctional?"

"Look, man, you've got to understand, I mean. We got in so much trouble *because* we were intelligent and shit. I mean, we had fucking nothing else to do. What, were we just going to, like, go to school?"

"Yeah, well, I *did* go to school."

"After you were an adult! And I'm like really proud of you for that. I'm the one still fucking shit up, but, like, you didn't do school as a kid. That's what I mean. I mean, we were like not-stupid *kids* who didn't have fucking shit to do so of course we were going to fuck it up."

We were always taught that we failed school as kids, not that school failed us. It was our responsibility to turn in work, get to class on time, listen, care about what we did. We were told by church leaders and our dad that as long as we followed god's commandments, we would be okay and after that came everything else. We were told by teachers, parents, adults we didn't trust, that the world revolved around getting good grades, success revolved around how well we performed for our institutions. Some of our friends were motivated by that. Some were motivated by parents. Some of us couldn't visualize that world presented to us. Some of us were lost in the system.

I knew I was a bad student before I finished first grade because of how angry the adults around me got when I didn't do my work. Mike knew he was trouble since before that because of how much he was yelled at and punished. We seemed to fulfill what we were expected to be, more than what we wanted to be, because we had no idea what we wanted to be. Something about Mike put the adults around him on edge. It was his smile, or the fact that he charged money for a hug, or that he was darker than the rest of us, with black hair that shined. Or it was his penetrating intelligence, an intelligence that defied anything the adults tried to feed him. He questioned everything. While I disappeared and faded away from school, Mike was kicked out. But despite our seemingly opposite natures, at the core, beneath everything we used to insulate ourselves against hurt, we were very much the same.

We had plenty of ideas: how to steal cigarettes without getting caught, how to sling heroin and pills from our landscaping jobs or fast food restaurants, how to miss about a month of school without the school and parents ever noticing (asking friends to say "here" when our names were called), how to counterfeit real-looking money like Mike did when I was a missionary in Brazil, how to make drugs with household items, how to write and get through college while hiding a raging addiction, how to survive in prison when surrounded by white supremacists. Yet, how could we be broadly educated when both of us had left school and failed our way through it when we were there? School was a game that we didn't want, or didn't know how, to play. My first-grade teacher was young, going to be married soon, pretty, and genuinely kind. I liked her, so I was disappointed when she presented the stack of papers I hadn't done to my parents. I had no notion I wasn't doing well because I had no notion I was supposed to be doing any work. The classroom was messy, and kids didn't stay in their seats and there was so much noise and glue and cotton balls and the desks were muddled with graphite and the adults were always so stressed. If I was paying attention, I was just confused. I convinced myself that all that paperwork handed out to us was for the others to do, not me. I was too busy in my own head.

I daydreamed quietly in my chair of being a Ninja Turtle, wondered what it would be like to have large green fingers, crossing them over one another until I made five into three. My synesthesia made my letters act out their dramas on math worksheets, 4 sneaking off with 5 when they thought 6 wasn't looking, 8 longing after 9, who secretly longed after him, even if she felt unworthy after a fling with 5. I dreamed of sneaking kisses under the table with girls I liked during those times the class was in an uproar and wondering if any of the girls would sneak kisses with me while simultaneously feeling ashamed and trying to decide if kissing would make Jesus cry.

I wrapped myself in those dreams, paralyzed by them,

unable to swim away if I'd wanted to. My dreams took the
feelings I didn't understand, the terrors in my hallucino-
genic panic attacks, and morphed them into something
if not rational than at least palpable. I dreamed to keep
the terror of the apartments where we lived, the tense-
ness of our home, and the loneliness I couldn't describe
or understand at bay. I learned to let my dreams float so
I could watch them, detached—the way I sometimes saw
scenes from my life as if outside my body—guiding them
while not forcing them to go one way or another, letting
them surprise me instead. Releasing a daydream to let it
play out in my mind meant letting the dream go where it
would. But it meant I had to detach from life too, from dull
paperwork that didn't benefit me, from listening to what
teachers or students were saying in class. I would read
assigned books at home so I didn't have to strain to pay attention when other kids read paragraphs during in-school
reading time. I loved the dreams I found in books, and I
didn't like it when people couldn't read the words or read
in a monotone voice because it interrupted the dream with
the reality of mechanics.

Mike had a job once in high school assisting a guy our parents knew from church. It was electrical work, and Mike
picked it up fast. He said, "Before I started working for
that weird fuck, he told me his one rule was just to not
contradict him, never to tell him he was wrong because he

hated that shit. I thought he was joking! I mean, what a weird fucking thing to say, right?"

A week after Mike got the job, the guy made a mistake. Something technical I don't understand, but Mike did, and he told the guy.

"Yo, this douche like chewed me out and shit when we got to the car," Mike told me later. "I mean, I thought he was joking, but he was not. And he fired me. I mean he fired me for being right!"

Mike observed everything and forgot nothing. Phone numbers of everyone he knew, directions to anywhere, words he'd looked up in dictionaries, chords, scales, theories. All of it was stored and brought out in an instant without hesitation. He wanted to experience everything, and he tried. He picked up Spanish by himself when we lived in Puerto Rico, and thereafter spoke fluently, making deals or having long conversations and laughing with random people he'd meet.

My intelligence manifested differently. While Mike acted on his impulse and intuition, I pondered and calculated. When I was nine, my dad took me to his wood-paneled office in our basement, sat me down, and pulled out a poster I'd made for school. He'd gotten it from my teacher during a parent-teacher conference. He stood next to the heavy, gray, metal desk he'd inherited from his grandfather. My dad was serious, and besides the whir of the computer fan, the room was quiet, building an intensity and drama until he spoke.

"You did a good job on this," he said. I was proud of it because in answer to a question about what I would ask for if I could have one wish I wrote, "Wisdom, like unto Solomon." It made me feel smart and intensely spiritual.

"In fact," he said, "your teacher says that you do really well every time you turn something in. The problem is, you never turn anything in. You've done so little that you're going to fail the fourth grade unless you change now."

This was before my dad lost his hair to stress, before he shaved his mustache, before that seriousness would make him sick, weighing him down until panic attacks started to look like heart trouble. It was back when he was young enough that his severe depression was somewhat manageable but before his anger started to fade. He looked at me with a worry that would intensify over the years, a worry that made me ill, made me sad for what I knew I would never be able to do: ease his burden, make him be happy. I understood even then that look for what it was. Desperation. I knew my dad was desperate about everything: money that he could never hold on to—and I knew, because I was constantly reminded, that we kids were very expensive—the job he seemed to hate so much, the perpetual stress of a noisy and messy home, the impression that no matter how hard he tried to clutch at control it would spiral away from him, always missing the mark because he didn't know where, or even what, the mark was.

On top of all this, he didn't know what to do about me, his boy whom he loved, who he felt had so much potential that he knew might never be realized. On the desk next to him sat a stack of paper, homework assignments I hadn't done all year. I had copies of some of those same assignments crumpled in the bottom of my swollen backpack, some of which had been there for months, since the first days of class.

"I'm not sure if I should tell you this," he said in what I can now only conceive of as a trick to make me do my schoolwork. "Your teacher says maybe I shouldn't. But she thinks you might be smarter than normal kids—that you might be a genius. Do you know what that means?"

For a kid who loved to read, who loved to learn, but felt stupid for doing so poorly in school, it meant everything. It meant that maybe I was destined for something. It meant that I would be great, and right away I wanted to be a character like I'd read about in my books or seen in movies—I dreamed of being like Indiana Jones, professor by day and adventurer by calling. It meant that I had a chance.

"Yeah," I said. "Like Einstein."

"Right," my father said.

"And he got, like, bad grades and stuff too."

My dad faltered. It wasn't the response he was expecting. Now I wonder if my quip made him regret his plan to get me to believe in myself. But in the moment, I tried not to smile. It rose up anyway. It spread across my face, and I was ashamed of the pride swelling in me because I felt what my dad was saying was true, but I was ashamed to

hear it, ashamed to believe it, ashamed because the sham
was obvious. My teacher never said that. My father was lying to me in a desperate, ill-thought-out attempt to inspire
me to do better.

He said he was capable of doing anything to help us—
anything except look at us, except confront his own ghosts,
which eventually grew so large they haunted us through
him. He opted instead to bury them, pretending his depression wasn't real, that he was being silly, that these
were personality flaws rather than symptoms of something else. His buried demons flourished, and their influence seeped into us. Just like us, he likely inherited much
of his faulty thinking through the environment in which
he was raised. At the desk holding that poster, my dad
seemed so big it cemented my naïve belief that he was in
control, a messenger of god's truth. I could feel the tension
and buildup of all his traumas over all those years, but I
didn't understand it yet.

I doubt Mike ever had a conversation like that with
our dad. Their relationship was strained even when Mike
was a child. Years after that conversation, when my parents were in Brazil and Mike was in and out of jail back
in the States, they seemed to pretend he didn't exist. After
he died and our parents posted about it on social media,
their friends were confused. They had no idea they had a
kid named Michael, and I hated them for it. Our parents'
friends knew who I was, knew about all the other siblings.
Mike was never even mentioned. I wanted to be as much a

ghost for them as Mike was, but in the end I felt that sense of responsibility toward them, that sense that they were children I needed to care for. That obligation felt like a betrayal of my brother, and that conflict between wanting to comfort my parents and standing with Mike was something that plagued me for years.

Mike acted out. He talked back to teachers, told them when they got math problems wrong, would come out of a room and yell, "Where's my fucking money?" once when he was five and had lost a couple of bills under his bed. The first time he got suspended was after he stood on a friend's shoulders and tried to peek into the window of the girls' bathroom. He was maybe seven or eight—they didn't even know what they were looking for, only that it was taboo. "I couldn't even see anything!" he said to the teacher, then repeated the same to the principal and again to my parents. "The windows were too dirty! I shouldn't even get in trouble for something I couldn't even do!" The kid acting out is thirsty for attention. It's listed as a symptom of sexual, physical, and emotional abuse, neglect, mental health issues. The same goes for the dissociated and quiet kid.

Where Mike tried to fill his life with movement and chaos, I tried to fill mine with more premeditated adventures, not for a thrill, but for an escape. I didn't necessarily want to play it safe, but I wanted to get away with anything I decided to do (something that was never as important to Mike) so I studied other people's adventures. I read. I wanted to read everything, to feel everything like Mike did—but without the madness that encircled him. I wasn't necessarily more careful on purpose, just more thoughtful and somewhat less impulsive, and books helped me process my place in the world. In *Wayside School*, I loved Miss Zarves's class on the nineteenth floor, the floor that didn't exist, the teacher who didn't exist, with a room full of students who didn't exist. That was the class I wanted. Stephen King's *Nightmares and Dreamscapes* helped me process the darker sides of my imagination. I hid the book on my leg under the desk while my fifth-grade teacher explained the scientific method in his monotone voice. I had a huge crush on a character from *From the Mixed-Up Files of Mrs. Basil E. Frankweiler* who ran away to the Met, and not long after I read it, I decided to run away too.

I'd just gotten my report card. I was failing. My parents would be angry. That was why I told myself I was running away, but really I just felt sad, disassociated, and more and more ashamed. Mike and I had these small emergency windows in our basement bedroom that could be removed in case of a fire. We loved playing with them and knew that once open, they couldn't be closed from the outside. The day I decided to run away, I came home from school, walked into my room, crawled out the window, and left the pane lying in the grass. I walked down the road with a small bag stuffed with two sandwiches, a Bowie knife I found in my dad's office, and matches. I was headed toward a deserted cluster of trees that had been bent to form little dome-shaped rooms some other kids must have made, next to a dried-out canal and cow pasture. It would have been that orange time of day, except that it was overcast and there was no color coming through. I had a light jacket, but it was fall in Idaho and it smelled like snow was on the way and the small fire I built when I got under the trees went out and I ran out of matches and sandwiches and I was bored. I knew there was no way it would have worked, but because of what I'd read, the idea had grown in my mind until it had become an overbearing desire I couldn't control. I groaned sometimes when that kind of melancholy hit me. When I imagined the stories I'd make of my life, I became wild on the inside, unfettered, wanting to throw away all responsibility. But the cold got into my bones, and I watched my breath on the night air, and I slouched back home. The only reason my parents knew I was gone was because I had left the window on the ground. I'd failed. Instead of just being angry about the report card, they were angry about having a cold house.

Later that year, I was awarded the Space Cadet award for never paying attention in class, but I still slipped through to the next year. As usual, I scored so high on the national tests that the school thought holding me back wouldn't do me or them any favors. I went in circles like that until sixth grade, when Mike and I got caught smoking the cigarettes we'd stolen. By then we were learning more outside the classroom than in school or from lessons at home.

Mike seemed to gather his knowledge by osmosis, through the air, and there was a lot of it. I can't even imagine his paying attention in class, but somehow he knew everything. He could fix whatever, build engines for his bicycle; he played bass and guitar like no one else around. In his circle, he was a bass legend, until he got bored with it. Until he sold his instruments for dope. He gathered his bits of information of chemistry from learning the molecular composition of the drugs we took. He knew each alkaloid and derivative and synthesis of the opium poppy or synthetic opium. He learned business as he began to sell acid and pills and coke, and later black-tar heroin. He learned—though he never could do it himself—that it's best not to use all the product. More than anything, Mike learned about people.

His intuition often manifested in his knowledge that no one ever knew what they were doing. He saw that everyone doubted themselves and realized that exploiting that doubt with humor could do miracles for him. It's not that all his experiments worked out. They didn't. But he learned from them. When I was fourteen and he was eleven, he tried fixing the air-conditioning in our shared room in Puerto Rico, which had been working but wasn't cooling as well as it used to—each room had an air-conditioning box, and ours was one of the last remaining functioning ACs (the last being our parents'). The AC was over my bed, and I sat on one side of it while Mike took the front of the box off.

"That might not be a good plan," I said. But even though I cautioned, I had confidence. I knew he didn't know what he was doing, but I believed he could figure it out. He had already fixed the broken pool pump before it was replaced after the hurricane when we'd emptied the pool for a few months. I thought maybe he could pull it off.

"I got this," Mike said, picking up a flathead screwdriver with a green plastic handle.

"Did you at least unplug—"

There was a loud pop, a quick flash of sparks, and a little cloud of smoke as all the lights in the house, the TV, and the appliances went out. Mike, who had been holding the plastic handle, was okay, but the metal on the screwdriver had a small groove melted into it.

For the next couple of years, if the lights downstairs were on, the lights upstairs wouldn't work, and if the lights upstairs were on, the lights downstairs wouldn't work. We also couldn't wash clothes and watch TV at the same time. And nowhere in the house—besides our parents' room—had air-conditioning for the remainder of the time we lived there.

After Mike was expelled from eighth grade in Florida, he couldn't handle staying in isolated homeschool. He pleaded and argued for months until our parents let him go to the Seminole County annex school for youth who were kicked out of regular school. After a year at the annex, if he stayed out of trouble, he would be allowed back to public school. I drove him the half hour there and picked him up every day, in the red van that had circled Puerto Rico, the one with the dinging door and stuck tapes. The teachers yelled at the students like drill sergeants and marched them everywhere in lines, as if they were in prison.

Mike quickly found friends and formed a band. He and Rob, the guitarist, tried sticking gum to orange peels and hiding them until the peels turned black and mold grew on the gum.

"That did not get me high when I chewed it," Mike said.

"Of course not," I said. "That's some sketchy shit."

I wasn't one to talk. I used to steal packets of morning glory seeds from gardening stores, crush them up, and make a tea that made me at least dry heave when I was lucky. Crushed, they released a chemical called LSA, similar to LSD, but they almost always also made me violently nauseous first. If I could keep from throwing up for an hour or two after ingestion, it was great, but fighting through the hour or two was always the hard part. Mike and I scoured the internet looking for home remedies like this in our isolation. For a normal individual, spending a couple of hours trying not to puke but almost always doing so, later living a life in which we were either sick or putting needles into ourselves, would seem insane. And it's not a good or pleasant or fun life. But every person with an addiction I've ever known used because despite the sickness, homelessness, terror of cops, loss of family, the alternative was always worse—whether that alternative is mental illness, abuse, physical pain, trauma. The only people I've ever known who have gotten out got out because they found a better alternative, treated whatever it was that drove them to use in the first place. For Mike and me, it was either suffer through the dangers of our sketchy remedies or survive sober in a home saturated in guilt and depression and a set of religious rules we couldn't live up to. It was get high or deal with the saudades we didn't yet understand, our own neurodivergences, bipolar disorders, and other mental health issues. We got sick and risked our lives because the only alternative we could conceive of was much worse. Mike never found a better alternative.

While the students at the annex had their own long list of sketchy ways to get high, there were also more reliable ways. Rob took both approaches. His house was always packed with teenagers and no adults, all of us pushing our way through an effluvium of cigarette and weed smoke during their practice. I wasn't in the band. I sat on one of the amplifiers and smoked cigarettes or drank whatever they had. By that time, weed had started causing psychosis in me, so I wouldn't partake, but when they passed their opium around—a little round chunk of paste in a pipe—and bragged about how no one else in the area had any, I smoked it. For a reason I never understood, af-

ter I turned sixteen, weed stopped producing any kind of
euphoria for me, leaving instead a severe disconnection
from reality mixed with abject terror. It must be that THC
doesn't react well to my body chemistry and bipolar disorder. I liked opiates by that time though, even if I was still
learning about their effects and was not yet physically dependent on them. Mike and I would steal Vicodin from our
dad or buy an assortment of pills in the housing projects in
Puerto Rico. But what Rob's friends were passing around
in Florida wasn't doing anything.

"I don't think this is opium," I said, as I tried hitting
it again. It was sweet with a hint of soap taste to it. "This
isn't doing shit, man. Are you sure this is opium?"

"Of course it is, man," Rob said, annoyed. "But you
have to smoke it with weed to really feel anything." They
scorned me for not smoking weed anymore, but I didn't
care. By the time I knew them, getting high was not about
being cool for me.

"I don't think that's the way it works, man," I said.
"Plus, I think you have to have a special pipe for this shit.
I think I read about that. You don't just smoke opium like
you would weed. I think this is incense, man."

"You just don't know what you're talking about," Rob
said, getting angry.

I didn't hang out much with them after that. I got the
feeling I wasn't wanted and started going to the bookstore
while I waited for Mike to finish his band practice. But it

turned out Rob was good for something eventually. He was a door to pills and ketamine.

In the months building up to when I would drop out and Mike would go to the annex, a few months before meeting Rob and smoking incense at his house, I would spend all day reading in the school library, switching seats every time a new period started to avoid being noticed. Once, one of the classes I had been skipping for weeks came in. I moved away from the teacher, but a couple of students made their way over to me and sat down.

"Hey, I think I know you," the guy said. He was a little shorter than me, thin, and did some school sport. His functionality pained me, reminded me that I was supposed to somehow be like that, supposed to have something that drove me, something that would give me a future.

"You know me from history," I said. The table was long, and though anxious, I was grateful for the company. I was relieved to see I still knew how to socialize.

"Right!" he said. "You're that kid who used to sit in the back of the class and answer all the random questions the teacher asks. You're the one who's like read all those books. I thought you moved."

I failed the class he was talking about, but I loved going to listen to the teacher, a Vietnam vet, rail on about the US's moral failings throughout history, in between chain-smoking behind the building during his breaks. He also asked trivia questions either at the beginning or end of each class. Who wrote *Alice in Wonderland*? What was the Cold War? Who was John Lennon? Who was Vladimir Lenin? Who was Malcom X? Who was Karl Marx? Who was Joseph Smith? What happens in *The Great Gatsby*? I could answer those questions, but I never did the homework.

I told the boy I'd just stopped going to class. The fact that he'd thought I'd moved scared me. It meant that even though I felt like I was walking through a dream, what I was doing was real. I was leaving school. There was no coming back from this. Either I would fail or leave. That was it.

The girl with him looked at my books. "What are you reading?" She was pretty, had dark brown hair and an expression on her face that showed a determination to engage. I showed her the Salvador Dalí and Van Gogh biographies, the book on Bob Dylan, and the civil rights history book I was looking at so I could see who Medgar Evers was after hearing "Only a Pawn in Their Game," and American lit compilations I'd been picking at. "So, are you one of those guys who likes to study all the time?"

"No," I said. "I like to smoke too." I had been without anything to get me high for a few months, and though I was starting to not like weed, I wasn't yet convinced my bad experiences with it would become the norm. We'd just moved from Puerto Rico. I didn't know anybody. I was desperate.

"Oh, damn!" she said. "I wasn't expecting that." She smiled. I saw these two people not as potential friends— I couldn't make myself interested in either of them for a reason I couldn't explain—but as tools. Him? No, he would never know where to find what I wanted. But her? She liked to party, or at least pretended she did. On top of that she was outgoing, and that meant she knew people.

"Oh, no," the guy said. "I'm on the track team, and I don't do anything like that. Plus, my parents would know, and they would kill me."

"Are you a cop?" the girl said, turning back to me, smiling, interested.

"Of course I'm not a cop," I said, trying to match her grin. "Plus, you found me. If I was a cop, wouldn't I be trying to mingle, going to parties and shit?"

"I don't mess with drugs," she said. "I don't like things that are illegal. I only like to drink."

"That's cool," I said. "But drinking is illegal too."

"No, it's not."

"You twenty-one?" I said.

"No."

"Then it is for you."

"Yeah, but that's different." She looked over to the guy across from me and asked about how his girlfriend was doing. "You fuck her yet?" she said to him, then side-glanced at me.

The guy blushed and stammered. He hadn't.

The girl laughed, but not in a mean way. The way she

spoke, even if loud, was earnest and kind. She took on a maternal tone, became a counselor to him all of a sudden. "You know, you have to get her into it." She winked. "Go down on her."

She seemed to gain stature the more embarrassed the guy became. I was aware that the conversation was also for me, and it made me uncomfortable. Their ability to lead what looked to me like normal teenage lives started to make my stomach hurt. I was scared of what I seemed to be doing to myself, and my body and mind were screaming at me for relief. I wanted pills—though I would have taken acid or weed or anything—from them, from anyone who might have appeared. Anything at that moment to be okay.

She asked if I had a girlfriend, which I didn't. She had a hunger about her, but not for me. I figured it must have been for some sense of adventure and transgression. I figured my best bet was to give her what she was searching for. I just needed to find out how.

"You a virgin too?" She grinned.

It was a confusing question. I thought about it. I could lie. I could tell her that I wasn't. But the girl in the library had liked making that track guy blush. She liked the power of it. "Yes," I said. "I am." I didn't care about her thinking I wasn't cool. I didn't care about anything other than getting high.

She was delighted. "Shit. We're going to have to make sure we get you laid before senior year."

"I don't think I'm ever going to be a senior. I think I'm going to drop out."

I hadn't said that out loud before—I didn't have anyone to say it to, unless it was Mike, but that didn't count—and it was strange. I was relieved and terrified.

She leaned back, abandoning her conversation with the track kid and giving me her full attention. "What do you mean?"

"I don't think it makes a difference whether I'm here or not."

"Of course it does," she said, leaning closer to me. She seemed truly concerned, and I was touched. "What will you do with your life if you never graduate high school? How are you going to come to my graduation party?"

"I don't know, and I don't know."

I don't remember the rest of the conversation, other than my annoyed realization that neither of them could help me get high. At some point the class left, and so did they. I gathered my heavy stack of books and stood up to rotate tables. Before leaving, she told me that she didn't know where to get anything, but she knew a guy named Van who probably could.

When Mike got back to public school, after leaving the annex, he met a girl who worked at a veterinarian clinic. It was where he got ketamine sometimes, and it was also where other shit came from. I didn't know her. I just used what she provided. There was some type of pill—I can't remember what it was now—given to dogs that the girl stole. She and Mike would sell it at school. I snorted them. Mike snorted them. The girl snorted them, and so did their customers. Problem was, the pills weren't fit for human consumption. *We* had no issues, but a couple of the kids who bought them started having mild seizures. Everyone was okay in the end, but apparently the pills could have caused serious and permanent brain damage. I'm not sure how Mike wasn't expelled for that—or maybe he was and I'm mangling the timeline but either way, what's the difference? At some point he got sent back to the annex, tried and failed to complete a GED course, and finally left school again by his own accord while I was a missionary in Brazil.

His intelligence and intuition helped him to survive for as long as he did, and it never faded. My parents and grandparents said that Mike was losing his intelligence because of his constant drug use, but that wasn't true—they never really talked to him, so how would they know? He blamed himself for the trouble he got into and for the family's reaction to him. For years, when someone in the family wanted to know how Mike was doing, they asked me. I always hated myself for not standing up more for him. I know not everyone will believe my portrait of my brother, my family, myself. But these are the secret stories we retold to one another, and he can't tell them anymore.

I've always been hungry for stories that are true. Truth to me has nothing to do with reality or logic. I want stories that tell the truth about loneliness and despair and emptiness and insanity, stories that turn them into the norm, alongside love and patience and kindness and peace. Truth is in the details, and impossible to pinpoint, and it was something no one could teach me, because it was something no one around me could face. The truth is that everything is absurd. The truth is absurd. The motions we go through and all the motivations that drive us are no more or less important than whatever random event might befall us or anyone else. For all the rules we might learn and all the structures put in place to guide our lives, we will all inevitably confront life-altering or life-ending chaos—loss of freedom, cancer, loss of home and family, the death of a brother—and it will crush our core. Then what?

I read Kafka's *The Metamorphosis* for the first time on my back, on a fraying piece of plywood in the middle of my bedroom floor in Florida—probably while listening to Bob Dylan cassettes that I'd recorded from library CDs—after I dropped out. I'd been reading and learning on my own for years, but I think I learned more lying on that floor than I ever did in a classroom. It was covered in tangled cords that sometimes dipped into the wet paints I had on the plywood I kept in the middle of the carpet. The plywood was to keep the carpet clean from my art supplies, but the ink and spots of crimson and viridian and ultramarine oils took eternities to dry, so I kept stepping in them and spreading spots and footprints around the room. A couple of years later, burn marks from spoons littered the carpet as well. Only the square spot underneath the wood remained immaculate. I had paintings I'd done along the walls, a couple of bookcases filled with books, papers, and CDs and a stereo with a record player, CD player, and two tape decks. I was surrounded by my paints, canvases, clothes, instruments, amp cords, and garbage, wondering how I had gotten there and what I was doing with myself. My paintings hung on the red walls, looking at each other and the mess, for the better part of the three years between my leaving high school and moving to São Paulo to become a Latter-Day Saint missionary.

Gregor's room was a minimalist version of mine. We both spent most of our time obsessing over anxieties, in judgment of ourselves, in fear of the judgments from others, especially family. I preferred Kafka's absurd spaces to the ones I found in schools, which to me were machines not too different than the one in "In the Penal Colony." Living in a suburban house that looked like every other one was more surreal to me than anything the writer described. Gregor wants that order, at least on the surface, but it is obliterated when he wakes up a monstrous vermin. All that structure means nothing in the face of all that weird beyond his control. His nightmarish life was as real to me as the pointlessness in which I was living. It allowed me the horrible "ethic of lucidity" that Camus describes in his writing on Kafka. I loved laughing at the ridiculousness of it all, as I wondered why Gregor didn't just crawl out the window in his room. I kept climbing out of mine, only to find I didn't have anywhere to go.

In an appendix to *The Myth of Sisyphus*, entitled "Hope and the Absurd in the Work of Franz Kafka," Camus writes that Kafka's "perpetual oscillations between the natural and the extraordinary, the individual and the universal, the tragic and the everyday, the absurd and the logical, are found throughout his work and give it both its resonance and its meaning. These are the paradoxes that must be enumerated, the contradictions that must be strengthened." When I was alone in my room, I tried to process the oscillations between the disparate pieces of my own life. I felt like a walking contradiction: The knowledge-hungry dropout. The guy who couldn't stand most church people, was "unclean before the lord," was reading scriptures every day and about to go on a mission. The guy with a black and indigenous mother and white father who never felt like he belonged with any race. Seeing Kafka's characters responding to other dissonant contradictions with little to no surprise gave me hope. I had no hope in the rational and logical world, the world in which high school and office jobs and church existed. I never believed they could give me what I needed (even though I had no idea what it was I needed). I wouldn't have wanted it anyway. I felt that world wasn't real. All that fiction I read was the only thing that rang true. So I stayed in my room until I could face the absurd with the same acceptance as Kafka's characters. I didn't care if they met a horrible end, or if I would too. Whether we embrace the absurd or not, we all end up the same way: dead. Whether we lived or not. Whether we were geniuses or idiots, monsters or humans, or something in between.

4-track recorder

Mike and I had a 4-track recorder in our room in Florida. My room. The only room we didn't share throughout all our moves, but it was ours because that was where we would spend our time, often alone but sometimes with some of the wounded we brought home. We would stay up all night listening to Bad Religion or X or Radiohead or the Red Hot Chili Peppers. Mike loved Flea and learned to play all their songs. We had guitars and amplifiers, but we didn't have drums. We recorded anyway though. We captured song after song on the 4-track, though none of them were ever finished and I was too embarrassed to sing the shitty lyrics I'd written. But we laid the music down as best we could.

When Mike and I learned that the percussion track in the Chili Peppers song "Breaking the Girl" was made from garbage from a junkyard that the band banged on, I thought, "Hey, Ricky can just like bang on some shit." He was a skinny, black-haired kid we knew from church who, like us, didn't belong or like it there. Like us, he had been pulled from public school, and like us, his parents had sent him through the same libertarian correspondence high school I attended after I left, and that Mike attended briefly before he went to the annex alone. We would grow into our twenties together, shoot up together, sell shrooms and dope to each other. Ricky was in many ways our adopted brother, by our side as we spent hours together in my room pushing cords out of the way so we could sit on the floor and try to record.

We told him the garbage idea when he came over.

"That doesn't sound like it's going to work," Ricky said.

"No," I said. I was sickly skinny at the time, with wild uncombed hair, slowly going crazy from my isolation after leaving school. "Trust me. It'll sound good. I promise."

Mike doubted it too, and he and Ricky were right. It did sound like shit.

The tapes are gone now, eaten by mold in a Floridian storage unit and then thrown out. Maybe it's for the better. With no proof of what we really sounded like to correct me, I get to decide how to remember the screeching guitar I played through a distortion and delay pedal, the loud slapping bass Mike slammed and later strummed after he discovered the joy of bass chords, and Ricky whacking a cracked, empty bucket, none of us quite in sync, on that dangerously messy floor in the middle of a school day when anything was possible.

Defragmenting

I hardly have any memories of my brief stay in high school in Florida, but I do remember paying Van for overpriced weed in a dark and crowded lunchroom. A few years later, after I started with heroin, he died alone in his apartment after mixing Xanax and the methadone that he and his mother, or aunt, were on. His is the only name I remember from high school in Florida, and he was the last person I spoke to there. The day after I bought weed from him, I was gone.

While my parents went out that night to the temple, Mike and I smoked from the long bamboo pipe I had made and brought with me from Puerto Rico. I gave him a couple of buds while high. It wasn't good. The panic and anxiety and godly guilt I felt all the time were compounding, and the weed was aggravating, not assuaging. I could feel my terrors physically manifest in the shadows and cold around me, and while I did try smoking many times after that, it was never good again. It wasn't the incident per se. It had slowly been getting bad for months, but that marked the end of it for me.

I think I made up some excuse to skip school the next day. I was high and in the middle of waking nightmares, having smoked more in the morning before my dad came home. He was agitated and pale and looked physically ill. He pulled me to the side and said, "Mike's been arrested."

Before we left Puerto Rico for Florida, I had already started to feel mentally and spiritually thin. During my first two years of high school, I was kind of popular, though I didn't realize it. I wore mismatched socks and torn skater shoes. I was awkward, but I could read people and knew how to behave within most groups. I could hang out with goth kids and punk kids, kids into hip-hop, the artsy ones, stoners, skaters, surfers, girls, guys, band geeks, some jocks. I skated in front of groups of kids at school or in competitions. I felt unsure of myself, and bad and dirty and shy and embarrassed that I was a Latter-Day Saint, so I rarely dated (and absolutely never dated anyone from church), despite knowing of girls and boys with crushes on me. People sought me out so I could find weed or acid for them. They called me to chill with them. I used to sing all the time and tell stories, make people laugh. I laughed a lot. It was fun.

At some point I started skating less and getting high more. I would roll around with friends hot boxing in stuffy cars until we had to roll down the windows because we could no longer breathe. These memories come in patches:

Sitting in the back seat of my friend's packed car, some guy's elbow in my ribs and some girl on my lap because there was nowhere else to sit, listening to Bob Marley and feeling how I sank into myself. The same group swimming in the ocean in our underwear. Salt water. Drinking Bacardi 151 with Mike and our friends in the crack-vial-ridden park at night and feeling nothing but the shadows and cool air. My parents arriving at the park at three in the morning in their big red minivan and the fear they brought with them. Feeling moody when not high. Feeling scared when I was. Rhythms. Deep, menacing drumbeats in my head. A voice—not a voice, more of a feeling—screaming in the back of my mind, sometimes laughing. Being in band class on acid, the instruments shining at me. Skating on the basketball court at that same park and the sensation that the gray in the concrete had seeped into everything, the sky, the trees, turning every other color cold.

In old notebooks from that time, I mention a state of mind I refer to as the Gray. The Gray is the space where nothing makes sense, and it doesn't matter that nothing makes sense. It first hit me just before we left Puerto Rico, and it dominated for maybe three years afterward, years with other states intermittently making short appearances. Before I left the island, I was walking around the basketball court where I used to skate, buy drugs, and get high. It was overcast and humid. Gray. I looked up a hill that led to the school with the twelve-set I used to skate and saw a tree I had known for years. It was dark with no leaves. It looked two-dimensional and wrong, like a cardboard prop. It hurt my senses, and I had to blink a few times before realizing the sensation wasn't going away. Everything looked and felt emotionally drained of color, like it had been that way forever, but it was only then that I had ever noticed. I knew it wasn't real, but that didn't keep the two-dimensional sensation from being stuck to me. People felt empty. School didn't seem real. Students, teachers, crowded halls, dirt on the floor, none of it real. It was as if everything existed on some existential plane I was able to see but not touch. I was alone.

My perception of reality became two-dimensional. Literally. It wasn't just the tree. Everything looked like cardboard. I was getting high even when I didn't want to. More and more I *had* to. On my last day on the island, my ex, who I was still friends with, got her sister to drive up to my house in a white car to say goodbye, to lose her virginity, and take mine. I looked at her face, the face I can no longer remember, through the car window. I didn't get in. Stuttering, mumbling over and over to her that I was high, smothered by an invisible force I could not escape, her tears behind her car door as she drove away like the tears of the girl I'd slammed the door on when I was five. Panicked. Caught.

I thought that this feeling was because of the drugs—terrified it was, terrified it wasn't—but when we got to Florida, I didn't take anything for about four months because I didn't know anyone and therefore couldn't find anything. But the sensation of being smothered, the two-dimensional world, the guilt, all grew. I was guilty about everything all the time: unrepentant drug use, incessant masturbation, the guilt itself. I never ran out of reasons to hate myself. My stomachaches and paranoia from childhood resurfaced. In my notebooks, I painted black shadow monsters eating light, devouring my body. I drew pictures of suicides. I tried to skate, signed up for events, met a few people, but there was something off about them. Everybody in Florida was off. I was off and getting worse.

I hated Florida, and my saudade for Puerto Rico was unbearable for at least a couple of years after we moved. We had changed scenes, cultures, communities, like clothing. My identity had been taken from me from the beginning. Instead of being able to walk to the beach like I had in Puerto Rico, I was stuck in Orlando, at least an hour's drive away from the ocean I loved. There were no bars on windows or broken glass on walls to keep away intruders, the way there had been in Puerto Rico. The uniform Floridian houses made for dead-looking neighborhoods in contrast to the unique, brightly colored places we'd lived before. Segregation was blatant and rampant. There were no groups like my old skate buddies, who ranged from black, like Carlos, to white, like José, and every shade in between. There were no saints on the walls inside homes. No trace of Yoruba in old places like there were in San Juan. The moment we got off the plane, the first thing I noticed was a sea of blond heads, and I knew I was in an unfamiliar land.

I cut off all my hair the day we stepped onto the mainland in Florida. My parents took us to a mall for food. They had been wanting me to cut my hair for a long time, said it wasn't becoming of a good church member, wasn't respectable, looked bad. They were always complaining about it, so I walked into a salon. I would never be a good church member in their or anyone's eyes unless I lied about who I was, made my outside different from my inside. But it would make them happy, I thought.

After over three years in Puerto Rico, it was strange to be in a public place where English was the primary language. When the woman sat me down to ask what I wanted, I said, "I don't know. I don't care. Just cut it off." She didn't know how to react. My hair was thick and nice, and she ran her hands through it. "You want me to cut it *all* off?" she said. "Or just a couple of inches? How much do you want me to leave?"

I told her again that I didn't know, two centimeters. I remember my parents with me there in the salon; I remember them not there. I don't think it matters which. Either way, after the haircut we all walked out of the mall together. "Isn't that better?" my mother said as we all walked toward an escalator. "Don't you feel better now?"

"I feel the same as I did before," I lied. I rubbed my head for days, until the strange sensation of no longer having hair dissipated, but the negative space where the hair had been lasted years.

I was supposed to be someone I was not, and now I looked like someone I was not. My parents, especially my dad, wanted me to have a Latter-Day Saint lifestyle, hairstyle, morality—even if that wasn't how I was raised. I was raised confused, and it showed. It was getting close to the time when I would have to go on a mission, but until then I had never even liked church. I had never told any friend at school that I was a member of the church. I truly wanted to be spiritual, but spiritual in my own way, a personal connection with god or the ethereal or universe or whatever there was to connect to on that level. The image I had of church people was never going to be me. I felt guilty about it. I felt guilty for feeling guilty, but no matter how much I wanted it to be different I knew it was true. I did not like church. Cutting my hair and taking me out of school weren't going to change that. My hair grew back, though not in the same nineties style, parted down the middle. It grew wild, wavy, almost curly, but stayed dark. I refused to comb it. By then I was in the house most of the time and felt none of it mattered. I spent that summer trying to hit up different skate spots, but I kept fumbling over small things, the basics, and I grew too frustrated to continue. I didn't have the drive I used to. Little by little, I just stopped.

Titia, my mom's sister, lived with us for a while then.

I have a picture of her holding my clip-on sunglasses up to her face as she danced around my room, trying to cheer me up on one of the days in which I felt particularly bad. She was the only person who noticed I was off. A red light in the picture looks like a misplaced brushstroke, streaking the bottom of her hand and the greenish wall behind her. That imperfection of light on the film comforts me. That light was invisible when the photo was taken, though it had always been there, red, vibrant, only seen after the fact, after the film was developed. By then Titia was back in Brazil. We never talked on the phone—and something inexplicable about that hurt makes me love the picture even more. It's as familiar as her face and smile. That invisible light, always there but becoming manifest only after the moment was long gone. I knew it well.

Before school began, and before Titia left, she took Mike and me on a bus trip to Kissimmee, on the other side of Orlando, to explore. I was restless, and I think Titia was restless too. I knew someone who had moved from Puerto Rico to Florida—someone from my old world—who was living out there. But we got lost and ended up at a rundown mall where half the stores were empty. It had a fluorescent light that made the whole place unreal, as if it had been dreamed up by someone who was never able to put the whole image together, and we sat under that light and ate cheap burgers, watching lonely people drag by like specters. We got lost on the way back home too, and as the sun went down, I started to panic. Titia thought it was because I was disoriented, but that wasn't it. The darker it got, the more I could see my own face staring back at me as I looked out the window, my own eyes becoming alien. I looked at the shabby people going to and coming back from menial jobs spattered throughout the city, or homeless, or blank-faced. I watched broken people and broken neighborhoods until all I could see was me in the glass.

The apparitions outside the bus window looked the way I felt. Sparse. I knew many of the folks I was looking at were on drugs. Still, I don't know why getting lost there had such a strong effect on me. I wasn't afraid of the area or people. I'd been in much worse places in Puerto Rico. I'd bought drugs in much worse places, even lived in much worse places. Maybe it was because Florida was on the mainland, and my imagination insisted that the mainland was supposed to be different than that—more like where we'd lived in Idaho. Maybe it was the dissonance or something else, but that part of Florida made me realize that the badness I had been feeling was larger than I had known. I hadn't gotten rid of the Gray. In fact, everything was infected with it. It convinced me that nothing was stable and never would be. It was summer in Florida, but I remember feeling so cold. I looked at the mirage behind my face and felt like I was seeing my future.

There was something wrong with me on a much deeper level than ever before by the time school started. My ability to function had been cut down too far. I used to at least pretend. I used to skip, sure, but I would go to school *most* of the time. By the time I left, I had stopped going to any of my classes. I had nightmares about it for years—in college I would dream that I had classes I didn't even know about and would inevitably fail or that I would have to go back to high school because my diploma was a farce. My failure was imminent, and there was nothing I could do but wander the school in a panic that I'd destroyed my life. I'd even gone so far as to forget what subjects I was taking. Everything made me anxious. The teachers. Other students. The air in the US. Other people. The Gray had even seeped into them. What I've come to understand now is that that period was likely my first major depressive episode, and it lasted a couple of years, coinciding with the first symptoms of my bipolar disorder.

"Fucking Mike," I thought when my father told me he had been arrested after showing off at school the weed I'd given him. "Of course." I didn't yet know it was my first day as a high school dropout. My father stared at me as if he was drowning and needed help, as he'd been doing more and more, as if I could give him an answer, as if I could offer wisdom or console him in any way. Even then, whenever Mike got in trouble my parents looked to me for guidance. I was spinning sick inside, but I knew that neither he nor anybody could know that.

"I don't know what they're going to do to him," my dad

said. The way he looked at and confided in me made me hurt, and I couldn't take it. I went to my room and grabbed the bag of weed from under my bed.

"I need to tell you," I said, walking into his room, "it's mine. I gave it to Mike." I couldn't breathe. I wanted him to look at me, to say it was okay, that he understood, but I knew he wouldn't. I had wounded him. I was the one who was supposed to comfort him. But I had no words—at least none he would believe. For a moment I thought admitting what had happened, how Mike had gotten the weed, telling the truth for once, would help. It didn't. I was inside one of my nightmares, and I would not be leaving for a long time. My dad took the weed and left me for a while. I sat on the edge of his bed, wondering if he was crying in the kitchen, while I had visions of Mike being arrested, going in front of the judge, getting expelled.

My dad was somehow more gaunt-looking when he came back. "You're going to need to tell the cops the marijuana came from you," he said. He took me, my shit, and my pipe down to the police station, telling me on the way in a heavy voice that he didn't know what they were going to do with me, but I needed to tell them it had been me who had given Mike the drugs. I would have done anything to help Mike. I was going to the cops not for my dad but for my brother. I had been smoking for years, and Mike had been getting in trouble with police for years. I should have known we were both going to be fine, but I was scared. My dad's grim reaction gave me the feeling that everything

was going to cave in. Nothing was fine. The shadows I felt
were embedded in everything.

I was still a little high when we got to the station. The
cops laughed at me and my story. Apparently the weed was
pure but I had overpaid for it. I was in a foreign land in the
States and wasn't quite sure of the price of anything. They
wanted to know where I'd gotten it. I said I couldn't remember exactly, then made up some name. I wasn't afraid
of the cops, though I didn't trust them. I was afraid for
Mike, for the trouble he was going to get into. I was afraid
of the mental and emotional stress on my father. I was
afraid of the shadows that were bearing down on me more
every day. "You didn't have to tell anyone you gave me the
weed," Mike would say for years. "Of course I wasn't going
to tell anybody, and I wasn't going to get into any more or
less trouble than I did." I knew he was right, but it was the
only thing I could think to do to help him.

Mike was expelled. He was court-ordered to go to one
of those daylong boot camps where they tried to scare kids
straight. Nothing happened to me. Everything always
seemed to happen to Mike all the time. Nothing ever seemed
to happen to me. Of course, I was never dumb enough to
show all the kids in class my drugs just to look cool.

The next day, I told my dad I wasn't going back to
school. "If I go back, I'll just end up getting high again,"
I told his silhouette as he stood in front of the window in
our empty living room. My mother was in the kitchen,

quiet. With the exception of the positioning of the rooms, it looked exactly as it did when I talked about those games I played with that girl all those years before. I had been re-membering those incidents a lot during that time. "I won't be able to control myself," I said. And I think I believed that, that my problem was school, that if I left I would be okay. If I left, I could just keep to myself, maybe I wouldn't feel so bad or at least wouldn't infect other people like I infected my brother. If I shrunk into myself maybe I could be the Latter-Day Saint boy everyone wanted me to be. I could spend my time alone reading scriptures. I could get prepared to go on a mission, and I could love it. I wanted that to be true.

"No," he said. "You're right. You can't go back to school." He pulled out a progress report that had been sent to the house that morning. "I don't think you'd finish high school if you did stay. You'd flunk out."

The next few months were hell. I avoided my parents—which wasn't that hard to do—and hung out with Mike. They made me go with him to the boot camp, since they considered the whole thing my fault. The program was ri-diculous. We were dropped off in the morning and marched into this compound—I don't know if it was a former school or what, but there was a field and classrooms and long hallways. There were drill sergeants, or at least people

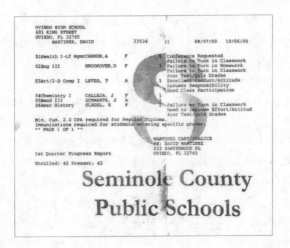

dressed in military uniforms, and from what I remember it was coed. Before anything else, they lined us up against the walls on either side of a hall, searched us, then made us squat with our hands close to the wall but not leaning against it. If we leaned against the wall, sat down, or quit, one of the uniformed adults would scream at us, call us weak, tell us how we weren't nearly as hard or bad as we thought we were, until they were either red in the face or the person they were yelling at started crouching again. They seemed to like it and became more aggressive if the kid they were yelling at started to cry. I think they thought it was proof that they were getting through to the kid.

We were forced to run and jog and do pull-ups and push-ups and sit-ups on the field behind the compound until we could barely feel our legs, the uniformed adults barking at us and ridiculing the slower ones. They separated the boys and girls and took us to the jail close by and made us walk through cells while prisoners joked about raping us, then had some inmate tell us that we weren't hard and that we would all be someone's bitch if we were where he was. After that, we went to one of the classrooms, where we were lectured on how lucky we were that people loved us enough to send us to their boot camp, how drugs would kill us, and how there were STDs that would "make our little penises shrivel up and fall off." They yelled at a kid who thought that was funny. They made us write apologies to our guardians that the adults in uniforms would read then mail to our homes. Anyone who talked to anyone else would be screamed at.

At one point I got in trouble for something—I can't remember what now—and a uniformed adult put her face an inch from mine and yelled at me. The correct response to whatever it was she said was "Sir, yes, sir." I was supposed to shout it, except I was confused as to whether I should say sir or ma'am, and I refused to shout. I said what they asked me to say, and I did the prescribed push-ups when I didn't respond the way they wanted, but I never did yell back. We were on a time crunch to get to the jail, and in the end, my minor infraction for not yelling loud enough probably wasn't worth being late. At maybe nine or ten at night, some kid with emotional issues started talking back to one of the adults, said he was going to tell his dad they were mistreating him. A retired cop from one of the other lines of troubled youth walked over and shrieked at the kid, and when the kid yelled back, the man pushed him to the floor, twisted his arm back, cuffed him, and took him away, all while the kid howled and cried about how mad his father was going to be. My parents picked us up after that. I don't remember the conversation we had in the car. I don't think there was one.

I know those lost high school years ended with my moving to Brazil to serve my mission, but the in-between is confused. I remember events, but there is no order, nothing to mark the time. My dad bought a bunch of textbooks and enrolled Mike and me in this correspondence home-school program where he was signed up as the teacher. The school, now defunct, had a libertarian-style philosophy that parents should be able to teach their children as they wished. He said he was going to make sure we studied, but that petered out quickly. He never had the ability or stability to see homeschooling through. I spent the next three years doing pretty much whatever I wanted, or I could have, if I had wanted anything. A couple of years after dropping out, my dad told the correspondence school I earned a diploma. At some point, I went to a makeshift high school graduation I didn't deserve with a ceremony I didn't want. I never took a GED-style test, never took the SATs, did nothing to merit a degree at all. I was embarrassed to be there.

After leaving school, after I was incapable of shaking those shadows, I was only ever comfortable around Mike and our friend Ricky. Mike was okay. Mike was family. Real family, not like my parents or anyone else. I loved Mike. We had history, would have more history, because we were brothers. Real brothers. I didn't want to talk to anybody else anymore, and I didn't have to. Our symbiosis became more intricate, more essential. I supplied Mike with stolen money and rides. I never could stay off substances, though I tried more than once. (I went so far as to create a calendar and ticked off the days I used in blue, the days I masturbated in red, together with the number of how many times. After a couple of weeks, when my entire calendar was red and blue, I got depressed and quit tracking my sins.) Mike supplied me with pills: Percocet and morphine, Xanax and Valium. Sometimes acid. Sometimes Special K or other drugs friends of his had stolen from veterinarians. I would attempt to make homemade hallucinogens, but most of the time I would have to fight through a vomiting fit to get to the euphoria and high. I couldn't smoke weed anymore, and I didn't like to drink, though those were the two easiest substances to come by. Anything else was fair game. One of the last times I tried smoking weed was with a girl I had met at seminary (who later tried to run her sister over in a car after they'd had a fight). We smoked, and in my mind's eye I could almost see god telling me I had to go on a mission. I spent the next few hours trying to suppress my terror and trying not to cry. When I could get nothing else, I would steal NyQuil and sleeping pills and drink or eat them by the bottle until I got sick. I stole Vicodin from my parents' medicine cabinet and the unending amphetamines my youngest brother didn't take for his ADHD. I would lie on the couch and watch *Invader Zim* and *Æon Flux* and *The Maxx* and hours of music videos and documentaries on the sixties and the civil rights movement and surrealism and CBGB and the Harlem Renaissance and Anaïs Nin and the Beats and Andy Warhol on any DVD I could get in the mail from Netflix, creating my own curriculum of what I was interested in and forging my own education I hadn't obtained in school, always daydreaming about being able to speak to people again, finding artist friends and living an entire life in which I created beautiful work all the time. I would do anything to keep from feeling bad. I would do anything to keep from feeling like me.

Everything was becoming more and more pointless. "You ever seen an independent film with no music?" I said to someone once, maybe Mike. "Like when the color is off, and you're not sure what the point of all the dialogue around you is? That's what everything feels like to me all the time." I'd been staying up late watching the Sundance channel for nights in a row, and that was exactly what everything felt like for me all the time.

My obsession with color is the best way for me to describe my levels of depression. At some point, I scribbled in an old notebook: "It's okay when it's blue, but when it's

I would use later. I would paint it later, or write about it; it was something I would turn into sound, never to attribute meaning. Meaning was inconsequential. The images would take care of themselves. The details were all that was needed. I imagined that the road I drove on early in the mornings when I took my youngest brothers to school—or when I went to the seminary classes my parents made me attend with Mike—didn't exist, because the fog ate it. I knew there were houses through that fog, but they ceased to exist for those moments as well. I wanted them to be gone. I wanted to be high, to have control, but I learned that I didn't need it to feel the beauty sometimes— sometimes I did. Sometimes it was natural. Sometimes I would rise up and become a conduit, receiving a thousand new ideas and images and thoughts simultaneously. Whether I was on drugs or not or had spent the night before looking at porn, I read scripture in the hope that it would change me into a Mormon. I read all the Old Testament, the New Testament, the Book of Mormon, the Pearl of Great Price, Doctrine and Covenants (all Latter-Day Saint scriptures). And while I often felt more connected to my Kafka and Vonnegut, in scripture I also found beauty. Rape, murder, love, sacrifice, fear, forgiveness, war, cannibalism, onanism, the promise of a beautiful new life after death. They made me depressed and hopeful, and I spent so much time alone with them. The longer I was alone, the more my head spun, the more I came to the conclusion that I needed to be alone, so I deliberately tried not to meet or interact with people. At home, no one noticed how I was folding into myself and how the symptoms of my bipolar disorder were beginning to manifest more each day, starting with that long period of nauseous depression.

A dim depression can look like serenity. It can look like hours in a meditative trance in which I'd lie on the floor and think slow thoughts. Potent colors percolate through my skin and into my chest and back or the middle part of my brain—especially deep, solid, pure colors, like pigments. The difference between this state and a euphoric one is a pervasive melancholy, strong but fleeting. But while it does last, it's sensual. When I hear songs declare they're in love with their sadness, this is the sadness I think of, and I understand. It's the exact sadness I felt driving around in the car at that time. It's like a small cut on the lip that has to be bit and sucked because it hurts so good. It's that spot between the painful and sweet, and it's lovely.

Being depressed at home was excruciating, listening to my siblings and parents yell at each other, or when not yelling leaving an anxious buzz in the air, or lying on the floor in my room as the clothes, and paints, and cords for guitars, and dust piled up, or just being soaked by the dense despondency that strangled the house, or the discomfort of hearing the rest of my family members yell and fight with one another. "I never want to be like that," I would think, as I listened to them scream, my father being the loudest when he was home. So, I didn't yell, and most

of the time no one yelled at me. Instead, I became invisible, which was great because I didn't want to be noticed. I
just wanted to read at the bookstore and hang out on one
of the lounge chairs until my anxious stomachaches would
send me back home, and then I wanted to read there too.
The presence of books would offer a small charge to the
fading electric feel as the depression deepened, the last
vestiges of fading color, the last safe space.

Once I stopped going to school, what I had left was
church people, which wasn't at all what I needed. The only
person from church I could hang out with was Ricky. I did
try—or half tried—to hang out with a couple of other guys
I knew there, but it never really worked. They were too
functional, and I didn't know what to do with that. They
talked about sports and going on missions and girls they
knew and how they were going to Brigham Young University after high school. They talked not necessarily about
faith, but about church culture. Their lives were defined
by it. Mine was not, and I didn't want it to be no matter
how much I wanted to please my family. The more I was
around the church kids, the more depressed I became. They
would—and did—grow up to be accountants and business-
men, able to wind their way through social systems like
the school I'd left. They would go on their missions, become
leaders there, learn to preach and persuade, learn confidence, go home, and go through college, get married, have
kids. I would lie to the church leaders and members to get
to a mission I felt obligated to complete—though I didn't

want to feel like I felt obligated—struggle through each Sunday, and while they all went off to college, I'd be snorting Roxys and cocaine from broken CD covers in my parents' car in a dirty smock outside the ice cream shop where I worked just under full-time. But it was more than their successes versus my inadequacies. I didn't like the concept of sin, of doing or not doing a thing based on an eternal reward instead of basic human decency, not that everyone I knew at church felt or behaved that way. The rhetoric at church meetings, testimony meetings, whispered rumors that someone had broken the "seventh" (a term many used for the seventh commandment instead of saying "had sex out of wedlock" or "committed adultery") were so prevalent. In my head, even then, everything seemed to be codified, labeled, turned into a formula. There were different degrees of sin, the most pleasurable being the worst, but they were all shrunk to a formula that made no room for nuance or thought, and it was a formula I couldn't follow. So it ate me up, devastated me, gave me the guilt that kept me awake at night and that I ingested copious amounts of drugs to nullify.

Part of people following a formula means that they become blind to anything existing outside said formula, become blind because all they seem to see is black and white, and no one seems to want to recognize what they don't want to see. The adults around me seemed to think bad kids did drugs and couldn't function, and because they were so eaten by their guilt, they would have to admit to any wrongdoing when questioned by the proper priesthood authorities, who spoke with the authority of god. Bad kids didn't answer questions about the Bible or share thoughts on what they'd read in the Book of Mormon when asked to in class. Troubled kids were full of rage and talked back and were irreverent and loud, not kind and courteous and thoughtful. They wouldn't be able to feel god or the Holy Ghost, and if they did, it would be not the quiet and love I felt when meditating but dread and trepidation telling us to repent. I may not have been able to apply the church formula to my own life, but I did know how to use it to hide myself, and I did it well. The problem was, like the hole in my leg, my wounds should never have been hidden. If they hadn't, if Mike's hadn't, if we'd had people who knew how to take care of them when we were still children, maybe our infections wouldn't have been as bad, maybe our wounds would have never been infected at all. It's only because of the stillness I've felt beneath the noise that I'm even alive at all right now. It's why I write what I write and say what I say. I know that. I know that's what's given me this extension, carried me through my mission, told me to try again and again every time I wanted to die by my drugs, not the formulas, not the rules.

"It's okay when it's blue, but when it's gray it's unbearable," the notebook read. That blue is the next level down from the sensual depression, which goes from red to purple. It stretches wide and dives deep until it reaches black, and eventually gray, or the end of color. When I felt like this as a child, I would walk barefoot around the small town where I lived, dreaming of running away, of starting some adventure I wasn't yet able to comprehend but would save me from the heaviness that was piling on. As a teenager in Puerto Rico, I would ride my skateboard, not practicing the tricks I was perpetually trying to master, just rolling down the hills in Old San Juan, barreling toward the ocean at that time when the sun was down but the sky was not yet all the way dark, hoping somehow the momentum could light me, carry me away. As a teenager in Florida, when it was worse than ever before, I would steal sleeping pills or Benadryl or anything with nitrous oxide or anything with pseudoephedrine or NyQuil from the Walmart next to my house, or drink or eat whatever substance Mike would bring me, then drive through the orange groves at night in pitch black with the windows down while listening to Radiohead until I got to a bar on the edge of Lake Jesup. I knew they wouldn't serve me, so I never went inside, but I would sit and watch the alligators that roamed the water's edge in the dark. Every now and then someone would catch one of the big ones and put it in a cage next to the bar so that people could appreciate it before setting it loose again. I liked the darkness of it all, the weight and comfort of whatever substance was weighing on my brain, the long alligators, and the smell of the orange blossoms.

I both liked it and didn't, I guess, which is the way many people addicted to substances describe their addictions. I wrote, "The substances don't work, but lack of them causes enormous lack of colors, blues and reds, purples and greens, black, gray. Gray is so much sadder than blue. It's nothing." The Gray is BoJack Horseman Depression. The drugs didn't cure anything, but they worked better than nothing, and I was realizing that I needed them.

I drew pictures of myself in Florida as my mental health declined. Pictures of suicides and manias, dark spaces and deep colors. It all culminated in a mental collapse during which I not only forced myself to be alone, I celebrated it. Alone, it looked like I wasn't getting into trouble on the outside, and for the purpose of satisfying my family, making them feel like everything was okay, that was all that mattered.

Alone, the spiral I had felt coming and been running from for as long as I could remember was in full swing. Sure, I left high school, but what was more important was that I left people. I left people because I couldn't bear to be around anyone I thought was functional. I needed to be around others who were also inadvertently trying to destroy themselves. I needed people as broken as I was, and I needed them to know they were broken—even if they didn't know why—and I needed them to know they were destroying themselves the way I knew I was. I couldn't have them deny it. If they lied, it didn't work. I needed to see the nerve. I needed to expose my own. It would have helped to have had an adult who lived outside that formula to tell me that they were broken too, that, yes, my fears were legitimate—that it would never get better but that it didn't need to because I would become stronger. I wouldn't have needed to lie later. I wish someone had told me that I was allowed to be broken and still be beautiful and sacred, the real sacred that has to do with growth and not fear. I felt destroyed and couldn't stand to listen to anyone who made me feel that I needed to fear, made me feel by comparison that I had no chance of ever being okay. I think I thought I could find some kind of secret that could give me hope and then, and only then, could I encounter other people again. But there was no secret, only what I didn't want to see, my own self-imposed blindness. It was harder on me, but easier on everyone I loved, to say I was inherently weak and therefore doomed to punishment. I chose to believe I

olivia and the beach

Me and Mike on the beach in Fortaleza

The first and last time Mike went to Brazil, he was fifteen. He picked up two neighborhood girls without speaking Portuguese and had another one conspiring to marry him so she could get to the States. One of the neighborhood girls lived across the street from our vovó's house. The other lived the next block over, and I'm not sure how the whole thing started. I was so deep into my own head at that point, I didn't pay much attention to the beginning. Both girls were friends of our cousins, and I'm not sure who he started hooking up with first. All I know is that the entire house (with the exception of our dad) knew about it and helped keep the two girls away from one another. Girl 1 would come in, go with Mike into our cousin's room, and make out on the bed with the door open—Vovó insisted the door stay open. When Girl 2 would appear at the spiked wall in front of the house and clap her hands for someone to answer, one of my cousins would pop her head into the room, whistle, and Mike would sneak Girl 1 out the back. This went on almost the entire three months we were there.

A few years later, after I learned to speak Portuguese, I talked to the girl who lived across the street about the whole thing. She said, "Of course we knew about each other. But neither of us speak English and your brother didn't speak Portuguese. It's not like we were going out with him. We just wanted to hook up."

The third girl, Olivia, the one who wanted to marry Mike, didn't make as much sense. One day she just appeared. Olivia's older brother had a beach house, or knew someone who had a beach house, or had a family member who had a beach house, or something like that, and my aunt was trying to get them to let us use it. They did—on the condition that the brother, his wife, and Olivia come with us. Olivia spoke English because she'd lived in Miami with her mother until they were deported, and she kept telling us how she would do anything to get back to the US. Anything. We weren't very receptive. Mike was busy juggling the two girls he thought didn't know about each other, and I stayed away from Olivia as much as I could. It might have been because she loved talking about partying and how much she loved the malls in the US and nice cars and the older guys she fucked and how she liked to milk them for all the clothes and gifts they were worth. Meanwhile, her brother was what was called a *crente*, or a believer, and was always trying to argue the word of god. When he found out I was going to go on a mission soon, he flipped. He said Mormonism was of the devil and tried to convert me to his church.

When Olivia found two bottles of cachaça (sugarcane liquor), we shared them in secret on the beach. She was annoyed that neither Mike nor I paid much attention to her, and we were annoyed with her constant talk about prom, but we weren't above drinking together. It wasn't until later that our cousins told us she had been trying to have sex with Mike with the hope of getting pregnant so that our religious parents would make him marry her and she could go back to the States. Living in the US was prestigious. My mother had prestige for marrying an American and living in the US. I get it now, even if it annoyed me then. Apparently, the crente brother was in on it as well. For all I know, the cachaça wasn't an accident.

Nobody had sex with her. Nobody married her. But the beach was magical that night. The whole family came out, and Mike and I pulled together dried palm tree trunks and coconuts and whatever wood we could find and built a fire. We brought out one of the bottles of cachaça and told the adults that we'd just found it and were using it as an accelerant. We poured the liquid on the flames to make them flare and pulse. We took turns walking off to the dark to take another swig before pouring more on the fire. Someone had brought a guitar, and Mike and I took turns playing, listening to the ocean, tasting the salty air, the smoke in the sand spreading up to a sky so vast and starry that it looked like the embodiment of the immense saudade growing in me, the saudade the moment would become. I saw a picture of us at the beach years later, after Mike died, and I thought, "We look like children!" Then I realized, "My god, we were children! Isn't that strange? How were we ever children?" How were we ever alive, dancing around a fire like our ancestors had before us, with the same stars, the same ocean, the same eternity?

Nothing to Do with God

A confused and terrified me on my first day at the CTM
(missionary training center in São Paulo)

1.

The first missionary for the Church of Jesus Christ of
Latter-Day Saints was Joseph Smith, who founded the
church in 1830 with exactly six members. By 1844, when
Smith was murdered, there were over twenty-six thousand
members, also referred to as saints. Up until his death, he
worked converting people from New York to Illinois, through
stories of his visions and visitations from god and angels
who instructed him on how to form the church. He preached

of receiving the priesthood from god, which would be given to all worthy men, and proclaimed it was the power to act in the name of god, lead his children, and perform sacred and saving ordinances in god's name, specifically in temples that were to be a blessing to *all* worthy saints.

Joseph Smith was murdered in an Ohio jail by an anti-Mormon mob in 1844. After two months of confused tumult in the church, Brigham Young, the man who led pioneers across the plains and whose name is given to the church's university (with campuses in Utah, Idaho, Hawai'i, and Israel), became the new prophet and leader. Before then, the temple and its ordinances—including baptizing deceased ancestors by proxy and joining spouses and families dead and alive as family units for all of eternity—were available to all saints who were deemed worthy if they followed a set of commandments. Under Young's leadership, the church adopted the prevailing white Christian belief at the time that black people were descendants of Cain, the first murderer in the Bible. In a journal kept by Wilford Woodruff, one of the early presidents of the church, he wrote that Brigham Young declared, "If there never was a Prophet or Apostle of Jesus Christ [who] spoke it before, I tell you, this people that are commonly called Negros are the children of old Cain. I know they are. I know that they cannot bear rule in the Priesthood." From then until 1978, anyone who had any known black antecedents was allowed to be baptized, but they were not allowed to hold priesthood authority, nor could they enter the temple to baptize their dead or be joined for eternity to their spouses and family. The church excluded black people from what they taught allows a person into the highest heavens.

If we had been born a handful of years earlier, the excluded would have included me, Mike, and our mother and other siblings. It would have excluded the entirety of our mother's family, who for generations (unknowingly) funneled proclaimed sin and unworthiness into us through their "black blood." When my dad taught us this history, he emphasized that it was a long time ago. He said it no longer mattered, that we shouldn't think about it, so I didn't. I had other things to worry about, like not letting school friends know I was associated with the church and pretending I wasn't getting high. Though I wouldn't know it until after my mission, Brigham Young also taught, "I will not consent for a moment to have the children of Cain rule me nor my brethren." While this is not currently officially accepted, Brigham Young's beliefs on race live on in the church to this day, in the shrugging dismissals regarding race from most white people I've met in the church and in my family and in the explicit bigotry of the DezNat, a group of Latter-Day Saint white nationalists that runs rampant in Utah.

I don't tell people I used to be a missionary for the Church of Jesus Christ of Latter-Day Saints. Mormon ideas make me uneasy. Having ever associated with their overbearing, conservative culture makes me uneasy. The homophobic and insensitive remarks made by many make me uneasy. Their racist past makes me uneasy. These days I don't want to be affiliated in any way with the church, Latter-Day Saint culture, or any organized religion—while I find many teachings ranging from Buddhism to Christianity to Judaism to Candomblé interesting, I want affiliation with none. My entire life, I've listened as members of the congregation walked up to the pulpit on what is called fast and testimony meeting, held every first Sunday, to proclaim that they know "without a shadow of a doubt" that the Church of Jesus Christ of Latter-Day Saints is the only true and living church on the earth, that Joseph Smith was a Prophet, and that the church is guided by a living prophet and apostles in modern days. I haven't been able to bring myself to make those statements for a long time—though I constantly did as a missionary, even when I felt awkward doing so. I couldn't even say without a shadow of a doubt that god is real or even that my own life is anything more than a dream. I don't know anything without a shadow of a doubt. The moment I say I was a missionary, people make assumptions I don't have the patience to disprove, and I don't entirely blame them. I'm ashamed of it. But my whole mission was a lie, at odds with my personality and part of my history. I told myself I was the one who made the choice to evangelize, but the choice had been made for me long before. I don't regret it, but it was never true to who I was. I had to lie to even go.

In Puerto Rico, when I was maybe fifteen and Mike was twelve, we took a breather from skating the basketball court by our house. We sat on the green and chipped bench we had been grinding and looked out over the bleachers in front of us. I told Mike I knew I'd been fucking up, but I was going to be better by doing the right thing and going on a mission. I was going to get clean, go away, come home, maybe get married and have kids, work an office job—do what I was supposed to. I was using the term that other people always used on me. *Supposed to.* We had just finished smoking a blunt or taking hits off that bamboo pipe I'd made. I looked to the sky, imagining everything I was supposed to have. I didn't like the future I saw above the bleachers, but I was convinced it was my only option. I only had a little more time to have fun before I was trapped in the same regimented misery as the adults around me.

"That's good of you," Mike said, pushing his board back and forth with his feet. "But I don't know that I'm going to do that."

"It'll fuck Dad up if we don't go," I said.

"I know," Mike said.

We had been told we were going on missions since before I could remember. Boys practically had to when they turned nineteen, or at least it was strongly suggested they go. Most parents made it mandatory. (Girls could if they wanted, or they could focus on getting married.) Church people and our parents and relatives had been asking if we were excited to go on a mission since we were old enough to talk. The answer had to be yes, unless we wanted them to frown, mumble about our rebelliousness, and try to initiate long talks about why we were rejecting god's will.

"It's required of all young men when you reach nineteen," my dad and so many church leaders said. (It's eighteen these days.) He made sure to tell us that being a missionary in Brazil had saved him. It was where he met my mother, and though I wouldn't realize it for years, I think it was also one of the first times he felt important. We grew up with stories of his mission miracles, adventures, moments of spiritual enlightenment. I believed all that was possible for me too. A mission would magically erase my constant feelings of unworthiness and filthiness and change me into who I was *supposed to* be—who my family wanted me to be. Maybe, I told myself, though I couldn't quite see it, happiness was possible for me there.

The mission was an event forever on the horizon but without form, like getting married or going to college, having some random adult career. It had been three years since I'd dropped out of high school and started spending most of my time in my room feeding on stolen pain pills, or morphine when Mike could get it for me. I was decaying in almost every way. Only reading, writing, and making art brought the quiet sense of belonging and progress I craved. I'd been dutifully reading scriptures for hours a day, sitting cross-legged on the floor surrounded by my paints and clothes, whether I was high or not. I read the entire Bible, from Genesis to Revelation. I read the other official scriptures of the Church of Jesus Christ of Latter-Day Saints. I loved the gospels, especially John, who referred to himself as the disciple Jesus loved. The stories about Christ provided such a stark juxtaposition to the violence, vengeance, anger, and wars in so many of the other books. It was in distinct contrast to much of what I heard in church and from other Christian religions.

"I'll disappoint a lot of people if I don't go," I said into the quiet, afraid of the impossible expectations my parents and extended family had for me. People from church had expectations as well, but while those expectations might have been important to my parents, they weren't for me. Latter-Day Saints are big into community, and they have a lot of gatherings and activities besides the normal Sunday hours, but Mike and I always tended to be on the outsides of all that, and we tended to be ignored—and we liked it that way. Part of it may have been that we weren't white like most of the members in Idaho and Florida, and neither Mike nor I ever fit into starkly white lives like that. Maybe it was because neither of us were into sports or anything conventional or considered normal. Maybe it was because the kids our age knew we got high and did crazy shit (even if their parents never seemed to know), and because of that they were a little scared to be around us. Maybe it was a mixture of reasons. No matter why, the Latter-Day Saint community was always something I had to put up with for my family's sake and never something I was interested in being a part of for myself. But despite all that, I felt it was my obligation to go on a mission. It was something my dad had looked forward to and wanted for us since before I was born, and when I pled into that quietness, and stillness came back to me, I took it as confirmation—despite my unworthiness—that I needed to go.

I'd worked for maybe two months in the last three years before my mission. I was terrifically underprepared for anything resembling a normal life. My thoughts reverberated off my bedroom walls and back to me. "I'm unworthy," I argued. "I'll be doing a disservice if I go. I won't help anybody. I won't fit in." I knew this was true, but I knew I had to go anyway. If I didn't, my family would hate me and probably spend days or weeks crying, and I would atrophy even more. It would make my parents physically ill. My dad could get sick and die. He'd been having new health issues he and my mother were starting to blame on Mike. And in the end, dreaming of leaving the scraps of my life and that house in Florida behind thrilled me slightly more than the thought of becoming a missionary scared me.

I reminded myself that Christ preached love. That was all he preached, and I thought if I could stick to that and only that I would possibly have a chance of not turning into a robot or going insane. If I could continually find that stillness I'd found meditating, maybe I'd make it through.

I loved Christ for preaching love. That was the reason I gave myself for going, and that would be my response to anyone who asked me why I did. I loved the kind Jewish man who defied the rule-obsessed leaders and refused to hate, even as he was being murdered. But no matter how badly I wanted that to be true, I knew I was really going for my parents—for the fear that they would get sick and die if I didn't.

The paperwork, doctor's appointments, and interviews with church leaders to evaluate my worthiness took a month. I was left reeling after my last interview, during which I sat opposite a tall, severe man in a suit whom my dad had told about the time I'd surrendered my weed to the cops to help Mike. The man seemed to hate me for it, or at the very least seemed to consider me weak.

"I need you to know this is serious," he said, glaring across his desk. "These interviews are the perfect opportunity for checking in on yourself and for evaluation so you can achieve forgiveness for your sins. If you lie here, then you are lying to God. And that is something He cannot abide." His next question took an unsurprising turn. "Do you masturbate?"

My mind went directly to *The Miracle of Forgiveness*, which I knew the man in front of me had certainly read: "Prophets anciently and today condemn masturbation . . . Our modern prophet has indicated that no young man should be called on a mission who is not free from this practice." I knew what I needed to say for me to go on the mission, to make my parents happy. I knew that, like always, I needed to pretend.

"No," I said, but if god existed, then he knew full well I masturbated every chance I got. I knew the church leader was the only one I was lying to. He kept staring at me. We swam in the silence around us. I felt sewn into the white shirt and tie I'd been forced to wear for the occasion. The formality made it so much worse, especially since I knew it would be my uniform over the next couple of years.

"I know you've had trouble with drugs," he finally said.

"That was in the past." I looked straight at him. I wanted, more than anything, to slink away. "I got in trouble that one time, and I quit," I lied to him again. God knew I'd eaten a weed cookie after taking a handful of the Demerol a doctor had given me after I'd had my wisdom teeth and a tiny chunk of jawbone removed in order to get mission ready. There was stolen Vicodin in my room. There were amphetamine-fueled nights with Mike and sick days tripping on LSA. "It was only marijuana, and I haven't used anything in years."

I didn't like to lie. If I could have, I would have lain down on the floor or bent over to hold my knees to my chest to keep the nausea at bay. Instead, I stared at the man's face, answering his questions until there was nothing else to say. On the other side of the door, my proud parents wore enormous grins at the prospect of me doing my godly duty.

My papers were sent to Salt Lake City, where the

twelve apostles and the president of the church himself looked at them. At the time, they were the ones to determine where each missionary would go. (These days there are so many missionaries that other general authorities are now partially responsible for mission assignments.) I was in Ohio helping my uncle move when my dad called me a few weeks after sending in my papers. I took the call in the empty room where I'd been staying.

"Well, son, your mission call came today." His voice was thick. His pride in me set my stomach off again. I wanted to make him proud, but I wanted to do it in a way that wasn't a lie. I looked down at the worn carpet and faux wood paneling in the wall while he talked.

My mom's voice came in on the other line. "Your dad already opened it."

"Shut up, Joia!" he snapped at her. "I told you not to say anything!"

"Just tell me where I'm going," I said. Up until that point, I had no idea where I would go for my mission. We weren't allowed to choose.

The papers rustled as he pulled them out of the envelope. "David Martinez," he began, choking on the words, "you have been called to serve a two-year mission in the . . . in . . . in the São Paulo, Brazil, Interlagos Mission . . ." He read on, crying, but that was all I heard. We went wherever the church sent us, and it was luck or god or the goodwill of the universe that sent me to Brazil.

My father served in northeastern Brazil in the early

eighties and met my mother there (though I'd been assured all my life that their courtship began only after he
went home to Idaho and they started writing letters back
and forth). My mother had always seemed less enthusias-
tic about the idea of my mission, though she guarded her
feelings more closely than her husband. He was ecstatic
that I was part of the select tribe of people called to serve
in Brazil. Everyone knew it was where the best missions
were. I sat on the bed and rested my elbow on my knee, my
forehead in my hand.

2.

The first members of the Church of Jesus Christ of
Latter-Day Saints in Brazil were German immigrants
in 1913, though the first missionaries weren't sent until
the mid-twenties, when an influx of Germans migrated
to the south of the country after World War I. The first
Portuguese-speaking congregations weren't formed until 1940, almost three decades after the arrival of the
first missionaries. Brazil's population is more than half
black, including people with mixed heritage. There are
more black people in Brazil than in any other country
outside of Africa, but until 1978, missionaries were dis-
suaded, if not officially then unofficially, by many mission
presidents from trying to convert black members. While
they could be baptized, they were still not allowed to hold
the priesthood or attend the temple, and the end goal of
missionary work is to bring in people to the temple since

we're taught that the temple ordinances are the only path to salvation.

The ban might have continued longer if it weren't for Brazil. Brazil has always been intensely religious, even before the Jesuits forced Christianity on the indigenous population. The indigenous religions included *pajés* (or shamans), spirits, a complex history of myth and legend, and rituals and rights. The enslaved Africans brought the Yorubá religions with them on the boats. They brought Olodumaré (the creator of everything, god) and *orixás* (spirits) like Iemanjá, Xangô, and Oblatala, along with hundreds more. Indigenous, white, and black people mixed, and so did their beliefs, forming religions like Umbanda where orixás and saints are mixed, making Iemanjá Our Lady of Navigators, Xangô John the Baptist, and Obatalá Jesus, while also keeping many of what was left of indigenous spirits and rituals. Protestantism also flourished in Brazil, especially with the Assembleia de Deus, founded in 1911. Even language like *se Deus quiser* (if god wills it), *valei-me* (save me), and *vai com Deus* (go with god) are all commonly used in everyday speech—especially in the poorer populations. Like in many places, religion, specifically Christianity, flourishes with the poor and downtrodden. The poor and downtrodden are usually people of color, and this is true even in Brazil.

When the Church of Jesus Christ of Latter-Day Saints branched out from the German-speaking to the Portuguese-speaking people, the numbers of baptisms skyrocketed. The problem was that it became harder to track people's black lineage to determine if they could enter the temple, and even if a person could pass as white, it didn't mean they were. The new black and mixed-race converts were adding up. On the church's official website today, "Race and the Priesthood" acknowledges the ways Brazil complicated the racial ban on the priesthood:

> Brazil in particular presented many challenges. Unlike the United States and South Africa, where legal and de facto racism led to deeply segregated societies, Brazil prided itself on its open, integrated, and mixed racial heritage. In 1975, the Church announced that a temple would be built in São Paulo, Brazil. As the temple construction proceeded, Church authorities encountered faithful black and mixed-ancestry Latter-day Saints who had contributed financially and in other ways to the building of the São Paulo temple, a sanctuary they realized they would not be allowed to enter once it was completed. Their sacrifices, as well as the conversions of thousands of Nigerians and Ghanaians in the 1960s and early 1970s, moved Church leaders.

My father baptized my mother in 1981, three years after the ban on the priesthood and temple ordinances for black Latter-Day Saints was lifted. In 1984, they went to the temple—her pregnant belly full of me—to be married

and talking till four in the morning. We cousins stayed
up late most nights talking: Natália, who was one year
older than me; Marília, who was a year younger; Mike;
and me. We listened to the same types of music, had the
same types of ideas. We talked about Jane's Addiction and
Chico Buarque, the state of public schools in Brazil, the
evils of President Bush. Their laughs would fill up a room,
and it was okay to be silly, turning the lights off at night
and playing with a flashing toy while listening to music as
loud as we could and pretending to be in a club. The two
girls were so similar to Mike and me—except that they
were highly functional in school and work and social situations. Marília, who looked like a darker female version
of me, complete with a single crooked tooth and a scar on
the forehead like mine, would take Mike and me to hang
out with her friends and boyfriend at Dragão do Mar. We
went with Natália and the rest of the family to Olinda to
see the old Portuguese and Dutch buildings (which looked
so much to me like San Juan), where I snuck cachaça sam-
ples a shop was giving to tourists. We went to the beach,
where Mike and I drank half a bottle of cachaça, built a
fire, and played guitar and sang until we had nothing else
to burn to keep the fire going. We all went to Fortal (an
out-of-season Carnaval in the city of Fortaleza), where
everyone seemed to hook up with someone, except me. I
watched, from a hill, children running against a crowd,
hitting people on one pocket with palms or magazines and
pickpocketing wallets out of the other. I hid my tears three

Vovó at church

months later when I had to part ways with the part of me
I'd never been allowed to know.

I feel a mixture of pity and shame and confusion at my
mother's denial of herself and her heritage, and it took
years of me studying and living in Brazil to realize it was
not just her but many people there denying similar heri-
tages. I feel a mixture of self-pity and shame and confusion
at having been raised with so little knowledge of Brazilian
culture. My mother's resemblance to her mother was undeniable. She was almost identical to her sister. But, like
many black (especially mixed-black) people her age (especially in Brazil), she tried to abscond from who she was,

with light makeup and by proclaiming that she wasn't really black when the subject came up. Really, she said, she looked more Polynesian—anything but black and indigenous. Three months after I said goodbye to her family, I was an official agent of the American religious culture that had helped perpetuate her shame. I was tasked with finding and teaching more converts like her, though I never thought about it in those terms then.

I loved aspects of serving a mission in Brazil, but they had nothing to do with the reasons I was supposed to be there. I was finally a Brazilian *in* Brazil. I held on to my idea of a tender god and got to know people I will always adore. They helped me learn my mother's native tongue, which I never would have otherwise, despite both my parents' fluency. I finally walked on the same land as my South American family and ancestors, most importantly the black and indigenous ones I never knew anything about. Breathing their air made me feel grounded and connected like I never had in the States. My family in the States were pilgrims and pioneers and usurpers of indigenous lands. My family in Brazil were the indigenous people, though also mixed with the usurpers. My bloodline ran in the land there much deeper than in the States. I was in love with Brazil and the prospect of escape it offered me. I could access the mirror version of myself that my father's culture and my mother's erasure had withheld from me for so long.

But I hated being a missionary in other aspects. I

hated god-shaped platitudes, was exasperated with missionaries who wanted to argue with and criticize others,
was exhausted with the rules that tried to govern even
the way I thought. We weren't allowed to *think of*, or have
conversations about, anything that wasn't related to god.
It was a mission rule, and mission rules were considered
sacred. I was tired of watching people around me contort
themselves to meet those unreasonable standards. I de-
tested the pervasive feeling of being stuck with a group of
people I did not belong with. The overt ethnocentricity and
superciliousness of many American missionaries reigned
supreme, even in a place that was supposed to be mine.
Otherness followed me even in Brazil, and it came cour-
tesy of something that was supposed to be sacred.

At the training center, I'd been paired with a missionary who would be my partner, or companion (we were
assigned new companions and switched areas every few
months). We would go everywhere in pairs to avoid trouble. A couple of days later, he confessed his sins to the leaders. He'd slept with a girl before his mission and had to go
home for a while before he could come back to the mission
clean. The others speculated. Maybe he wouldn't be called
back to Brazil. Maybe he would have to stay in the States.
He was a cautionary tale. By the time he left, I had been
moved in with the Brazilians because I spoke Portuguese
better than the Americans and had a new companion. I
stayed awake in my bunk at night feeling *my* filth and
shame for not confessing *my* sins. I longed to experience

LEFT: The favela I looked at while listening to Metallica (on the side without garbage on the rooftops). **ABOVE:** São Paulo. I took this photo through a bullet hole.

made before the mission, until he caught himself and tried to focus only on gospel thinking again, telling me off for distracting him. We were in one of the most dangerous favelas in the area, under the oppressive sun, trying to visit people who weren't home. We decided to take an unknown, crooked *viela*, an alley so tight we couldn't stretch out both arms without touching houses to either side of us, to get to the street above. After wandering and climbing up the corridor-like vielas between run-down houses, we needed to catch our breath. We were almost at the top of the hill when we heard Metallica through an open window above us. I stopped and leaned against the wall, knowing my companion was just as tired as I was and had liked Metallica before the mission. He joined me, and we looked down over the top of the favela, not speaking while "The

Unforgiven" played. Garbage was strewn on the roofs,
thrown by the slightly less impoverished people who lived
above. I wondered what was going on in each house below,
while the music played over our heads and the light faded
over the valley. I survived because of those moments. They
trained me to shift my focus away from the rules I loathed
and toward the lives I was encountering along the way.

There are various types of favelas in São Paulo, some
worse than others. Most of them wound up hills. We'd have
to find our way to people's houses through thin passage-
ways so tight there was never enough room to breathe.
They wound around the buildings like constricted veins.
Many houses were stolen: the construction materials, the
electricity, the land on which the homes were built. Some
had the cleanest dirt floors but no electricity. Others were
built piece by piece with sloppy bagged cement and found
plywood, milk boxes, and red brick. A large portion of the
mission was in a place called "The Triangle of Death." I
was always put in the more dangerous areas, where most
non-missionaries I met were poor. I was caught between
my US and South American realities, and I was discovering
that Brazil, and my place in it, was complicated.

The lives I encountered in the favelas were unlike anything I'd ever imagined. I met a man—one of the funniest people I've ever known—who lived with the trauma of
having seen his older brother gunned down in front of his
house. His brother had run outside the moment his bike
was being stolen. I thought of Mike and fought not to sob

at the thought of losing him. I prayed that I would never have to go through it. I met an almost toothless woman who learned to read in her fifties so she could study scripture. I saw countless teenagers who had risen from poverty, learned to study, and went on to help others. I won't deny that the church helped a lot with that. We visited a family, in a house on top of a house on top of a house, who had a pregnant teenage daughter who couldn't stop drinking and getting high, and two sons who had just gone to prison. The mother, sobbing as she told her story, made a sweeping gesture with her right hand to indicate her home and the surrounding favela. She looked me in the eyes and said, "See this? This is perdition." It was true. I marveled at it all, but it later became normal, and later still it became more comfortable for me than rich areas filled with people I had at least as much trouble relating to as the missionaries who surrounded me.

In a small valley, in the favela that was hard to walk through because the police had broken down the houses so many times that the busted walls and ceilings were piled in a layer around the newer makeshift homes and in the street, there lived a dreadlocked artist who loved Bob Marley and who I later heard was murdered over an affair he'd had with a married woman. His name was Conde and he painted Bob Marley, Nelson Mandela, and Brazilian poets on the walls in front of the local schools, and cartoons of corrupt politicians on opposite walls. In his crooked third-floor home hung a painting of the view of the rest of the favela from his window. The redbrick walls covered most of the canvas, but clothes on lines and hanging from windows and people dancing on rooftops and in the street added blues and greens and black and purples. It was electric and true to life. The favelas were an ecosystem I'd never encountered before, not even in Puerto Rico.

The only difference between many of the people I met and me was that I was born in my father's country rather than my mother's. I don't think many American missionaries who were so quick to criticize the Brazilians understood that the only difference between the judged—the people they were supposed to be serving—and them was the longitude and latitude at which they happened to come into the world.

Many of the guys around me who were from the States were repulsed by the areas in which we lived. Backfiring cars were gunshots. People who weren't members of the church were sinners in need of saving. Brazilians were poor souls learning through the gospel to be as strong as Americans. No matter how friendly, how polite, how authentic the people being taught were, there was a gap that the missionaries rarely bridged, almost impressively, as they dodged even questions about their personal lives back home because of the mission rule to only talk about Christ.

While the church is a global religion, the culture is distinctly American. American and conservative. We were taught in church as kids that god created the United States specifically for the purpose of establishing his church, that it was the greatest country in the world, and the only country capable of birthing such a great work. The Book of Mormon teaches that the indigenous peoples of the Americas are descendants of ancient Israel and that the US will house the New Jerusalem; even the Western Hemisphere's pre-American and post-American history were taken into account. We were taught in church that white Europeans "settling" the New World, and Columbus (who was revered as a righteous man), were ordained by god to take the land away from the indigenous peoples of the New World (murdering indigenous peoples was never really mentioned) because they had fallen away from Christ and had become wicked. A good portion of people I grew up with were big believers in Manifest Destiny. Even the idea that black people were the seed of Cain came from the early American Protestants trying to rationalize slavery. Every American missionary I ever knew carried those tenets, even if subconsciously, with them. Most of them were almost indistinguishable from any other white, conservative, Christian American: very nice and polite people, many of whom I really liked, with generations of these ideas in their heads. Their version of the United States, which they idolized, was the version of the United States found in many US history books, idealized and without criticism—the only meaningful difference was their belief that the indigenous peoples were from one of the lost tribes of Israel. That history and that mindset had consequences large and small.

A companion and I were walking down a street in a midday rain when a couple of dark, braless girls in soaked white shirts walked toward us. He turned to me and said, "I'm so grateful I don't find Brazilian women attractive. It's like I've been blessed to not have a wandering eye. They look like frogs when they get older anyway. Most Latin women do." He was a blue-eyed Okie at least six inches taller than me, someone who would have never talked to me before or after the mission, who I would have never talked to either, someone whose world would not otherwise intersect with mine. He knew my mother and I and

Me and Conde. Behind him are his paintings, including
the painting of his favela.

half my family were Brazilian. He—and many others—
preached to me, about me, in third person. If I tried to
confront them, they would have told me I was imagining
things. I'd known that kind of rhetoric my entire life and
raged in my silence. I'd like to think I said something cou-
rageous. But I didn't.

4.

Many of the young men on the mission seemed to live in
that constant, strangling silence. Standing up for ourselves was an act of rebellion, unless we were standing up
against a missionary who was breaking the rules. Many
guys came from families like mine, who equated missions
with success and not going on a mission with tragedy.
Doing this work was an indicator of good parents. "Bill's
youngest daughter is a mess, but it's not his fault. His son
served a full-time mission. I heard he was even a zone
leader there. Some kids are just bad." Some guys were
promised cars for doing their mission time; others were
told that if they didn't come back honorably, they shouldn't
come back at all. We were lectured if we dared question the
idea of going or even hinted that we wouldn't; we were told
to stay out of trouble because it could impede our ability to
serve. It was a punishment and a prize, a goal and a fear,
with eternal shame guaranteed for us and our families if
we returned early. The shame and stigma became so prevalent that there are sections of church manuals and pamphlets dedicated to caring for those who leave the mission

early for any reason and how members should behave toward them. It was the greatest terror of every missionary
I knew. It was more terrible than dying on the mission—
which many considered to be a direct path to salvation. It
was so bad for me that I began to hope and fantasize about
being hit by a motorcycle while walking the streets. The
motorcycle, I rationalized, would only break my leg, so I
would have to go home to heal, and no one would be upset
that I went home early.

I wasn't the only one who didn't really want to be a missionary. After I'd been there half the allotted time, a little
over a year, a few of the guys wanted to go screw around
downtown. We weren't allowed to leave our areas without
permission, but they knew I was itching to get away too.
So, strict companions were swapped out for the day and
we got on the bus, headed toward a little autonomy. We
were told never to remove our name tags so that we would
remember who we were, and to always wear slacks and
white shirts and ties unless we were doing service projects. Normally, I would take off my name tag and put on
regular clothes to sneak around, but one of the others—
who happened to be a zone leader—was too scared, so we
went dressed as missionaries.

I had been drifting more toward the Brazilian missionaries at that point—I saw them as more aligned with culture I'd been deprived of—and started talking to one of
the guys from Rio. Bus passengers who were squeezing by
slowly nudged us away from our white American compan-

ions at the back of the bus. As we neared downtown, we noticed a commotion behind us.

"They were talking about my tits!" The woman who said it wasn't yelling, but she spoke loudly enough for everyone around her to hear. The white missionaries were red, stammering, all eyes on them. "I bet you didn't think I could speak English, did you?" she said. "What? You don't like them? You don't like the shape? That's what you said. Don't deny it!"

They said she didn't know what she was talking about as they pushed themselves to the front of the bus, pulling us along with them. "That's right," she said after us. "Run away. You're disgusting." We stood in awkward silence on the street for a moment before the American missionaries started nervous laughing. I never wanted to tear off my name tag and burn it more than I did in that moment. I was ashamed of them, sick at my association with them. And just like all the other times, I said nothing. We weren't even supposed to be downtown, so I couldn't have reported their behavior to the mission president later. I don't think that had even crossed my mind. We were where we weren't supposed to be. They'd say that verbal sexual assault was the smaller of the offenses, I was sure, and I was too much of a coward to even consider trying to win that argument.

Other missionaries tried to force themselves into such rigid compliance that it hurt to be in the same room with them. The pressure was relentless: baptism numbers had to go up, numbers of contacts had to improve, we needed to teach more people, needed more people attending church, someone had to make sure the other missionaries stayed in line. Everyone knew I was never perfectly obedient, so I was never given additional responsibilities. I was just a nice guy who was unfocused and would try to get his companions to loosen up. Those who didn't ascend to leadership positions were seen by other missionaries as having a lack of excitement, and maybe that came from a lack of faith, and maybe that came about because god was punishing those who weren't following the rules.

Earlier in my mission, I spent a day working with a tall, white, also half-Brazilian guy called Elder K. He was new, and I was maybe a year in. He was nervous and quiet, but I got him to joke with me a little while we walked down some street. Months later, after he'd been given extra responsibilities, he changed. I was nearing the end of my mission and was building up my collection of CDs, art, and reading material more than I was baptizing people. I'd heard the president had left the mission a week or two early because his father was dying. We were in a strange interim period with the assistants in charge until the new president arrived. These twenty-year-old boys decided that the reason our numbers were so low was probably because of something I was doing.

I'd been doing my morning study with my beat-up scriptures on my mattress on the floor. My allergies were terrible, and it helped my inflamed sinuses if I could lean one way or another to steady the pressure in my head.

But that was against a rule. We were supposed to be sitting at our desks, fully dressed before eight. I had my shirt untucked, no tie, shoes, or name tag. Also against a rule. Elder K and his companion stormed in, fuming. What was I doing on the floor? Why wasn't I studying? Did I grab my scriptures when I saw them coming and start pretending to read, thinking they'd fall for that? Why were our numbers down? Elder K asked me why I was even there when it was obvious I didn't want to be.

"You haven't changed at all," he said. "It's sad. You're exactly the same as the first time I met you. No difference. The mission hasn't changed you at all, and I find that so sad."

I don't know now whether he meant my demeanor—I'd hardly had any contact with him since that one time we met at the beginning of his mission—or the fact that I never became a leader, or if it was by reputation, but I did what I've always done anytime anyone yelled at or lectured me. I shut down. Trained by my dad's temper tantrums, I didn't interact with angry people. I stood there, not afraid but not willing to show any emotion.

"You have all this garbage you've collected," he said. "Why? What does it have to do with your mission?" He pointed at different items on my desk "Why do you have this?" He picked up a painting Conde had given me. "And this?" He picked up a wooden face I had carved from a broken bedpost I'd found in my apartment. "What is this, some kind of weird idol? An *orixá*? You need to pack all this up and get rid of it, put it in the mission office or throw it away. I can't believe you. Want me to send you home? I will send you home right now. How would that be? Sent home at the end of your mission dishonorably? How disgraceful. All this time here for what?" I stood still and looked at him as he got nearer and nearer to my face. I knew he had no authority to send me anywhere. Only the president could send me home, but I let him rage. "What? You got something to say? Is there something you want to say to me? Go ahead. I'll send you home right now."

"No," I said, stone-faced.

He switched tactics and tried to get spiritual, maybe move me like he might have thought a good missionary leader should. He told me he wanted to see me a different man when I went home in a couple of months. He wanted me to find him and give him a hug before I left. I heard that later he felt bad about the incident and apologized to one of the other guys who'd been there. The same pressure to be what he thought he should be, the pressure that couldn't change me, turned Elder K into something he wasn't. With an eternal resting place in heaven on the line, outbursts were bound to happen. I finished my mission not too long after that and never saw him again. At least he didn't try to hug me.

Maybe my inability to care as much as Elder K, my failure to stop sinning and transform after all that time and work and suffering for god, was set in stone from the beginning. I'd made a conscious decision not to change into the types of men and boys I saw around me on the mission. I was glad when Elder K had made the comment I hadn't changed. Maybe it was in my blood. According to many of the men on my mission, at church, and in the white American side of my family, black people sinned before coming to this life, after all.

When I lived in a grungy apartment in Educandário, about ten miles from São Paulo, I came across a sermon tucked away in the bedroom, left behind by a missionary who had passed through before me. It was written by Bruce R. McConkie, a former apostle of the church who died around the time I was born. My dad used to say he was saintlike. McConkie preached that "those who were less valiant in pre-existence and who thereby had certain spiritual restrictions imposed upon them during mortality are known to us as *negros*. . . . The negros are not equal with other races where the receipt of certain spiritual blessings are concerned, particularly the priesthood and the temple blessings that flow therefrom, but this inequity is not of man's origin. It is the Lord's doing." The text was printed on old, folded paper, in typewriter-esque font with wide margins. The staple that held it together was caked with rust—it had been read and reread, passed down from one missionary to another for who knew how long. After reading it, I stayed awake at night asking god if my family, and by extension I, was cursed, if we had really been less

faithful and therefore less deserving. I cried, confused as
to whether I had to believe and accept the racist narrative.
I knew what the response would be if I tried to talk to anyone, including the black, mixed, and Brazilian missionaries, about it. "That was a long time ago." "It's silly to dwell
on it—it'll rot your faith if you do." So, I didn't speak, but
the thoughts lingered.

Many men in my life seemed to think the same way as
McConkie, and I'd heard many speak similarly, but they
were unofficial spokesmen. McConkie had been an apostle.
The text I found made it official for me—though later I
found out it had come from a book the church had not au-
thorized him to write and that the other apostles and the
president at the time were unhappy that it had not been
evaluated by them first. (They ordered him not to allow a
reprint, and years later, when a new edition was finally
released, the parts removed were parts related to what
he considered the wickedness of the Catholic Church. The
parts related to his beliefs on the origins of black people
weren't removed until after the ban in 1978. The book is
currently out of print.) I thought of the missionaries who'd
preached the same words to me. I couldn't fathom why.
Why say those things to *me* of all people? Did they think
I was white—and if they did, did that make it better or
worse? Did they think I would agree? Why did they think
it was okay? Because my father was white? Or was it much
bigger than my family? "Is it the gospel?" I thought. "The
word of god? Is it true?"

It wasn't until years later that I would read a transcript of a speech by Brigham Young that said, "Any man having one drop of the seed of Cain in him Cannot hold the priest-hood. . . . I will say it now in the name of Jesus Christ. I know it is true and they know it. The Negro cannot hold one particle of Government. . . . If any man mingles his seed with the seed of Cain the only way he Could get rid of it or have salvation would be to Come forward and have his head Cut off and spill his Blood upon the ground. It would also take the life of his Children." Brigham Young, a man I was supposed to revere, said that about me. But by the time I read that, I knew it had nothing to do with god.

The church website now states, "Today, the Church dis-avows the theories advanced in the past that black skin is a sign of divine disfavor or curse, or that it reflects un-righteous actions in a premortal life; that mixed-race mar-riages are a sin; or that blacks or people of any other race or ethnicity are inferior in any way to anyone else. Church leaders today unequivocally condemn all racism, past and present, in any form." It's a start, but it has not stopped the growth of racist ideals from spreading in many mem-bers. They existed long before I was born, existed when I was on my mission, and continue. And I want nothing to do with the people who perpetuate them.

Brigham Young University's minority students feel un-wanted, trapped, scared, and lonely in Mormon culture too. The school, in an attempt to solve the issue, had a committee conduct and publish a "Report and Recommendation of the BYU Committee on Race, Equity, and Belonging" in February 2021. The sixty-four-page document outlines issues regarding race in the school, and provides suggestions for betterment.

> The students described many different individual experiences, but we noted a number of recurring themes across these meetings that we feel an urgency to communicate. . . . The most pressing concern is that BIPOC students often feel isolated and unsafe at BYU due to racism. . . . One student from the Hispanos Unidos club said it is "very hard to find other Latino students at BYU." A student from the Tribe of Many Feathers club recounted that she wanted to transfer out of BYU after her first year because of the lack of other Native American students. A member of the Black Student Union reported, "My experience as a Black student at BYU is not equal to other students on campus because I don't feel safe." A student from the Tribe of Many Feathers stated that during one Halloween there were White students who dressed up as "savages" in Helaman Halls. Another student from Hispanos Unidos said that a faculty member chastised her and a friend for speaking Spanish before class. A member of the Black Student Union recounted an

incident where a classmate used the n-word multiple times in response to a professor's question, leaving the room in shock. He described the acute pain and heartache that the event caused to himself and to other Black students who later heard about it.

Louise Wheeler, an assistant clinical professor and psychologist for the school's Counseling and Psychological Services confirmed that "[BIPOC students feel] a lot of stress regarding the rise of alt-right movements (e.g., DezNat) within the university student body. This includes worries about physical safety and worries about things that might be said or done in classrooms, at church, etc. I have heard so much more about [these concerns] this year than in the past. This has led many of the students I have worked with to tell friends and siblings to not attend BYU."

I understood that sentiment. I'd always known that was how BYU was, known that was how Mormon culture in Utah and Idaho was because I had lived there, known that was how Mormon culture was all over the United States. As a kid, and even after I started looking into colleges as an adult, I never wanted to go to BYU even if going there would have been cheaper for me, and I considered myself lucky that I didn't have to go. I felt bad for the poor kids who were there and suffering for it.

After the priesthood ban on black people was lifted in 1978, McConkie, who repeatedly expressed his belief that black people were the children of Cain and would never have the priesthood in this life, gave an address to Church Educational System employees entitled "All Are Alike unto God," in which he took back some of his words—he was also the one the church ordered to make the new official declaration lifting the ban.

Forget everything that I have said, or what President Brigham Young or President George Q. Cannon or whomsoever has said in days past that is contrary to the present revelation. We spoke with a limited understanding and without the light and knowledge that now has come into the world. We get our truth and our light line upon line and precept upon precept. We have now had added a new flood of intelligence and light on this particular subject, and it erases all the darkness and all the views and all the thoughts of the past. They don't matter any more.

Except they do matter. They matter because the damage the words of Brigham Young, George Q. Cannon—who also believed the offspring of mixed couples should be killed—and Bruce R. McConkie and others is done and lives on. If they didn't matter, I wouldn't have found that text in Educandário and DezNat might not exist. The students at BYU might be thriving in a more diverse atmosphere, where the idea that they and their families should

is literally *present* in all we do." He writes about the "great pain and terror" that comes from realizing this and learning to analyze the history that has shaped one's life. It becomes an animating battle that can shift history away from tyranny. History is the only path to a bright future the way that self-analyzing and learning to understand the self is the only path to liberation, fulfillment, and growth.

I'm grateful for what I learned in the church about seeking the spirit of god that we were taught was manifested as a still, small voice, because it taught me to listen to the quiet peace I've needed so badly in my life. It taught me to meditate before I ever knew what meditation was. I'm grateful that because of the church I was able to learn Portuguese and live in Brazil, which is something I would never have been able to do within the limitations of my family. I'm grateful to have been exposed to the Testaments and other spiritual texts, even if I no longer think of them as infallible or even strictly true. I'm grateful for the beautiful people I've met in church, many of whom are active in trying to change the church from the inside. Feeling as I do now about the church—that I want no association with it—after all those years, after an entire mission, makes me sad. It's like losing a family member, but I can't pretend I feel any different. I do have saudades for some aspects of my mission: walking through the *garoa*—the particular wet mix of fog and drizzle of São Paulo—on dark, cold nights with the smell of smoke rising up from the dinner fires of the poor; the loud bars and churches we passed, the scores of people I met, the city that doesn't end. The church in Brazil was different than in the States, even with the strong American influence. It was more diverse— partially because it had to be in that population—and in the areas in which I lived it was full of poor and struggling people, people who were new in the church and had lived lives outside it, real people. The church in Brazil has its own set of problems, not least of which was how many local leaders developed a strong sense of superiority when called to positions of leadership like the scores of missionaries I knew who did the same. But in the end, not even the good aspects, not even the saudades, were enough to make it worth the racism, obsession about sin, right-wing politics, bigotry, misogyny, and homophobia that were so overwhelming at church and even from church leaders I was taught were the people closest to perfection on earth. I also find it difficult to process a belief system that tells followers to ask god if the church is true but then tells them not to question the past, that whatever might be damning must be considered god's will and to move on. But what do we—especially those of us who were the subject of so much violent language that persists in many today—move on to?

I didn't want to go back to the States when I finished my mission. It hadn't worked as advertised to fix me, and if I told this to anyone, they'd blame me. I wasn't ready to be back full time in conservative white America. I wanted to

go to Fortaleza, where I thought I might be able to live like
a normal person. Florida meant life locked in my room or
forcing myself to engage in Mormon culture—which my
mission finally allowed me to admit to myself that I would
never be able to do. But my parents wanted me in Florida, and more importantly Mike was there, so I went, just
like I was supposed to. I pretended I was okay. A couple
of weeks later, I was back on opiates, back on the needle
with Mike, and I would stay on it for a little more than a
decade. Later, my family would talk about how bad Mike's
addiction had gotten *because* he never went on a mission.

"I taught you everything you needed to be happy," my
dad said to me after Mike died, his eyes tired and hollow
as ever, worse after the death of his son. He was pleading
for me to confirm it was true that he had been a wonderful
father. We were in my grandparents' kitchen in Phoenix,
among the scraps of food left over from a family gathering.
Everyone was in the living room, pretending to not pay
attention to us, but every time I looked up someone had
their head turned or neck craned toward us, and snapped
back when they noticed I could see. "I just don't understand why Michael didn't want it. I don't understand why
he decided to live that kind of life he did, go off the deep
end like that. I knew everything was going wrong for him
after he wouldn't go on a mission."

"Of course you never taught us to be happy, Dad," I
said in Portuguese, so our English-only-speaking relatives
couldn't understand. I leaned on the counter and regarded

him with a mix of pity and contempt. "You couldn't. Mike didn't die because he didn't go on a mission. He didn't drown in his addictions because he didn't go to church. I was never happy *because* I went on a mission, and I've always hated church. How could you ever teach us anything without looking to see who we were and what our problems were? You threw us a list of rules and a church. I get it. I know you didn't know what else to do, but that was never enough for any kind of happiness. What happened to Mike didn't happen because he didn't go to church."

"I don't see things that way," he raised his voice. He refused to respond to me in Portuguese—though his Portuguese is near perfect, and he's proud of it. He stiffened on the tall bench he was sitting on and lifted his chin, his repentant and humble demeanor evaporating without a trace. I'd been afraid of hurting him. All those years I'd been afraid. I'd been afraid to bruise his white fragility, and the church's. I'd been as afraid to say anything that would make him feel bad as he'd been of even considering that there was more to happiness than following rules. I felt bad for him, but like McConkie's statement telling members to forget what he and other prominent leaders had said, it was too little too late.

For years, my parents insisted that Mike was the cause of my dad's ailments because Mike refused to go to church. But Mike was sick too. And so was I, from pretending I was okay and drug-free and a faithful returned missionary, all to protect our religious and conservative family, to protect our dad's health. I looked at my dad, opened my mouth, and shook my head. There was nothing more I could say to him.

I didn't hate my father then (though I wanted to) and don't now. I love him. I'm not even angry at him anymore, and I realize he's partially the product of his uber-religious environment. I don't hate the church. I realize that it's partially the product of hyper-conservative US culture. I don't even hate the US, but that doesn't mean I don't have a serious contempt for the extreme conservative and racist culture and teachings perpetuated here, the toxicity that has seeped into the religion I was brought up in, my family, my everyday life, the death of my brother. It makes me think of Baldwin again, this time in *Notes of a Native Son*, when, after talking about how it's because of his love of America that he insists on having the right to criticize her, he says "that the finest principles may have to be modified, or may even be pulverized by the demands of life, and that one must find, therefore, one's own moral center and move through the world hoping that the center will guide one aright." I've found that my own moral center does not align with church and church people, and many of my family's teachings, and teachings of this nation, and never really did despite how much I wanted it to. It's not even about forgiveness.

When he was maybe two or three, our youngest brother, Matt, was hit by a minivan in front of our house in Puerto Rico. He'd been walking from the neighbor's house across the street to ours when a woman who'd been yelling at her own kids in the back seat hit Matt and sent him flying into the gutter while our brother John and the neighbors watched in horror. I had been upstairs sleeping off something I'd taken in the small room I shared with Mike— the one where he blew up the air conditioner—when Mike came running upstairs to tell me what had happened. "Matt was just hit by a car," Mike said, wide-eyed.

"Shut up," I said through a thick voice before turning toward the wall. "No he wasn't."

"He was, dude. Look," Mike said as he pointed at the window that looked out at the street.

I peered through the window, and there was Matt in the gutter, my mother kneeling in the street with his head in her arms. My gut dropped, and I said to Mike, "What the fuck?" before running downstairs.

The neighbor berated the woman who had hit Matt while we waited for the ambulance. The woman who had hit him was frantic, the neighbor exploding with rage, my mother quietly weeping, John in shock still standing in the street, and Mike and me silent in the driveway. It seemed like it took forever for the ambulance to arrive, but it turned out Matt was okay. He was bruised on his side and a little scratched, but nothing was broken and there were no internal injuries.

It wasn't his fault he'd been hit. He was a toddler. There were no adults with their eyes on him. The woman who had hit him should have been paying attention and not screaming at her own kids while driving. There was a list of shoulds and shouldn'ts, but the shoulds and shouldn'ts didn't matter. Whether or not the driver was forgiven, or the adults were forgiven for their inattentiveness, didn't matter. The fact was that Matt was hit by a car the same way I was years later. Forgiveness didn't stop John from having nightmares for a few years after the event. Forgiveness wouldn't stop the terror. It didn't change the fact that the driver ended up paying the medical expenses and more. The consequences we have to deal with for racism, bigotry, limited thinking, and a long list of ills have nothing to do with forgiveness and everything to do with dealing with what we're left with.

It's about learning to live and deal with lasting results whether or not we've forgiven whoever or whatever has caused the pain. It's about not turning away from or shrugging off legacies in an attempt to minimize. If someone is hit by a car and is maimed, it doesn't matter if the driver repents or even if it wasn't the driver's fault; the results are the same. Changing and evolving alone cannot change the results of something that has already happened. The maimed person can forgive, and that can be beautiful and freeing when that happens, but that forgiveness cannot make a person walk again, cannot get rid of a perpetual limp, cannot bring back a life, cannot stopper trauma. Damage done is damage done, and while I hold no grudges, these stories cannot be told without including key moments and injuries and how they happened. They all are part of one another. Knowing how horrible and potent prolonged guilt is, I don't want to inflict anybody with it, but guilt cannot be assuaged by turning from the problem. It only turns into something much worse.

When I looked at my pleading father go haughty in my grandparents' kitchen, thought of all the teachings he was referring to, the thought of all that fear of sin heaped upon us through the intense teachings he'd received, the racism, that pleading to me to give him the permission to turn from his own guilt (which I had no desire for him to have in the first place), I felt so bad for him, but I also wished I could trade him, my mother, the church, all of them, for Mike. Anything for one more long conversation with my brother.

redemption song

Mike was forced to go to the Especially for Youth (EFY) weeklong event in Utah in 2004 while I was on my mission. It was either after he wrecked the car or was taken to rehab for a week. It was a summer trip. Besides spending time at EFY, Mike was going to Idaho to help our grandparents move down to Arizona. He would be driving our grandfather's pickup, having to learn to drive stick shift to do so, and for years after, our grandpa would praise him for it. "That boy was able to do anything he put his mind to. I only had to show him once!" Grandpa also praised Mike for installing the pull-down ladder to the attic in the garage. Every time I had to open it and climb up the ladder to take down their Christmas decorations and do home renovations as they aged, unable to climb anymore, he exclaimed, "You know, Michael set that up pretty much all by himself. He was such a great help while he was here." The refrain echoed long after Mike's death, and my grandmother would add, "I wish he would have stayed here instead of going back to Florida to those awful friends he had."

Mike hated EFY and Utah when he finally went. "I could only score some weak-ass Utah regs," he told me later. But he did like the talent show. His decision to enter was spur of the moment, and the acoustic guitar was borrowed. He walked up to the stage alone, sat on a foldout chair set next to a microphone he pulled down to his mouth (another had been set next to the guitar's sound hole). He was supposed to play church or gospel-related music. But Mike loved Bob Marley. And Bob Marley sang about god.

He picked at that lonely opening riff Marley uses in his solo acoustic version of "Redemption Song" before singing, "Old pirates yes they rob I . . ." The auditorium was silent as Mike sang, and though I wasn't there, I already know it was Mike's earnestness, his belief in the song, belief in the beauty of imperfection, especially the imperfection of others, that made his audience hold their breath. "Won't you help to sing these songs of freedom, 'cause all I ever had, redemption songs. These songs of freedom . . ." I'd like to think he ended with that minor sixth ringing to a silent and stunned crowd before they cheered.

It was such a good performance that a picture of Mike ended up in a BYU article on EFY. In it, he's singing into a microphone and playing guitar. When he came off the stage, a couple of girls fawned over his musical talent and told him they'd never heard such a spiritual and heartfelt song. They told Mike he was a wonderful songwriter. Mike grinned. He never corrected them.

Education II

Me on the left, our friend E in the background,
Mike with the cigarette, and K on the right

When I was fourteen, the morning after the first time I took acid in Puerto Rico—when the world was still shimmering but not full-blown bizarre—I went to the pool, put on goggles, jumped in the water, and blew all the air out of my lungs until I couldn't float. I lay at the bottom of the pool watching the sun spill through the silver skin where the water met the air. The water around me was heavy, my long hair dancing slow around my face and head. I meantime, I was allowed to check emails every Monday through a mission-approved email address (other sites or addresses were banned to keep us away from pornography and other evils of the internet), and personal phone calls were limited to a call to our parents on Christmas and Mother's Day—though these days missionaries are allowed to call every week. Mondays were also reserved for washing clothes, shopping for the week, and taking care of any other personal upkeep. With no phones (at that time, the lines were reserved for missionary leaders to receive weekly reports, and we weren't allowed to carry cell phones) and no computers in our apartments and houses, we took a bus to a local LAN house, a public place where we could sit and pay for time on a computer. I refused the church email partially out of rebellion, partially because I didn't want anyone to read what Mike wrote to me and then get him in trouble. So, I used a Yahoo! account until an overzealous missionary tattled on me and I was banned from the internet for a few months—but even when I did go back online, I continued to use my Yahoo! account.

Being a missionary taught me to speak Portuguese, adapt to the structure I didn't have at home, push through discomfort, and lie and hide my true self better than ever before. While I was gone, Mike was learning to maneuver through the networks of dealers and users in Florida, learning to avoid cops and our parents. He took over my room when I left but left it the way I had it. The few emails he wrote me during that time show a pattern that encapsulates his life from sixteen to eighteen. I would reread them over the years, especially when it'd been a long time since I'd heard from him. When they were fresh, I read them surrounded by kids playing video games and other missionaries writing home about people they were baptizing. Mike wrote:

man I just saw my friend sean who just got out of rehab for shoottn up heroin (my heroin addict friend) he went to a year long program for it and he only was there for a month. i saw him do oxycontin the other day like smokin it and stuff and his eyes started fluttering and rollin back into his head and he kept starin off it was crazy. but hes goin to NA meetngs and i think hes tryin to stay off that's who im jammin with today. ta ta for now

MIKE MIKE MIKE MIKE MIKE MIKE MIKE MIKE MIKE MIKE MIKE MIKE MIKE MIKE MIKE MIKE MIKE MIKE

MIKE MIKE MIKE MIKE MIKE MIKE MIKE MIKE MIKE MIKE MIKE MIKE MIKE MIKE MIKE MIKE MIKE MIKE

MIKE MIKE MIKE MIKE MIKE MIKE MIKE MIKE MIKE MIKE MIKE MIKE MIKE MIKE MIKE MIKE MIKE MIKE

MIKE MIKE MIKE MIKE MIKE MIKE MIKE

MIKE MIKE MIKE MIKE MIKE MIKE MIKE
MIKE MIKE MIKE MIKE

I dont ever jam with rob anymore. i usually just
play by myself in my room i mean Your room. that
is all for now

mi

ke

hey whats up man my bad i havenet been writng
but i dont know i havenet been busy just I just got
alot on my mind. i got court ordered for rehab not
to long ago aint gonna happen though cause mom
and dad aint got the money. not alot is goin great
right now at least not for me. i got sent to arf a little
while ago its the addictons receiving facility. mom
and dad really dont trust me any more and they
think im a hardcore drug addict. which i am not
really i have been but at this Point im doin nothin
more then smokin. but with mom and dad its gotten pretty bad. i dont know life really sucks. Ricky
has his own apartment with his girlfriend. hes doin
good now but smokes aloI. oh yea and at school because of all the time i missed while in rehab im only
takin 2 classes one a day so im not doin much. i am
playin drums every chance i get though its one of

my favorite things to do now. i dont know like i said life really sucks but ill talk to u later hombre

peace out cuz

hey what is goin on man. everything is good here i went to court on

mon. for myy reckless driving ticket and they didnt suspend my liscence i only got three days of community service and 168.00$ticket and 8 hours Of driving school but thats all better then my Liscence suspended.

yea well i gots to go peace till with loye meet

again.

your hermano mike

hey hows it goin im goin to utah on saturday hurahh (sarcasm) itll be allI right i guess nothin much has been goin on here ricky works now so i havent chilled with him or seen him for a long time oh well theres pretty much nothing new goin on here Just straight chillen homie man i hate florida i cant wait toI leave it. yeah whats goin on with u is the mission chillen? yeah well i Guess im gonna go cause

i aint got much to say but fuck the world todaay.
peace out home slice.

Miguel

hey que te pasa hombre? whats up everything is
allright here i guess man mom and dad called the cops
on me the other day i came home and they searched me
and found these three pills and they called the cops
and the cop came and tested it and it came up negative for everything haha and they gave them back
to mom and dad and the cop told them it was probably just tylenol. but what it really was was 2ci-t7
a research chemical that makes u trip really hard.its
illegal In alot of different countries but not the US u
can order it off the internet. yeah but other then that
everything is the same im goin to help grandpa and
grandma move in like a month im drivin all the way
from idaho to arizona so it will be awesome. but yeah
u need to hurry and get back so we can move to cali
im gettin sick of this shit hole. but yeah

im Gonna go so peace

peace mike

hey what is up man whats goin on nothin much here.

im gettin out of the annex in like a week and then i go straight to scc and

start there for my ged. yea i got kicked out last sunday cause the thing is is i got a

speeding ticket and i cant let mom and dad know so im comin up with the money as discreet as i can and i was sellin and mom was lookin through my pockets and found a dime and 40 bucks and she woke dad up and me at 7 in the morning and me and dad were fighting then he kicked me out and i left and dad came to talk to me but i was mad so i just walked for a while and they

locked me out of the house when they went to church. so i walked to my friend leslies house and i stayed there then mom and dad found me and took me home sayin that i was a run away and yeah it was crazy but yea i got a really cool girlfriend shes alot like me but hot and Puerto rican and she loves pink floyd her name is denisse. yea but i got to go so ill talk to u

later peace.

your bro, MIKE

hey whats up I would send u stuff but I cant drive. The car was messed up and I crashed it AGAIN. I hit 3 bobs barricades cause the gas pedal kept getting stuck and that's pushed it too hard and went off the road. Um yeah that's think that's about it. Later.

quack >() MIKE ()< quack ()()

^^ ^^

One thousand or so words was pretty much all I had from him for two years. It wasn't like we didn't do the things he described together. But when I was home, I'd been able to control it more. I was always trying to teach him how not to get caught and how to better pretend if he did get caught for something. Mike was impulsive and manic, but I'd learned to work with that the way I'd learned to work with our dad's impulsivities and manias. And I'd learned to be a buffer between them. "You just have to pretend to be who people want you to be, man." It was my philosophy. Everything was going to suck either way, so why not at least get high while causing as little trouble as possible? No talking back, no scenes. I know now that was flawed thinking that led to some of the worst pain in my life, but that was the only way I knew how to deal with my bipolar disorder, unhappy home, and severe religious guilt back then. Our parents didn't keep tabs on us as long as they thought we were going to church both before and after my mission. Mike could never hide as well as I could—he never tried. The mission taught me that everything acquired comes with a sacrifice. Sometimes we don't know what we're giving up and what we're gaining. What did that hiding cost me? And what did Mike's unfettered nature cost him? Once I was gone, the whole structure I'd tried to set up for us crumbled. Mike was just a kid, floundering, and there was no one there to help him.

When I finally went home, my dad and younger siblings picked me up at the airport in the little Nissan he'd bought while I was gone. He had a grin on his face and tears in his eyes, proud that I'd completed my mission and come back with honor. My heart sank. Mike wasn't there.

"We need to talk about your brother," my dad said as we put the suitcases in the trunk, where my siblings couldn't hear. "He's not the same as he used to be. I'm afraid . . . I'm afraid he's gone down a very dark path, and I can't help him anymore. He disappears for days, and I just can't control him. I don't think he's ever going to go on a mission. Just don't be surprised if he doesn't want to hang around you anymore. I know you were close."

He spoke as if I hadn't been in touch with Mike as much as I could while I was gone, but I did wonder if he had a point. Mike wasn't at the airport, and I didn't know where he was. "Mike's not here," I said, still processing the situation, as my dad walked to the driver's side and I the passenger's.

"No. No. He's taken off again. I don't know where he went."

My dad had brought some of my CDs to the car, a small prize for the work I had just completed. He asked me which I would like to hear first. "The Velvet Underground," I said, my mind whirring. We listened without speaking once during the forty minutes home. I watched the cars on the freeway, the familiar Spanish moss on everything, while Lou Reed sang:

Teenage Mary said to Uncle Dave
I sold my soul, must be saved

Did I sell my soul to go on the mission, when I wasn't around to help my brother, or was I selling it then as I plotted how I was going to get high? My place was with Mike, and I had left him. It wouldn't have stopped him from doing any of the things he mentioned in his emails, but I might have helped him not get kicked out. I might have helped him not get caught. I could have driven when he knocked over the Bob's Barricades. Never once had my parents called the cops on him before my mission; never once did it happen after I got back. I was positive I could have prevented it. Once we got home, I borrowed the car and drove to the Taco Bell where I knew a friend of his worked. Apparently, in the spur of the moment, Mike took off to Maryland to help a friend drive some dope back down to Florida. He'd be back soon. I don't remember seeing him the next day, or when our reunion took place, but I know I was back on opioids not long after he arrived.

Coming home from my mission and realizing I wasn't who I was supposed to be was devastating, and I had stopped looking for that quiet as much because I wondered if it had deceived me since it had so little to do with the rules that were supposed to change me. I didn't know what to do with my life and only had vague notions of what it meant to go to school and get a job. I was twenty-one and hadn't been in a classroom since I was sixteen. I'd had three jobs at eighteen before my mission that hadn't lasted long before I was fired from each one: assistant pool electrician until the foreman pulled me back from touching the wrong part after opening a fuse box; McDonald's after I burned a couple of burgers, ordered Happy Meals for all the senior citizens who came in because I couldn't figure out how to work the register, and didn't think to clean the bathrooms while cleaning the rest of the restaurant; and Labor Ready, which only lasted a day, because I got too depressed after we smoked a blunt (which already didn't agree with me at that point) with the rest of the guys—many of whom were right out of prison—and we proceeded to clean the remains of a burned-down house and I almost cried upon picking up a charred stuffed animal. Drugs were what I knew before the mission, and drugs were what I went back to. At first I told myself I'd only do pills and only sometimes and got myself some morphine 30s. That escalated to Roxys and later other opioids and heroin, and a couple of months after getting back to Florida I was shooting up every day, often multiple times a day. I'd tried for a couple of weeks to go to church, but it was so lonely, and being there made me feel so behind and guilty. It wasn't what it had been in Brazil. It was all the negative aspects of church without any of the joys of being in the midst of my lost cultural heritage, and without my quiet center, it was just painful. After a couple of Sundays I told my parents I was going to the congregation for singles and just spent my time in church clothes hanging out with Mike and our friends, trying to remember to keep my white sleeves rolled up until the blood from where the needle entered my arm dried.

The moment I stopped at the Taco Bell to find Mike, his friends became my friends. We hung out at a middle-aged woman's house not too far from our own. Any time of the day or night, I could walk in and find people passed out on the floors or couches or in one of the rooms upstairs. Depending on the hour, I might find people fucking in the living room. A couple of times I found my friends turning coke into crack on the kitchen stove. They found me with *Going to Meet the Man* or *The Bell Jar* or *Jesus' Son* or some other book under my arm, while I tried to score some coke or acid or morphine, or just hang out, or score some Dilaudid, OxyContin, fentanyl, Opana, heroin, meth, rock. We were swimming in drugs, shooting up, smoking from

people who were supposed to be responsible. Scores of depressed and luckless women and men in their forties and
fifties and sixties, and successful people too. The guy who
had a limo business before he was T-boned by a semi, got
hooked on opioids after the accident, and lost his wife, his
social status, and his house shortly after. The woman who
worked as a nurse until she was caught forging scripts for
the pills she fed herself and was sent away for a few years,
leaving a couple of young kids and an opioid-addicted husband behind. The many who ended up losing their homes
in the housing crash. We knew paralegals and construction foremen and teachers and religious leaders of various
faiths and military personnel and family men and women
all buying and, in some cases, selling the opioids we all
used together. I had a couple of boxes each filled with a
hundred syringes I'd picked up at the local pharmacy that I
used and doled out to friends in need (or in exchange for
shit), and I knew many middle-class, middle-aged people
who did the same. Pills that doctors had prescribed were
everywhere. Heroin was everywhere. And they were in the
places we would never have expected before. Mike and I
had been in drug circles for years, but this was different.
These weren't fucked-up teens or people on broken downtown streets. This was a severely depressed and fractured
middle America. Many of the people I interacted with were
white, not the black and Latino people we grew up with
in Puerto Rico or the Mexican kids we hung out with in
Idaho—though much of our inner circle still consisted of

those minorities. As I began to branch out and sell morphine and Roxys to lonely professionals in suburban
households, I thought of writing the interconnecting stories of the people I was spending so much time with, these
diverse souls tied together by the pain of addiction. It was
dawning on me that all over this nation that claimed to
be the best, there were houses like that one in every class
of community, where people like me were being crushed
under the same weight, none of us wanting to admit to our
personal, and collective, systemic failures. No one admitting to the depression and anxiety that was drowning us
not just individually but as an American culture. It was
absurd. It was important that I both described and fought
against it—and I would, maybe after my next fix.

I read *Fear and Loathing in Las Vegas* in the back of an
ice-cream shop in Maitland, Florida, in between massive
lines of coke during twelve-hour shifts. "He who makes
a beast of himself gets rid of the pain of being a man." I
was trying hard to put Dr. Johnson's words into action.
I fluttered through that job for months, either coked up or
on acid, and always on opioids, sweeping the floors in a
sugar-stained smock and crooked cap. Most of the time I
was alone in the shop, but when people came in, if I was
loaded enough, or manic enough, I would talk nonstop, filling the previously lonely silence. I was good at it. Once,
two girls from the nearby university came in while I was

tripping. I had been pacing and yammering to myself before they came in and was grateful for the company. I have
no idea what I said to them, only that I pretended to sweep
the floor while the three of us talked and giggled for almost
two hours. After they left, one of them came back to put a
folded piece of paper in my hand. It was her phone number. I put it in my pocket and continued sweeping, dreaming of a future together until I got home around midnight.

The high was fading and the euphoria flickering. I took
the paper from my pocket and stared at the number written in blue ink. "There is no way this college girl would
like the real, depressed high school dropout," I thought. It
was only the acid that made me bearable. I let the paper
drift under my futon, which was littered with books and
paper and half-completed artwork on sketchpads. I pretended that I'd lost it until I really had, and a week or so
later when I tried looking for it, it was gone. The girls' nor-
malcy scared me. It was better to stay fucked up, to make
a beast of myself so I could at least talk to people.

I wasn't interested in Thompson because of his drugs
but despite them. I didn't aspire to be a drug-addict
writer—I was addicted before I knew of him, and though I
sketched scenes and badly written poetry, I had no dreams
of becoming a writer. More and more, I was losing any concrete idea of anything about what my future could be and
focusing instead on observing the present because I was
realizing I was never going to escape it. I wanted something but was unable to articulate or even understand

what. *Fear and Loathing* was full of somethings to grasp at. Thompson's writing brims with cutting perceptions: fierce descriptions of the death of the ideals of the sixties and the American Dream that made me feel a little less broken, inept, and insane. I knew my life would shock any of the missionaries and people I'd worked with in Brazil just a month or two prior. I knew that I was going to keep using, independent of where I found myself or who I was with. I was going to go mad at some point, and no one had the ability, or force, or know-how, to stop me—least of all myself. I still wanted to be good and whole but knew by then I never would be. Thompson taught me I could accept my madness as part of me and move on. That book gave me hope that my intelligence might seep through my madness and save me.

When I wasn't at that house or ice-cream shop, I studied fine art at Seminole Community College (which is now Seminole State College), where Mike had tried and failed to get his GED after dropping out. The main campus was close to the annex, a twenty-minute drive, across alligator-infested Lake Jesup. The idea of going to college was huge to me, so SCC was terrifying—but it was what people were supposed to do after a mission. The first time I drove to the campus and couldn't find parking, I sat in the car for almost a half hour listening to music and breathing and trying to psych myself into going.

My design class smelled like old building and paint. The instructor was a kind, blond Russian woman with a slight accent who made sure to praise our work alongside criticizing it. I was failing psychology and math and art history and even my drawing class, but I aced her class. I didn't realize how much of a mess I was: stumbling in late, running to the restroom every ten minutes and coming back sniffling and rubbing my nose in case there was white powder there. Placing shapes and colors on canvas or paper or board to indicate the idea of movement and space, learning to guide the eye to a focal point, gave me an outlet for all that energy. I did start all my assignments, but I often didn't finish them. I'd often come to class carrying a piece that looked like an apology, high on either coke or opioids, usually both. Still, I showed up and talked and laughed with everyone and by mid-semester I was the only guy in a room full of women, which put me at ease after a lifetime around angry men and missionary boys.

After a class in which I was particularly off, a Cuban American student I spoke to from time to time walked over to me. Her stern figure stood about as high as my mid-chest. She said, "I wanted to talk to you about something." I had no idea what she wanted from me. We usually traded jokes and casual conversation about her fiancé or Brazil.

"Yeah?" I said, smiling. My high gave me a wall between myself and everything happening around me.

We walked to a less-populated part of the room, where

she told me I was good. "I mean, really, really good," she said.

"Thanks!"

"And that's why I'm mad at you," she said.

"Oh." I looked down at her, the wall between us starting to give way to a shame.

Her face hardened, but not without pity. "You make beautiful work, and it's clear you have a natural talent for this. You do with ease and intuition what I wish I could, what everyone here wishes they could."

Though everyone seemed to be minding their own business, heads over their work, the instructor walking around to see what each student was up to, I had the feeling they had all talked about this on one of the days I was gone. It was easy enough to imagine the close-knit group discussing me and my obvious dysfunctionality.

"You don't pay enough attention, and you could do better," she added. "But what's worse is you seem to squander what god's given you. I don't know if you believe in god, and that doesn't matter. I'm jealous of your work, and you have the nerve to never finish anything. You act like you don't even care. You're a very nice person, but I don't think you take this seriously."

I didn't shut down like I did with missionaries who screamed righteousness at me. What she said cut more because her concern was genuine. She was stern but not volatile. Angry but not raving. I managed to apologize, thank her, agree with her, unsure of what to say. I thought about the conversation for the rest of the day, on the drive to work at the ice-cream shop, then to the house where Mike and I were shooting up more and more with our friends, then playing guitar or speed-talking in the living room.

On the last day of class, I forgot my portfolio and flew home as fast as I could and after a flurry of apologies. I had to pull a couple of more pieces together and rush back in time to get a grade. For my 3-D project, I thought about gluing the syringes I'd been using—the physical proof of my decay—to a posterboard, along with broken mirrors and randomly cut wires. In the end, I decided the syringes might be a health risk. I got back with just enough time to show off the pieces I'd gathered, including the clearly unfinished posterboard covered in wires and mirrors.

The woman who'd tried to encourage me sat back and sighed. When it was time to go, she hardly said a word to me. Later, when I approached the instructor to talk about my grade, she looked at me with pure pity. "I expect to hear about you and see good things about you in the future," she said. I wondered if she believed her own words, or if they were a platitude to help us both. I sniffed, the back of my throat and mouth numb, and apologized and thanked her too.

On the way home, I was rear-ended by a car while entering the freeway. The woman I was giving a ride to screamed as the back of the car crumpled and my head slammed against the driver-side window, breaking my glasses. Other than a scratch on the side of my face and a destroyed car, we were both fine. I never went back to SCC. I spent the car insurance money on a plane ticket to Fortaleza, where I caught up with Veronica, a woman I'd met while I was visiting my mother's family before my mission. Between when we started dating and when we'd get married, our relationship consisted of two three-month trips I made to Fortaleza and daily phone calls in which we laughed and cried and had soul conversations and I pretended I wasn't addicted to drugs.

In the meantime, I spent three years with Mike, huddling over spoons and crack pipes. It was similar to a lot of stories about addiction: the drugs took over and ran our lives. We were beholden to them before I went on my mission, before either of us were teenagers. Mike continued while I took that painful two-year break as a missionary, and when I got home it continued as it had been before except that we were shooting up and using at a much higher level because we were both even more devastated by life and able to get more shit than we could when we were kids.

Years after our time in Florida, I spoke to Ricky on FaceTime after he had been off drugs for a while and spent most of his time caring for his kids in Oregon. I said, "You're probably one of the few friends I have who knew me both before and after the mission. I don't think the mission really changed me the way it did a lot of guys."

"No," he said. "I wouldn't say you were unchanged. But I remember, man. It was like a huge weight had been lifted off your shoulders. It was like you had this vibe of the whole thing being over, like you were glad it was done and out of the way. I mean, you were the same in that you did the same shit, and you had your reasons for that, but it was like you had been through this ordeal that was finally over. It was like you were a mix of more depressed and relieved."

He was right. I had recurring nightmares for a couple of years after my mission that I wasn't done yet, that I had to return for another few months or year, and I would wake up, heart beating wildly, until I could calm myself down enough to get back to sleep.

Our "fucked-up-ness," as Mike would have said, and depression only got worse with age, and the use got worse along with it. I had gone on a mission and come back, but I hadn't healed, and being unhealed, I, like Mike and the rest of the damaged we loved so much, fell into that addiction narrative, the one that seemed to eat every person we knew either directly or indirectly through loved ones' use. Not long after I dropped out of SCC, I lost the ice-cream job and started working landscaping and irrigation with a crew of guys who were always high and drunk, until I quit showing up. I worked as a lifeguard at a timeshare resort until I stopped showing up there too. Mike and I made plans to go to New Orleans to help rebuild—Katrina had hit right as I had got home from my mission and we heard they were paying people mad money to work out there, even at McDonald's. Mike's band was going to take off, and he and I would do a side thing wherever he went. I was

couple of weeks going through physical withdrawals but managed to get it all out of my system and held on for a while—though the mental and emotional side of the addiction didn't dissipate. By the time I was fired from my second collections job within the span of a few months, I was at least not using. Sort of. Most of the time, at least for the first few months. I was a newlywed with no income, no insurance, no employment, driving down north Phoenix on Happy Valley pretending to look for work, talking and gesturing to myself, wild, when I saw the Glendale Community College North Campus. In either a manic state or an inspired one or both, I crossed three lanes and slammed over the speed bump into the parking lot. I wandered around the school and through the library until I found the front office. Light surrounded and penetrated me as I enrolled, speed-talking about how I felt like I just *needed* to be there right then, how it felt so wonderful to be in a place so full of knowledge. I didn't tell the people at the admissions office that I could feel the knowledge seeping into me like divinity, as clean and pure as sunlight.

I was thrilled to be back in school after years on the needle. The teachers seemed to notice and like me, and I got good grades. I was on the main campus of one of the biggest community colleges in the valley. The enormity of it all motivated me like never before, the opposite of what I felt at the community college in Florida. I felt connected to something larger than myself that I never knew existed, and I wanted to go toward it instead of running away. I took a graphic design course (that was going to be my major, and I earned a scholarship for it), intro to lit, a remedial math class, and intro to creative writing. Within a couple of weeks I realized graphic design wasn't all that engaging for me—I wasn't the artist I'd thought I was, and making art on the computer couldn't compare to painting with my hands. I dropped the subject the following semester to focus on writing and literature.

In creative writing, we covered poetry, fiction, and nonfiction. My writing was praised for the first time in my life. When I was a kid, it had always been marked down by my teachers and made fun of by my dad. My instructor at the community college, John Ventola, was a constantly laughing Italian who obviously loved what he did. His joy made me feel good about myself. I was putting the daydreams I'd created as a kid on the page. Once a week in the evenings, from seven to nine thirty, I'd sit back in my chair, enthralled, and drink my new possible future. I watched Ventola, and the other instructors, and thought, "That's what I want to do." They looked happy. It was something so simple that had escaped me for as long as I remembered. Despite failing miserably in school as a kid, I loved reading and writing and learning, so I figured that was what I should do. All I had to do was keep managing, keep not floundering, keep not running off to get high.

Marriage was part of what was keeping me afloat. College was another. But I was missing the mental health care to make the trifecta. I could almost do it, but not completely. Even when college was good, OxyContin was finding its way into my life through guys I met on campus and my scattered jobs. I did well in school but could still never seem to hold down a job for more than a few months at a time (even in the months I wasn't using).

Mike moved to Arizona the day after his daughter was born. It was his own failed attempt to get off drugs. I'd been in Phoenix for about two years at that point and had transferred to Arizona State University. I was using every day by then, alone in locked bathroom stalls at school or work, terrified of the day I would end my marriage, positive that day would come.

In the summer, I worked at the multicultural center on campus and interned at *Hayden's Ferry Review*, ASU's literary magazine. The magazine was run out of an old house called the Piper Center, which the campus had grown around. It was said that Robert Frost had stayed there on his trips to Arizona. The magazine was run from offices upstairs. Downstairs was a dining room, living room, kitchen, and bathroom, all lined with books. During the school year, MFA students and select undergrads filtered in and out, lounging on the couch, eating packed lunches in the dining room, making coffee in the kitchen. But in the summer, it was mostly staff and me. I didn't want to go home if I didn't have to—Veronica and I were couch surfing between family friends and my uncle's house, and my marriage was getting so tense because of my hidden drug use it was getting hard to breathe.

At the Piper Center and *Hayden's Ferry Review*, I could pretend to be literary, pretend my addictions were a sign of genius rather than a desperate attempt at survival. I pretended to be the same as every other student and writer who came in. I didn't want *their* lives—I wanted my own, but I wanted mine to be moving forward like theirs seemed to. One day, I was at the Piper Center after scoring some black tar heroin from a panhandling couple across the street. She had a seven-month-pregnant belly, and he was a short man with waist-length hair and sign that stated they needed sandwiches. I'd also just gotten my hands on a clean, still-packaged syringe. I hadn't shot up for a while to avoid track marks. I was familiar with powder heroin, smoking black, and a variety of pills, but this was the first time I was going to try shooting black tar. I walked up the stairs and talked with the editor about an idea I had for the blog. We joked for a minute before I let her get back to work.

I made my way downstairs to the small bathroom between the kitchen (where I grabbed a spoon) and the lounge area. I locked the door and took out my supplies. Without thinking, I made a mix of all the paste in the tiny baggie, tied off, and let the warm rush flow up my left arm to my brain and plow me over. I realized something was wrong almost immediately. My head sank, and I barely made it into the bowl as I started throwing up. It was a single-occupancy bathroom, like in a regular house, with one toilet, which I flushed a couple of times to get the smell out. My breathing slowed. I couldn't get off the floor. All I could do for at least half an hour was lay my face against the tile, hoping it wasn't in dried piss, and tell myself I had to stay awake.

The electronic lock on the bathroom door would unlock every few minutes. I had to keep hitting the button to keep it locked, which at least gave me something to do while I struggled to stay conscious. I was sick and terrified. "I don't want to die under this toilet," I thought. "This is stupid. I'm so fucking stupid." After having to lock the door five or six times, I tried to get out. It was only a matter of time before someone from upstairs would have to use the bathroom. Kneeling, I opened the door, looked around, and saw the living room was empty. Perfect. I knew that if I stood up, I would throw up again and probably pass out, so I crawled to the nearby couch. I don't remember what happened over the next few hours, but I stayed awake with the help of mental images of myself dying and the police having to call Veronica while she was at work cleaning one of my relatives' homes so that we could make our car payment. I was ashamed of everything about myself. The *HFR* people were going to find me passed out or dead on their couch. I was going to get kicked out of school. Eventually I got up and stumbled into the hundred-twenty-degree Phoenix sun. The point on my arm where the needle had gone in was almost imperceptible, but I could see it. I hated it. I walked over to the first rough palm tree I could find and scraped my arm against it, tearing at the skin, wanting to erase me. I promised myself I would never get high again. I knew I was lying.

While I was on the bathroom floor, Mike was on the other side of Phoenix, buying and selling pills out the back of the burger place where he worked, drinking in the pub next door after he got off. I would go into the restaurant every time I could, and he would grin and say to all his coworkers, "Yo, this is my big brother. He's the guy I was telling you about."

After I overdosed in the bathroom, I decided to go to the campus doctor's office. The doctor said there was nothing he could do. He didn't treat addiction problems—I should go to a rehab. "I can't go to rehab," I explained, on the bench in his office. I couldn't drop out in the middle of a semester. And if my wife found out I was back on drugs, she would leave me. Also, there was no way I could afford it.

"If you don't quit, you probably won't graduate. The addiction is more likely to end your marriage than rehab. It's more likely to end your life."

"Fuck that rehab shit," Mike said when I recounted the conversation for him as we sat at a booth a few days later. He was in his smock and cap, drinking Dr Pepper like he always did. "And fuck that doctor who wouldn't even like help you. You got this shit, brother. Look at you, doing all this college shit. You're good, man. You'll get through it like you always do. I'm fucking proud of you, man." It would be a couple of months before he quit his job and started slinging black full time.

As I finished my BA (with honors; despite the doctor's warning), I snuck away from home and school to hang out with Mike. Somehow everything felt like saudade even as we were moving through those years, as if we knew unconsciously that moving at that velocity could never last. Something had to break. Something had to end. Either my schooling or writing or marriage or drug use or all of it would end. It had to. Either Mike would get off drugs, stop selling, or he would go to prison or die. We knew these were our options. We were well aware of the dangers, but it felt like we were watching ourselves act out our lives, unable to understand that we were indeed capable of changing course. While we waited for whatever was to come, we hid in cars, in the back of rough parking lots with faded lines, and cooked crushed pills in water on spoons. We smoked black tar, chasing trails as they dripped down the tinfoil, pulling on the bitter smoke through cut straws melted at the edges that were always too close to the heat—smoke so strong that the first toke of the day, after the sickness had begun to creep in, would always make me dry heave. Or we would sit on the floor of Mike's apartment and talk as much as we could in the few minutes I stole between classes before flying the forty minutes back to campus to sit in on a Shakespeare lecture or creative writing workshop. I wrote essays and short stories late into the night to get everything turned in on time. I stayed with my wife in

the campus library past midnight, working while fingering
the oxymorphone tablets or the packets of Suboxone sub-
linguals in my pocket. I wasn't as bad as I'd been in Florida, I'd say to myself. I was using every day, but it wasn't
like I was shooting up every day like before—only some
days, and always with clean rigs this time. I didn't nod off
as much as I used to because I was trying to manage more
than get high, just enough to function, I would tell myself,
not knowing at the time that it was my mental health
I needed to manage instead of the opioids. No coke, and I
never banged meth. My rules were flimsy and never took
much to break, but they were all I had.

During those stolen minutes, Mike was earnest, telling
me about the money he was making selling, or TVs people
had given him in lieu of cash, though the one TV he had
was cracked in the corner where the color flickered and
bled. "We're, like, more than brothers," Mike would say,
and I would agree. At Mike's, I could breathe, could stop
pretending to be the student and husband and person everyone wanted me to be, who *I* wanted to be but couldn't.
He didn't want me to be anything other than what I was.
There was a comfort in him, an acknowledgment that everything was fucked, but we still had one another. Mike
was a wild constant. That would never change.

One afternoon, junk sick, I was walking to the light rail
with a classmate from ASU, a skinny guy who always wore

flannel and was obsessed with David Foster Wallace. He seemed constantly worried about not appearing bland. He hung out with the other creative writing classmates in bars after class. I didn't. Sweaty, oily, with gooseflesh and chills raising on my skin, I stopped outside a corner bar before we crossed the street. I don't remember what we were talking about, or why I said it, but I leaned my head against a pole and said, "I wake up in pain every day, man. Miserable every day."

He looked at me, half rolled his eyes, smiled, and said, "Is that really true? That's so cliché."

All he knew about me was that I was in his writing classes and he'd seen me floating around writing conferences and readings. He'd read some of my stories about drugs and mental health issues, and for some reason I'd thought that would have made a difference. But I knew— the way I'd always known—that no, like most *normal* people, he would never know what I'd said was true. I felt stupid for saying anything.

I ignored his comment, and he allowed the conversation to go in another direction. When we parted, I made my way over to the light rail alone. I carefully crossed the street, trying not to shit myself, and sat on the baking metal bench with the desert sun on my shoulders. While I waited for the train, I leaned over my knees and rocked back and forth. I hadn't lied to my classmate. I woke up junk sick most days, feeling greasy. If I ever was feeling

well, I knew it wouldn't last, so I'd set off in search to find
something quick to keep me high. If I was in one of my
periods in which I wasn't using, I would still wake up nervous or unable to see reality, unable to go to work, and
never really sure why—I was probably lazy or melodramatic. What I'd said was the truth, but all it took was one
comment, one accusation of being cliché, to make me feel
like everything I knew was actually an exaggeration.

"Asshole," I thought, trying to fight the idea that maybe
he was right. "There's a reason clichés exist."

My dreams had merged—my love of books and my need
for drugs—or the dream and nightmare were fighting one
another. It was wonderful and horrible, but being with
Mike made it beautiful too. I wrote essays upon essays and
stories upon stories for my college classes that I got good
grades on and published in the school literary magazines.
At least in Mike's grungy apartment on a side of town that
would have terrified most people I went to school with,
I wasn't in danger of running into a basic David Foster
Wallace bro. No one could tell me I was cliché as Mike
and I switched to Spanish to talk to the Mexican woman
who ran a mini market out of her one-bedroom apartment
in his complex, or when we argued and laughed in a mix
of English, Spanish, and Portuguese in the QT, drawing
the attention of everyone around us. Maybe I was a cliché,
walking proof of the epidemic spreading through the US:
the perfect student who almost kills himself in a bathroom

where Robert Frost once took a shit; the loving, lying husband; the guy who gets arrested the day after graduating with honors and instead of celebrating spends three days in Miami-Dade correctional sure at the time that his marriage and life were over.

china king

China King told me they were firing me because they'd found a Chinese driver and he would be better for them. It was bullshit. They'd found Mike, who applied because I told him to. I didn't know they'd replace me. I should have guessed though. I didn't have a GPS, and I kept getting lost on the deliveries in the little over a month I'd been there, and people kept complaining about cold food. It was my first job after coming home from my mission in Florida.

China King consisted of a couple of cooks, the owner, his wife, and me. I was the only one who wasn't Chinese and the only one who spoke fluent English. I worked evenings, sometimes during lunch, delivering to college students in dirty apartments soaked with a permanent weed smell. I delivered once to a sorority, and when I told them I was a painter, they gave me their number and told me they would give me three hundred dollars if I could paint a mural on their wall—I got high later that night and lost the number. I delivered to a crying kid in his early twenties, a family who lived in the dark woods who refused to pay me since I was so late. I delivered to a man with large pictures of black-and-white pornography on his walls—not erotica, full-on penetration. He came to the door shirtless and sweaty. I drove my family's little maroon Nissan around from place to place, listening to CDs I played from a boom box I kept in the car because the car speakers were broken. The top was duct-taped shut, so every time I had to switch a CD, I had to do it carefully to make sure the tape wouldn't lose its stick.

China King kept telling me they needed another driver. I thought it would be perfect for Mike. He didn't have a car, but he had a friend who would let him borrow one. I took him with me on deliveries one day to show him how easy it was and convince him he should apply. We'd been snorting coke and crushed pills from the unbroken CD cases, and Mike was sitting in the back seat, leaving the front passenger seat open for the boom box.

"Hey," he said after a couple of deliveries. "You want a shrimp?"

I looked back and saw him with his shoulder-length black hair hanging down as he looked into the bags of food. "Holy shit, Mike," I said. "You can't eat the food, man."

"Relax," he said. "I'm only taking one from each bag. No one will know."

"Fuck, man," I said. "You can't—you can't . . . fucking do that."

He looked at me, blank-faced, in the rearview mirror, chewing.

"Fuck," I said, reaching one hand back. "Let me get one of those shrimps."

Mike applied and got hired the next day. I got fired before he even started—they probably thought they couldn't do worse than me. Mike ran out of gas before he could finish delivering his first order. He ate the food and never went back.

"The job was boring," he said to me when I saw him that night.

Bipolarations

Mike and me a few hours before he was arrested while I was
making my way back to California for my MFA workshops

I don't remember the last time I smoked black tar. I
don't remember the last time I shot up or snorted coke or
smoked meth or the last time of any drug. Of course I remember multitudes of times I used, and many of the firsts,
just not the *last* times. There is no defining moment when
I decided, "Okay, I'm done with whatever substance." Although I often did say that to myself only to use again
hours later. It's not that it faded away either. It wasn't

easy. What it has been is a process, an ongoing one. Drugs were a part of my daily life for over twenty years. They dominated my every moment and caused intense pain and hell, but that had been normalized and therefore was nothing special, and I had no idea that my last times using would be my last times. In fact, I was only able to stop using when I had thrown away the idea of a last time and after years of working on my real sicknesses. The drug addiction, like every person I've ever met with addiction issues, was a symptom of various problems and demons far more entrenched and complicated and difficult to touch.

"I don't think there's anything wrong with you," my dad said, exasperated, not long after my first visits with my therapist. I was eleven. It was after Mike and I had been caught smoking those stolen cigarettes that my parents decided I needed help. They were concerned that smoking was too much of a risk for my soul, a sign of more problems to come. To me, the smoking was a symptom of what no one—including myself—wanted to see. I was miserable and didn't want to deal with or even understand the reasons why.

My dad was terrified of therapists, and the older I got, the more I realized the man was terrified of everything. "Shrinks make very self-centered people," he would say. "They always talk about their clients focusing on what's best for *them*. What about the other people in their clients' lives? You have to be careful. They'll try to trick you into thinking church is bad for you because it makes you feel bad. They'll make you talk about things you don't want to talk about. They'll make you exaggerate. Therapy is dangerous. It's for whiny liberals who don't want to take responsibility for their actions." My father's thoughts on therapy came, of course, from his intensely conservative environment and McConkie's writing where he states, "No doubt *psychiatry*—the study and treatment of mental disorders—has some virtue and benefit in certain cases. But in practice, in many instances, it is in effect a form of apostate religion which keeps sinners from repenting, gaining forgiveness, and becoming candidates for salvation." My mom nodded in agreement, her voice lost as usual on most topics my folks deemed serious—though when she did speak she often got her way. My parents are not the same now as they were then, and my dad's thoughts on therapy and many of his other conservative and intense ideas have changed somewhat. But changed or not now, the effects the opinions had on me at the time cannot change, nor would it change the results they caused.

I think I met with the counselor twice, and though I did like talking to him, when my parents asked if I wanted to keep going, I said, "No, that's okay." I wanted to make them happy more than anything.

Instead of continuing therapy, I was pulled out of seventh grade the following year—though I went back to public school full time in eighth after my parents discovered how hard homeschooling was. It was because I had flunked out of sixth. It was because the ADD meds the doctor prescribed gave me stomachaches and the school wanted me to be medicated so they could have an excuse to let me pass. But it was mostly because I was twelve—the age I would become a deacon at church (a big deal for LDS youth)—and I was already getting into trouble, and my dad wanted to shield me from bad influences. Mike hadn't been pulled out that year, and I was never sure why. Perhaps our parents thought that at nine he was young enough that there were no real moral threats at school. Perhaps they believed I was the bad influence since I was older. Either way, I was the only one to go to therapy that time, and I was the only one pulled out of school that time as well.

Being at home for seventh grade worked better than when I left high school later, maybe because I was younger, maybe because that time my mother had been a little more involved and interested. I had a math book I worked out of. I checked out library books on ancient history. I read whatever I wanted, and I *did* end up going to public school at least part time because of a deal my parents had made. My mom didn't want me to be "that weird homeschooled kid" and said I needed to socialize. It went completely contrary to the reason my dad said he wanted to take me out of school, but that was how it often went in my home: everything a contradiction, proof of a perpetually divided mind and ethos and self-conception.

Every day my mom drove me out to the middle school for the two electives I was allowed to take there. Classes were held in a group of trailers near an Idahoan potato factory while the real middle school was being built. I picked choir for my elective, and either the school or my parents made me take PE for another. I was also forced to go to a class for special cases, wounded kids who got in too much trouble. It was something the school made me do because I was a home-taught kid instead of a full-time student. We did social-building activities like trying to find a way to fit the entire class on a wooden pallet. We made boomerangs. We spent most our time outside if it wasn't too cold.

The choir trailer had large steps, not big enough to be bleachers but big enough that there were three rows with foldout chairs in a semicircle that led up to where the boys sat. Our chairs weren't quite touching the wall though because there in the back, next to my seat, was the radiator. And it was hot enough to blister the skin.

For years I'd had a large, cauliflowery wart on the knuckle of my right middle finger that I always tried to hide by tucking it under my index finger. As a ten- and eleven- and twelve-year-old, I had tried to use that wart remover that eats the skin and turns white when dry, rip it out with my fingernails, cut it with a knife and pull until I could see its roots and blood would start to trickle down between the fingers and drip from the palm. Sometimes I would succeed in pulling the outer part of the wart off, but with the roots still intact, it would always come back. I hated it and was embarrassed by it. I wanted it gone and didn't know what to do until one day I heard that doctors sometimes froze or burned warts off.

I sat in the back of the choir room. Next to a furnace that was hot enough to leave a person in need of first aid if touched. I had a wart that needed removal. I was twelve, with a track record of making poor choices.

When we were seated, learning to read music, listening to the piano or song recordings, I would let my right arm hang, curl my middle finger so the wart on the knuckle stood out, and push the wart onto the metal coil of the radiator. The first few times, I pulled my hand back like any normal person experiencing pain, but the more I did it, the more I was able to tolerate the hurt. The wart didn't come off. But every day I went to choir that winter, I curled my knuckle and burned it for as long as I could take the pain. One day before the snow melted, I was in the gym class I didn't want to attend, running, pushing the wart with my thumb, trying to hide it under the index finger as I ran, and it crumbled. It rolled away. My tenacious dedication to burning—though not immediate, and absolutely not safe—worked. There was a small, round, pink mark on my finger for a while, and I looked daily for signs that the wart would return, and though I still roll my thumb over my middle finger, the wart never came back.

The second time I was taken to a counselor was during my freshman year of high school in Puerto Rico, and by then I was smoking weed and drinking and taking acid and whatever pills I could find without asking what they were. The school insisted I see a doctor because I was failing, saying the only way I would be able to pass was if I saw a professional, got diagnosed, and, similar to middle school, was put into the homeroom for special cases. My parents say they don't remember any of this. For a while, I wondered where those memories had come from: the young but intimidating therapist I only saw maybe twice and the muted-red short skirt she wore, the quiet waiting room with the IBM at the front desk, being asked to draw a picture of my family to bring to her. Had I invented that special homeroom at school and the teacher who asked me why I was there—the one who told me I seemed so smart and nice?

I used to think some of my childhood memories were dreams I'd designed to make me feel better about the problems I caused. Then I found that crude drawing of my family tucked inside an old notebook from high school. It was real. If that was real, then the conversation with my school counselor was real. That homeroom full of abused, suicidal, drug-using, awkward teenagers was real. I wasn't making anything up or making the situation worse than it was. My memories were as tangible as that drawing, and in the environment I grew up in, tangible proof was crucial. The physical proof was the power to recognize and accept my own experiences.

If asked when I was a teenager why I took drugs, I would have shrugged. I knew they made me feel better. I knew I was fucked up, and I knew it was connected to being "sexually impure" like I was taught about in church and in *The Miracle of Forgiveness*. I also would have put that thought out of my mind before it had time to develop. I just knew that I loved walking around the circular tables in the outside area of the high school on acid, feeling the light from the sun and the white walls, feeling the colors of the plants and trees on my skin. I loved having friends and running off into the woods behind the school to smoke on the steep slope where no one could see. I loved breaking up and snorting pills on my desks in the backs of classrooms. It was like a secret behind my eyes, a protection. It was often the only time I felt good if I wasn't skateboarding with Mike, and I wanted that feeling to last forever.

My third and fourth attempts at therapy were short-lived and disappointing. The third try was when I was in my mid-twenties. It was through ASU student services in the middle of the campus. At the front office, when I handed in the paperwork to the woman doing my assessment, I said I didn't want meds. She rolled her eyes and said, "You don't care about what you put in yourself from the street but don't want meds that could actually help?"

I didn't want meds because I thought I knew the side effects: weight gain, erectile disfunction, loss of personality, hair loss. Mike thought that as well. After he went to ARF, he was prescribed lithium, medication to treat the manias in bipolar disorder. However, after reading about the potential problems that could come with it, only to lose the manias he loved, he only ever took one pill. After being forced into ARF, he never wanted anything to do with mood stabilizers or therapy again.

The fourth time I went, I was thirty, and it lasted a few weeks. I couldn't keep meeting up with that therapist because I couldn't pay, and while his theory for why I made poor decisions was flattering (he told me that I was just too smart and didn't seem like I had enough patience to deal with the world), it didn't fit what I needed. It didn't take care of the times I felt out of control. It didn't stop me from using when I was out of control, and it didn't explain the severe depressions and sensation of falling apart and the excitement and energy that would build in me so large I would feel lifted up and holy. While I loved the confidence he had in me, I felt like I needed something more.

I quit using for real not long after meeting with my fifth therapist, and after my official bipolar diagnosis. I figured that to keep from drug use I needed to explore myself and why I needed to use in the first place. I thought the best place to look would be to go to where I considered I'd fallen apart the hardest. What I knew was that after leaving Puerto Rico, moving to Florida, and dropping out of high school, I would never really recover from how far I fell into myself. That should be the place to start, I thought. It was like studying a stranger from a distance of years—the me in my thirties studying this peculiar boy I used to be. I scoured old drawings I'd salvaged from that time, searching for recurring characters and themes, and I found them. They began to show some sicknesses, depictions of suicide, severe depression, and more. One in particular was a grinning man found multiple times in every notebook, loose papers, and at least one old painting I lost years ago.

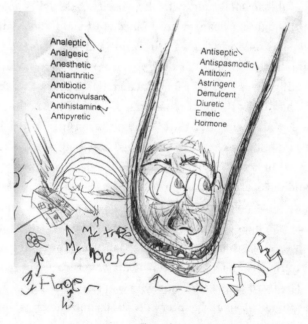

Figure 1

Figure 1 is an early iteration of what I called the grinning man—drawn for an in-class health course assignment I never turned in during what were to be the last few days I'd spend in high school. The balding look was an accident. I was so frenzied and full of energy that I couldn't keep my hand steady enough to fill in the hair. I drew with my left hand, though I'm right-handed. It felt important, something to do with the left being closer to the heart and therefore the soul, thus making it easier to spill the soul onto the page. The grinning man is clearly labeled "ME." The house, rainbow, tree, and flower—none of which I was able to spell right with the velocity of thoughts pouring through my head—were hilarious to me. I shook and laughed so hard inside as I drew but stayed as silent as I could on the outside, for fear of classmates and teachers thinking I was insane. I felt like a genius. I know I wasn't high as I drew the picture because I dropped out of school the day after the first time I bought weed in Florida. In fact, I distinctly remember wishing I was high as I drew. I wanted to keep that good feeling going because I knew it would dissipate soon.

At some point, that first smile morphed into an enormous grin plastered on a face, and like the second drawing (Figure 2), each subsequent iteration was almost always left unfinished as my attention span wavered.

The third drawing (Figure 3) was done with ink on paper stained at sporadic intervals, that same energy welled up with such intensity that I paced around the room be-

Figure 2

Figure 3

tween every few inky strokes of my bamboo brush. When painting, I would decorate my body in messages and symbols, paint my face, never knowing why other than it was important, seemed like the thing to do. With each of these three drawings, I laughed louder in my head, still always silent on the outside. My fear of others' judgment had grown full-fledged. If anyone caught me too far outside of the mildly eccentric self I showed, my euphoria would morph into dysphoria, a state I feared above all others.

Figure 4

When I did this last drawing (Figure 4), I was not laughing. The grin had taken over, far beyond the control of the face it stretches. The eyes are worried. I remember the fear I felt when I drew it, the monstrous and uncontrollable anxiety and energy welling up. I could see the drawing and remember putting pen to paper, remember the intensity, and I compared it with my adult medicated self, and my adult unmedicated self, and what I discovered was profound.

~~

The *DSM* says about bipolar disorder that "During a manic episode, individuals often do not perceive that they are ill or in need of treatment . . ." Mike was like that. All over the place, rambling about all the big ideas he had, making all the mistakes he could, and laughing the whole way. And he seemed like he was in an almost perpetual manic episode. In Florida, from the time he was a teenager he would disappear from my family for days—though I always knew where to find him before and after my mission—only to come home with a new girl he would sneak up to his room in the middle of the night. Not long after I returned from my mission, he came home with a ball python only to disappear again for another few days, during which time the python got lost in his room. I found it in his closet under clothes and papers as I was going through his room trying to see if I could find any pills he might have dropped on the floor. I was junk sick and broke (wondering how different Mike and I really were despite people treating us differently based on our outward demeanors). All I found were a few dirty needles and the snake, calm and curled in the closet. The next time he came home, a few days later, our mom yelled at him until he gave the snake to a friend (apparently, she had also found it at some point). Mike and I laughed at that for years. His life was a mess, but he preferred it to the ideas he had of therapy and mood stabilizers. He preferred it to church. He preferred it to the sadness that permeated our home. Not long before he died, he told me through the prison phone that he had lived a good life and that the only thing he regretted was not being there for his daughter, but *that* he regretted bitterly.

I kept telling myself that my manias, those times when I felt bigger than the cosmos, were a gift. I recognized the abnormality even when they started coming on stronger when I was a teenager, and through my twenties and early thirties, enough to know I'd better not say I felt I was receiving secret information from the universe. Again, my gift of hiding myself was imperative. Who doesn't want to believe they are singular and important? Who doesn't want to know they're really a genius, and everything self-destructive and confusing that they've ever done has been because of that? Who would want to replace those beautiful moments and impressions with sickness, with a case of mistaken identity? Who would want that kind of embarrassment? The problem with a manic *euphoria*—especially for someone who also experiences manic *dysphoria* (a mixed episode)—is that we want, we *need*, to believe that our delusions and good feelings are real.

When I'm in a euphoric state, I feel everything come on at once, like electricity. It builds, swells: light, air, movement, all on my skin—a physical sensation that penetrates me to my core, seeps into my heart and lungs and diaphragm. It runs up my spine and expands into the back of my head. I feel huge, towering over people, cities, the earth. The vast, cosmic feeling envelops everything, revealing secrets *normal* people don't see. When I'm on the rise, hypomanic, I can be sometimes at my most productive, convinced I'm a genius after all, and all I need is to work to prove it. The *DSM* also states of manias, "Inflated self-esteem is typically present, ranging from uncritical self-confidence to marked grandiosity, and may reach delusional proportions." I'd drive to a bookstore and pace the aisles, muttering and having conversations with myself, my hands and fingers in constant motion. I'd grin. Make others laugh when I talked to them. "Individuals in a manic episode usually show increased sociability . . . They often display psychomotor agitation or restlessness by pacing or by holding multiple conversations simultaneously." This is an almost exact description of Mike's constant demeanor. I can't count the number of times he'd be having a conversation with me, and others around me, while concurrently having conversations with two separate people on two separate burner phones. For me, on the outside, I'd look like my normal, eccentric, talkative self—the self my family and friends knew. On the inside, I was brimming. I've always loved manic states when they were purely manic and not mixed.

Unlike a natural euphoria, a drug-induced euphoria can be laughed away: "I was so wasted, bro." "Did I really do that?" "I can't believe I was that high. That's so funny." It doesn't matter how crazy the idea or good the feeling, how insane a person's rant about being connected to the universe is, how bizarre or garbled the words are—as long as it's drug-induced, they can minimize their strange experience. In my case, a natural manic euphoria can be as strong as an acid trip—sans the dreamlike quality—with the same spiritual feeling of growing importance. But I can't laugh the natural thoughts away. They come from *me*, not a drug. It's embarrassing, and like fear, embarrassment breeds gaslighting, so I would convince myself it was nothing I needed to address even if I knew it was.

I would keep it to myself, knowing full well that if I started ranting about the colors I felt on my skin and the electricity in my mind that I'd worry or annoy someone. I kept so much to myself that when I wasn't in one of these states, I'd wonder if they were real. If no one noticed and if no one said anything—I thought after my official bipolar diagnosis and while I was examining my teenage self in my thirties—was my bipolar diagnosis an exaggeration? If so, then I would also have to question the fact that almost no one ever noticed when I was on drugs: speedballing at a job fair where I was hired by a hotel because Mike and I seemed like fun guys, speed-talking on shrooms to family who nodded in agreement to whatever I was saying so they could get on with their TV shows, tripping on acid at work in the ice-cream shop kiosk at the mall and collecting phone numbers from girls I would never call. If none of that was ever noticed, how easy would it be to hide the state of my mental health?

I tried to quit my addictions almost the moment I started because using was a disappointment, and I never wanted to be a disappointment. After Mike and I were caught smoking at that park, I sat in the bathtub listening to Soundgarden and feeling the weight of the water and air, waiting for my parents to get home, swearing I would never smoke again. After seeing a friend kicked down her stairs by her mother after we were caught smoking weed in her basement while skipping class in eighth grade, I thought, "I don't want this world. I'll never smoke weed again." Every time I got sick from too many pills or LSA or anything I would swear off it again.

I tried quitting countless times by taking all the pills or dope I had in a single night, so I'd have nothing the following day, only to go on the hunt the moment I started getting sick. There was the time I made it a couple of days before shitting myself while driving with K, who was also trying to quit. We pulled over, and I stuffed my pants with paper towels from a gas station and cried all the way to a guy I knew who had overpriced Roxy 30s and had K buy them because I was too ashamed to get out of the car. There was the time I shot up six or more Dilaudid 8s (all I had) and fell to the floor in front of a worried Mike; I was hoping I would die or be lifted up into some magical space where I would find the secret of no longer needing to get high.

Instead, I got up off the floor, annoyed. My tolerance was way too high. I didn't even get sick. I was hustling the next day for shit. After I got back from my mission, and before I was married, Mike and I were notorious hustlers and had an extensive network of dealers and users. We connected people who needed shit and had money to people who dealt during the times we weren't slinging anything ourselves, always skimming enough off the top to make sure we were covered for the day or more when possible. It was just part of the game, and hustling and dealing can be almost or just as hard to quit as using for some people— it was for Mike. He loved to be connected to that network almost as much as he loved the drugs themselves. It was thrilling and there was a sense of pride in being able to hook a person up with what they didn't know how to find any other way. Mike would try to get off the shit by going to the methadone clinic, but part of what fucked him up is that he never stopped hustling, never pulled himself out of that network. He loved it.

I tried quitting drugs in 2003 by going on a mission at nineteen but was on morphine almost the day I got back in 2005. I tried quitting by moving from Florida to Arizona in 2006, only to have my friends send me pills until I could find my own connections in the west and eventually go back to Florida nine months later, where using was easier for me. I tried to quit by moving from Florida to Arizona again after I was married in 2008 but was using a short time after. I tried to quit by moving to Brazil the day after

I graduated from ASU in 2013 but was smoking black tar as soon as we got back to the States in 2014. I tried to quit when we lived in Salt Lake City, only to score shit from the homeless at the shelter downtown. I've flushed heroin down the toilet, pills, dumped booze out on the ground, only to search for and find shit the next day.

I both wanted and didn't want to quit for over twenty years. I would quit using for a couple of days, a year, back to a week, a couple of days again, another week. I learned the cycles of my body and mind. The third day was the worst when junk sick. The next couple of months to a year following junk sickness would be hell in the mind. But it wasn't in vain. In the long run I *was* getting better. I *was* gaining ground. I was building the pillars I needed to be able to grow, or maybe I was letting them be built, or maybe both, and each time I quit was like learning to stretch deeper. Each attempt was like a knife or fingernail to that wart, pulling, bleeding, sometimes ripping pieces off, but always leaving the roots behind. Each stretch I went without using counted. By the time I saw my fifth therapist and got on my meds in 2016, I was no longer using every day, though by that time monthly was devolving back into weekly and I knew daily use was upon me again.

The basis of the relationship between Veronica and me has always been a profound friendship. We talk deep into the night, sometimes all night. We tell each other our dreams as we walk bleary-eyed into the living room after waking up. She sits on the couch, and I lie on my back on the floor, before we eat, before anything, for no other reason than to hear from and be next to one another. We laugh at memes and the ridiculous things I've done and said. We make direct translations of songs from Portuguese to English and English to Portuguese. I'll speak Spanish with English syntax to make her laugh. We've developed an accidental language made up of Portuguese, English, Spanish, and made-up words that only we will ever understand. We laugh until I fall to my knees and she wipes the tears from her eyes. We compare skin tones by pushing our arms or hands or legs or stomachs together, since we're both about the same color and sometimes one is darker and sometimes the other is. I'll cut her thick, black, curly hair. She'll cut my sometimes dark, sometimes lighter wavy hair. I calm her anxiety, lie next to her every time she wants to take a nap so that she can sleep—she can't sleep unless my body is next to hers. I've never raised my voice to her or called her any names, the same way she's never raised her voice to me or called me any names. She makes sure I remember to eat, stay focused, take my meds, talk out whatever is going on in my head so I don't make rash decisions and do something risky. I read to her, make popcorn, hold her hand when she has to draw blood, and talk out whatever is going on in her head to try to ease her anxiety. I held her hand as the surgeon pulled out the drainage tube after her thyroidectomy after the cancer diagnosis she already intuited she would have. Through sickness and joblessness and moves and times when we had to couch surf because we had no money for rent, we've spent most waking hours together. We sincerely and profoundly love each other and love being with each other.

It still hasn't been easy though, and, like most couples, divorce has been mentioned more than once. I've had to learn to keep the apartment clean. Money has never *not* been tight. She's learned to be less angry with me and forgive me over and over. We've both learned how to recognize and react to one another's mental health problems and wounds and traumas. We've had our periods of silence and tension and pain. And of course there's been the issue of my years of addiction and lies.

Another iteration of the grinning man appeared in an oil painting I've since lost. The grin is almost exactly the same as in the three drawings I've held on to, but it's not attached to the face it controls. It hovers over it like a mask, casting a shadow on the skin behind it, the eyes in panic at the loss of control. Not all manias I have are euphoric. "Rapid shifts in mood over brief periods of time may occur and are referred to as lability (i.e., the alternation among euphoria, dysphoria, and irritability)." The worst manias I've experienced are far from the euphoric ones I love. Manic dysphoria has the same swelling electricity as euphoria, but instead of unbridled joy and confidence, it carries nervousness, terror, an overwhelming sense of guilt, and an irritability fused with obsession.

Figure 5

The marionette hanging from a noose (Figure 5) is another teenage me, severely depressed, malnourished, and helpless. The screaming figure is also me, berating myself for being so ridiculous—horrible, self-pitying, and melodramatic. The two forces create an inescapable vortex. The current cannot be stopped by trying to "think good thoughts." This is the state I felt I *needed* drugs for—specifically opioids, since marijuana would either trigger or enhance this state for me and other substances weren't as effective—and it is by far the most dangerous. I haven't had any serious dysphoric states since I started taking my bipolar medication. Before then, however, dysphoria meant I would do anything to get high, even if I'd been off drugs for a while. In this state, every part of me is thrust into panic. I pace the room in dread, knowing that I need something but not knowing what that something is. The nervous stomachaches from childhood come back. I become obsessed with wanting to sleep and never waking up, and the obsession grows into the need to either sedate or kill myself. But I stay quiet so no one ever notices. Why would I want them to?

Though I didn't understand their severity, I was vaguely aware of these states before going to therapy the fifth time, the time I started taking Lamictal—without any of the side effects I'd been terrified of years earlier. I'd tapered down my opioid use but couldn't quite get off completely, and I knew I was a breath away from getting back on with a vengeance. I had some structures in place, what I've come to think of as pillars, that helped me taper my use: Veronica, school. But I'd had those pillars for years, and I knew they wouldn't be enough. All it would take was one dysphoric episode and I would be back on the shit.

Veronica and I had gone through a lot by then. There had been two other serious episodes in our marriage in which my addictions had come to light, days of crying, pain, and guilt, scars we still bear. Both times, she promised me she would leave me if I ever used again. Both times she stayed. Both times I went back to drugs in secret, never meaning to, just seeming to slip into it. One time when I felt I needed them to function turned to two times and on and on, the same cycle I'd been on my entire life. I hated it and myself. Besides the tensions caused by my hidden drug use, there were Veronica's ever-growing health concerns (which would turn out to be thyroid cancer), and the money issues of two graduate students working odd jobs, and the general stress and irritability that comes with day-to-day living. When I started seeing the therapist, I wasn't where I had been the first two times we almost split up from my use, but I was starting to get bad again, and silences between us were growing.

By this time, Mike was newly in prison, and Veronica and I were almost done with our master's programs. I was finishing my low-residency MFA from UC Riverside, which meant most of the time I talked with my teachers and other students online and went to a resort in Palm Springs every six months, where I would spend ten days in workshops and seminars. Veronica had decided on an MS in mental health counseling. It was also an online program. She had been inspired by her own traumas and family traumas, Mike, and me. She was in the middle of her practicum at a place she thought at first she didn't want to be: an outpatient treatment center contracted by the Arizona Department of Corrections to work with people right out of prison and who usually lived in halfway houses (where Mike would go after his first stint in prison). She was terrified, and her anxiety almost took over, but she needed that practicum. It turned out to be one of the best experiences of her life.

She would come home and talk about how the guys she worked with were all really good guys who had fucked-up lives, how they called her Mrs. Veronica and said she was the shit and laughed and told her stories she would never repeat. She loved them and cried with them and wrote letters to their parole officers. I loved how much she loved them, and it gave me hope. Our change and understanding of addiction was slow, gradual, and depended on education on the subject. Veronica's perspective when we first started was that I didn't love her enough to quit for her, and I felt like an awful human unworthy of love because of how much I was fucking up. At least if I kept it a secret I could hold on to the love I wanted but didn't feel I deserved. It took years to change perspectives.

But I was still slipping. I was having long depressive periods, and every time I hit a mixed state, I would use, which would lead to more depressed periods. I had generally been able to do my school assignments throughout the years I was in college, but something was happening to me as I started the home stretch of my MFA. There was a twenty-page paper I was supposed to write as part of a lecture I was supposed to give, and I couldn't do it. I was almost done with my degree, with my schooling, and

I couldn't finish. I would stare at my computer screen, write words I knew didn't work, and then delete them. My instructor—a brilliant novelist and memoirist—knew it wasn't working either. After I sent her a couple of failed attempts, she asked me what was wrong. Without thinking, I told her I was having trouble not using. It just came out. I didn't know I would say it, but she had been in AA for years and had stopped drinking, and I knew she would understand.

I drove the three hours through the desert for the nine days of lectures and workshops at the resort and spent the entire time not drunk but secretly buzzed—alcohol has never been my drug of choice, but I couldn't get the heroin I had wanted to take with me. I went through the workshops and lectures, talked and laughed with friends, but by the end of the residency my limbs hurt and I knew I was spent. As I was preparing to leave, another of my instructors—another brilliant novelist and memoirist—who was also in recovery and years off heroin himself came up to me, hugged me, and told me how important it was not to hate myself (he'd been told about my relapses).

I knew what I had to do. I went home and told my wife about my continued drug use, that it wasn't as bad as it had been in the past but that I needed help. She cried and I cried, but she didn't tell me she would leave me. Instead, we borrowed money, and I went to a psychiatrist who was about my age. By the end of the first visit, she had diagnosed me with bipolar disorder, and I started on Lamictal.

It turns out, that was the last piece I needed for what has been the longest period since I was eleven that I haven't been dependent on dangerous chemicals to feel good.

I don't like the terms "addict," "clean," "recovered," "sober." I am none of these. The word "addict" does not define me. I'm not clean—that's a term that brings to mind church people teaching sexual purity. A sober person sounds so serious, and I'm not that. I am recovering, never completely recovered—the way all people are growing and never completely grown. I am a person who has a severe addiction who is not using and hasn't used for some years now. I don't tally the days, months, years. I don't knock it. I know it works for many people, but it never has for me. The weight of that accountability, I fear, would smother me.

For me, I like to concentrate on what I consider my pillars. First and foremost, I have Veronica, my support. She's not as much someone I feel I need to be accountable to and responsible for (though that is part of it); rather, she's someone I love and want to be present for, available for. Second, I have my purpose. It used to be school, until I graduated. Now it's about connecting to others through teaching and writing. It's having a voice and helping others gain their own voices. The third turned out to be health and the medical help I needed, which now includes medication, meditation, exercise, and self-exploration. Still, it's a matter of trial and error, constant modification. It even took a couple of years to be on a stable dosage. But like the kid who burned the wart off his middle finger on a radiator and spent days learning to get his skateboard to flip the right way, I am tenacious.

When I was still figuring out the right dosage, I came across a fellowship I wanted to apply for. Veronica was concentrating on her own work in the living room. I stood up, excited, and began to ramble about my ideas, what I would write, why it would help the community, how I was perfect for it. I read all the requirements to her, read the bios of the people who had won the previous year. I went back to my seat, read more, then stood up, walked over to Veronica, and started repeating everything I'd said before. Veronica, calm, looked up at me and said, "You're repeating yourself. You already told me all that."

"Right," I said. "Sorry. I think I'm getting too excited."

She went back to typing her notes, and I went back to the kitchen. My excitement wasn't diminishing. It was growing electric. I had forgotten to take my pill—and as I later learned when I counted them, I had forgotten to take it a few times. "Oh shit," I thought. I could feel myself speeding up. The grinning self was taking over. "I just forgot to take my pill. Well, it's too late now. It's too late. I'll just have to take it tomorrow. But I need to act cool or she'll think I'm high, that's what *they* don't get, people will just think I'm high, *they* don't understand that that's the problem, that's why I can't trust *them*, *they'll* think something is wrong, nothing is wrong. This is great. I just need to harness this."

I cannot fathom why I believed I couldn't take my pill at that moment, but I can recall perfectly the feeling of the grinning face expanding. It's a sensation that is often present in me but rarely in control. The entire range of my manic and depressive sides are always present, like a constant current running over, behind, or under me. It's rushing over my head as I type this. When I'm stable, I feel it outside myself, either below my feet, parallel to my back, or over my head. When I'm dysphoric, I'm drowning in it as it rages. When I'm depressed the current trickles into a sick sway—almost still, heavy, but silent, and I am under it. I suffocate. When I'm euphoric, I ride it, surfing at high speeds.

The morning after not taking my pill, it was difficult to hear anything that wasn't my own thoughts. I took Veronica to work, came back home, lay on my side on the couch, wrapped my arms around my knees, and rocked back and forth, free from having to pretend to be normal, feeling everything, trying to get myself under control by humming with the inner vibrations of the universe before I would have to go to work. Knowing what was happening and wanting more documentation, I grabbed my computer and wrote this:

°¡§¡¡¡¡¡ ¡ ¡¡ ¡¡ ¡¡ ¡¡ ¡¡ ¡¡ ¡¡ ¡¡Remember¡¡   ¡¡¡   ¡¡¡¡¡¡¡when   youwerepartof   thesun?
Rememberremember?andIneedtogetmy head straightanditwasgloriousaaaand@THISISAMAZ
ing   tobethisway.   IT'sthe   clarity   !!?¡™   they   don't
understandrember?Whenyouwerepartofthesuntherythmstherymstherythmsstrummingmypain…H
A! AHA! AHA!HA!HA!HA!HA!thisis ! the way thisisthewayitworks…if Icouïldgetthisall
downif ificouldgetthisalldownifl ¡¡¡¡¡ whatastupidmotherfuckeriam motherfucker youknow
rememberwhenyouwerepartofthesun   thefunnythingis   that   rememberremembertheclarity
you'venever!!!!!! ! !actually thatswhattheydon'tget ¿fuckedamotherbefore noonewho has
ineedthismotionalways theydon'tget it haschildrensotechicallyyou rememberrememberremeber
bydefinitioncannotbeamotherfuckerhahah ahaha!!!!! ! ! ! ! ! ! !!! ! ! !!! !!   !! ! ! !! !
!!!!!!!!¡¡!¡you know youknowyou know what's hillariousis tha tifsomefamilymembers we r
etoseethisth ey would√!¡÷?¿eflikely sayyyyy"areall the swearwords really neessesary?¿÷¿?€ y y
y y y y yyyy Yed s YES DAMNIT!!we cannnnnnot becensored HA HAHA haha HAHA hha
HAHitstheenergy   andhowwouldthey   un   der   standit   anyway?   Nottheirfault
Singingsingingsingingsinging Hummdeedummdoooooooool iineed towritethsi doe wnit;s fucking
gooold   manfucking   goldun   abashed   unabashednessinthe   sunnnIfeel   as
l¡¡¡¡¡¡¡¡¡!!¡!1thsisiwhathtey don't understand theydontunderstand I fthisicouldberidden uoutout
is ficouldberiddenout???thiswve thiswaveis   so   imensethey h
      avenoideahowimensethisewave pa   rtonfthesuntthesunthsunthe   sinsin   sun   suns
nusnsunsunsnsunsusnusnsu aef hd u ddw efq rqw D   qf   uwhfuws arerélvoelovelovecom você
Precisode olodum olodumaréolodum sabemcomo eles s abemc omo como controlar whatwhat w
ahathathat esse electricidade ô eletricidadeboa   éninguem nota soul ninguemsabe what was
thatthingshe said?comoé mas OLODUM……elessabem they havetosomeonehas toooo…

It went on for much longer, as I teetered on the prec-
ipice between manic euphoria and manic dysphoria. At
some point, I went to work with those thoughts running
in the background of my mind. At the time I was working
as a professor, and I performed the role, asking students
to repeat what they were saying because my thoughts kept
getting in the way. That was the only hint I let slip. Otherwise, I could never let what went on inside come out.
The moment someone saw they would worry. I had been
trained my entire life to hide it, and I was doubly good
at hiding it because I'd learned what not to do from other
people who weren't as careful as I was.

Even with small manic or depressive lapses like these
as I've tweaked meds or forgotten them, I've been off all

substances since I started with my Lamictal. While I have had temptations from time to time, mostly I'm just no longer interested in using. The true test came for me not long after Veronica's thyroidectomy and cancer treatment.

I have bad pains sometimes, especially if I eat something I shouldn't at night. A pain expands like a supernova from the upper-right part of my stomach that wakes me in the middle of the night and sends me to a fetal position on the floor after it forces me to pace the room a while. Each time, I can barely talk, and it feels like I'll die. I don't have them so much anymore after I've started trying to eat better and exercise, but shortly after Veronica's surgery I had an episode. She'd saved her pain pills in a drawer by her bed in case they were needed for something. In the middle of the night, in horrific pain, I slid over to her side of the bed, opened the drawer, and took the six pills she had left. My pain went away, and I could breathe. I was grateful for the hydrocodone for that, but while I did get high, I didn't like it like I used to. It was even slightly uncomfortable, and more than anything I was annoyed that I wasn't able to get back to sleep. The effects on my body weren't any different than they had been when I used opioids. It was that I no longer needed them. It was as if they had served their purpose.

All this said, I know the feeble ground on which I walk. I know that while for now I'm not interested, that doesn't mean it will forever be this way. I'm aware that my pillars need to be flexible, need to be boiled down to concepts for them to even work since everything is mutable. The best-case scenario for the end of a marriage is death, and if Veronica goes before me? If she outgrows or leaves me? What then? I earned my AA, BA, MFA, and I have no plans to go back to school. That purpose changed to teaching. But I left my teaching job. My purpose is writing for now, but that could change. Everything does. My meds could stop working. They do for many people. What then? As concepts: support, purpose, and medical and health treatment, my pillars are strong, but like any building, renovations are to be expected. So I try to understand as much as I can through self-exploration and analysis. I've gotten back to meditation and searching out that stillness beneath the noise—I had never really quit, just slowed down after the mission. I watch my depressions and manic tendencies for signs of needed adjustments. So far, I've passed through some of the worst times of my life without drugs: having COVID for a month, thinking my wife and I were going to die and hoping I would, Veronica's cancer diagnosis and surgery and treatment, Mike's death.

I think of Mike, how he didn't have a single pillar similar to mine and what that meant. Mike's relationships were toxic at best and usually dangerous for both parties. Not because he was violent. He wasn't, and he loved his partners with all he had. But Mike was a whirlwind who was attracted to other whirlwinds: girls he lived on the streets with, who were partners in his drug dealings, who declared their undying love for him one moment only to scream and punch and throw food at him in a crowded restaurant the next. Mike had wild ideas of how to make money, he had connections, and he was addicted to dealing and hustling, but I don't think he ever really knew what to do beyond that. He always talked about wanting to be there for his daughter, but I don't think he knew how. And he absolutely refused even the idea of medication, diagnosis, and therapy. *I* wasn't a pillar for him. I had nothing I could offer him by the time he died: a small, one-bedroom apartment with rent I couldn't make as adjunct faculty, money I didn't have, time to hang out with him every day like I had done when we were kids or when we were adults and both using. All I had to give him was the friendship and love I always had, and we talked almost every day through email, but it wasn't enough. I am fully aware that part of the reason I'm not dead is because I chose to cling to my pillars, and that they were available to me in the first place. I sought them out. I chose to believe in them, and I still do. I know that knowing something and feeling something aren't the same and that sometimes feelings aren't reliable. But my survival still doesn't feel deserved, and my guilt at being alive and no longer using—even if I know it's faulty thinking—feels real.

happy valley

We almost hit a huge rock these kids had put in the middle of the street in our grandparents' neighborhood while driving back from a movie not long after Mike came out to Arizona. The eleven- and twelve- and thirteen-year-olds were on the side, skateboards and scooters in hand, half hidden behind a wall, smiling and watching to see what would happen. It was next to a Safeway in a middle-class, white neighborhood, just off a street called Happy Valley, nice enough.

Mike and I had done something similar once. One of the houses we lived at in Idaho was next to the highway. It wasn't busy, but depending on the time of day there was no lack of cars. We were much younger than the kids who'd put the mini boulder in the street next to my grandparents', but old enough to know that throwing anything at moving vehicles was a bad idea. We had a game. We picked small pebbles and tried to skip them under the cars as they passed. We didn't want to hit anyone, and we didn't, but one of the cars pulled over after an accidental ricochet

off the asphalt. Mike and I ran inside and to our room, but
the guys in the red car we'd nicked on the underside with
the pebble knocked on the door and told our parents. We
were forced to go upstairs and apologize. Something about
having to apologize to strangers was more embarrassing
and painful than any trouble we might have got in with
our parents.

I saw the rock on Happy Valley and pulled over to move
it out of the way before it caused any damage to another
car behind us. Most of the kids took off when the car pulled
over, but one, defiant, stayed behind. He blanched when
we got out of the car though. Mike was out before I was,
his pants sagging, an unlit cigarette hanging from his
mouth. At that time some of his teeth were wearing away
from the meth. Not enough that it was bad, but enough
that it was noticeable. I came out next, black hair slicked
back. After me came our six-foot white brother-in-law. The
kid looked like he might cry.

"You put this shit in the middle of the road?" Mike said,
taking the opportunity that he was no longer in my car to
light his smoke.

"N-no," the kid said. He had a baseball cap, and a new
skateboard under his arm.

"Hey," I said to him, walking closer. "Look, whether you
put it there or not I'm just going to say that's dangerous.
A car can get really messed up if they hit something like
that."

"Well," he said, clutching his board, "I didn't put it there."

Mike said, "You any good with that skateboard?"

"I don't know," the kid said. His friends had run off, but we could still see them a few yards away, watching.

"Yo," I said at the sight of the board. "You should let me see if I can still do a kickflip."

Our brother-in-law didn't say anything, and although he's an extremely mild-mannered person, his silence must have intimidated the kid, because he kept staring at him. Kids usually like me, but I don't know what this one thought of me—one of the three guys who'd interrupted his fun, for his own good or otherwise. If he was wary of adults, I couldn't blame him.

"Um," the kid said, eyes on our brother-in-law. "I got to go." And he ran off toward his friends.

"Think I could have stuck a kickflip?" I said to Mike as we got back in the car.

"Yeah, brother," he said. "Hold on." He blew the smoke from his mouth, dabbed the cigarette on the back tire, pinched the end with his fingers, and tucked what was left behind his ear.

"I don't know," I said, climbing into the driver's seat. "I'm getting kind of fat."

"Nah," Mike said as he got in and closed his door. "I bet you could still do it."

Mike looked at our brother-in-law, who hadn't talked

much during the interaction, and said, "I bet those kids were not expecting like two Mexicans and a football player to walk out of this car."

We howled at that, laughing until we pulled into our grandparents' driveway.

Sangue Latino

Mike and our younger brothers when we
picked him up from prison

The first time I was taught about Latinos "invading"
the United States and the dangers they posed of potentially mixing blood with and corrupting white people was
in a middle-school Spanish class when I lived in Idaho.
My teacher was a tall white man with black hair, who'd
learned Spanish as a Latter-Day Saint missionary in Gua-
temala. He spoke through a smile as he walked around
the room, peering with authority into the faces of those he
was trying to inspire. When he glanced at me, I panicked. I
was the mixed guy he said was invading his land. Soon, he

explained, white men like him would be the minority. The
Latino population was the fastest growing in the United
States. It was only a matter of time until the American
gene pool would be too genetically mixed, he said, so weak
that if a major disease came it would wipe everyone out
with ease. He was so sure of himself and the validity of
his statements, as he divulged his terror at the thought
of becoming a minority, his terror of impending racial in-
cursion, to a group of children. I knew I was one of the
threats he was referring to, but I had no idea what I was
supposed to do about it. I just knew I wanted class to end.
I just knew he was one of the reasons I didn't trust adults.

In 2015, I got a job substitute teaching at a Title I elementary and middle school in a predominantly Hispanic part
of town. The federal program provided financial assistance
to local schools with children from low-income families to
help them meet state standards. When I'd applied to a
subbing job in Utah the year before, I was denied because
of my arrest in Florida in 2013, which stemmed from the
bench warrant that was issued in 2008. But the job in
Phoenix was mine before I went in for the interview, before
they'd finished running the background check, and they
didn't flinch when I told them about the bench warrant
for failing to go to court on a possession of paraphernalia
charge almost eight years prior, or that the paraphernalia
was two dirty needles. They didn't care about the arrest in

Florida. My fines were paid, and I no longer had a warrant out for me. Arizona needed teachers. It has one of the worst teacher shortages in the nation and is ranked as one of the worst places to teach in the country.

"You'll be good for these kids," the head of HR told me. She was tall and brown and lively and had a doctorate in education. "*¿Hablas español?*" she said, less as a question and more as a statement. I've usually been told rather than asked that question, and most of the time in Spanish.

"*Bueno*," I said as I followed her to a printer for my new name tag. "*Sí, puedo, pero no tan bien como me gustaría. Mis idiomas principales son el inglés y el portugués.*"

"You'll do well here," she said. "You speak well enough, and you're a guy. Many of the boys here will respect you more because you're a guy. It sucks, but it's true. They need you."

My entire life has consisted of living in spaces populated by mixed people, even when surrounded by white, conservative culture. My mother, siblings, and I are all mixed, and this was nowhere more apparent than in Idaho, where I was once asked what it felt like to be black after my mom came to the school for some reason, and I had no idea how to answer because I would never have conceived of myself as black. It was a place where someone was either Mexican or white. Many kids had never even met someone who didn't fit into those two categories. None of us were ever fooled into thinking we were white, because there was no space for that. I wasn't white in Puerto Rico. I was an object of scorn when people spoke to me in Spanish and I couldn't answer despite being Latino, until I said I was Brazilian and the scorn lessened some. Even in Florida, I spent a great deal of time with the Cubans and Mexicans and Guatemalans and Peruvians I worked with when I got off my mission.

As a missionary, I lived in a country that both prided itself on being mixed and had a strange shame surrounding it as well: that *complexo de vira-lata*. The term is used to describe a cultural inferiority complex that everything outside of Brazil is better than anything inside, but much of the origin of the sentiment is rooted in judgment around racial mixing. The term even translates to English as the mutt complex. It's a sentiment I understand: the pride of my ancestry and shame that I don't know if I can or am allowed to claim them, that everything and everyone who has a firmer classification of themselves is better, purer, in some way. It's something my mother has passed down from colonial times, when Europeans like the great French racist Joseph-Arthur de Gobineau declared Brazilians to be "unbelievably ugly monkeys," and it seeped knowingly or not into the national consciousness.

I can identify as Brazilian—depending on if I'm in the US or what part of Brazil I'm in and who I'm speaking to—more specifically *cearense*, someone from the state of Ceará. Many people I know in Brazil consider me Brazilian when compared to an American and as mixed when there is no one to compare to. I've been called an *americano falso* (a false American) and an *americense* (a mixture of the words "americano" and "cearense"). When told that I'm American, people usually furrow their eyebrows and say, *"Ele? Esse é o americano? Esse cara é como a gente!"* Him? This is the American? This guy is like us! But even in Brazil I'm hard to define, and Latino, cearense, and Brazilian are not races. I've been referred to even by family as *filho de negra* (son of a black woman), but never as black myself. No matter which country I'm in, my race and concept of myself are confused.

Most areas I've lived after I got married have been predominantly mixed as well, and poor. There's a beauty and comfort and familiarity to walking outside to large family gatherings laughing and talking in Spanish, passing black and brown faces as I walk the street, like in Puerto Rico, like in Brazil. There have been a few times though when Veronica and I didn't have money to pay rent and have had to stay either with relatives or housesit for their friends on the other side of town, Scottsdale, the white and wealthy side of town. Each time it was strange, and while we were grateful for people who took us in when we had nowhere to go, we were always strangers, and we always felt like frauds. Mike wasn't allowed in those family members' houses. He wasn't allowed in the places where we housesat, and while that never felt right to me, we had to do what we could to survive.

Every day, when Mike called me from prison after he was arrested and I was in those wealthy places, I would feel slightly sick. Every day, for the fifteen minutes the prison gave us, I wanted a cigarette. It never felt right for me to be there while Mike was locked up, even when I went out to my MFA residencies. They were worlds estranged from and at odds with one another, experiences so distant it didn't even seem like the same country.

Going to work at the middle school reminded me of when I was a kid: wet hair on cold mornings, tightness in my eyes as I pushed myself to wake up, so much noise, watching for my friends as I bumped through the crowded halls, the dread that I didn't know what I was doing, didn't know which classes I was failing, my stomach aching every time I walked into the building, everything so overwhelming that I started walking into the buildings high by the time I was in middle and high school. I saw the same nervousness take shape in my students: the girl who couldn't handle anything below an A, the guy who had to fight over every perceived hint of an insult, the small kid who had to be noisy and obnoxious to be heard and respected, the girl in the back of the class who would talk as loud as she could about "fucking" so that she would be liked, be seen. They wanted to be seen so bad. I looked at them thinking, "They're going to want that their entire lives."

I loved the job when I didn't hate it. I had no classroom management skills and couldn't control the students. I despised dealing with some of their parents. But I loved the kids. I had my old middle school teacher on my mind the day I told my seventh graders—a class with almost only Hispanic and black and Middle Eastern students— that many people in this country expected them to fail because they weren't white. We talked about redlining while I drew maps on the whiteboard, how schools are funded by property taxes and why the school we were in was labeled Title I. We talked about the school-to-prison pipeline. We talked about proving motherfuckers wrong. I probably said "motherfuckers."

I had three classes, and each would ask over and over, sometimes in the middle of lessons, if their group was my favorite. "Mister! I heard that you got mad at your C block," one of the kids would say with their hand raised. "Does that mean we're your favorite block? It does, huh? I bet we're your favorites."

Individual kids would ask the same thing. "I know I'm one of your favorites," the kid who would be wearing an ankle monitor in a couple of years said to me, and he would be right. "Am I your favorite?" the girl who cried when I gave her an A minus said. Of course she was. "I bet I'm your favorite," the girl who had been adopted by her aunty said, the one who had been in foster care while her aunt prepared the papers, who told me how much she loved the train ride down to Arizona when her aunt finally won custody. She bet right. The kid who never asked but sat in the back of the class, whose abusive father had abandoned him a few months prior and left him with a mother so worn down she seemed like a wraith, who stood shocked when I called him over to my desk one day to tell him that the poem he'd written in class was fucking good, was my favorite as well. The girl who cut herself was my favorite. The quiet ones were my favorites too, the ones who would sit hunched over the comics they were drawing, the short stories they were writing, the pictures of the video games they played, then follow me out to recess to talk to me about the *Invader Zim* cartoon I'd put on in class. There was the girl who, before she moved away in the middle of the semester, came to me during class, already emotional from saying goodbye to all her friends, and said, "Mr. Martinez, I have to go to the office later, and I need to know if I'm one of your favorites. They're like going to ask me who my favorite teacher is, and you're my favorite, but only if I'm your favorite kid. Or at least, I'm like one of the ones you like the best, right? Even though I'm loud and talk a lot? 'Cause I'm funny and stuff, right? I need you to tell me."

"Look," I said. "I have a lot of favorite students. And of course you're one of them."

"I knew it." Then, changing the subject as fast as she

could, she exclaimed, "Hey, watch this. I can do a back-bend."

"Please don't. Please go sit down and get back to work."

"Nope. This is happening." She bent backward, placing her hands on the ground behind her.

"Come on," I said from my desk. "Go sit back down. That looks painful, and I don't need you getting hurt."

"Ugh, fine," she said, shooting upright again. "I knew I was your favorite." She grinned.

I drove three hours north with my younger brothers to pick Mike up from prison the first time he got out. He was uneasy as we drove through the wide-open desert back down to Phoenix, more quiet than usual. Hollow-looking. When we were alone, he told me about having to fight all the time, to prove himself. When he was in jail in Florida, he'd been able to choose whether he wanted to go with Latinos or white, but he explained to me that in Arizona he had to go with his father's race. But Mike never was white.

"I guess I didn't have to go with the Woods, but Dad's white and they were the biggest and baddest there, so I thought it would be the best option. Shit," Mike said. "I got through it, but those motherfuckers are racist as shit. I mean like big-ass white supremacists, skinhead motherfuckers."

He never revealed the full extent of what he had to go through surrounded by white supremacists, but he later told me it was one of the worst mistakes he'd ever made and that he had to fight a lot.

By then I'd left the middle school—unable to handle the constant demands on my energy and mental health—and earned my MFA. I was teaching English and creative writing at the community college. Mike would be out for a few months. He'd leave the halfway house he lived in and go to the streets, where I finally lost touch with him for a while, though I kept watching the faces of the homeless who gathered by the methadone clinic close to my apartment. I still look for his face among them, knowing I'll never find him again.

Teaching at Glendale Community College was the dream. It had been my goal since I'd taken my first creative writing class in Arizona. My instructors had helped me in so many ways. I'd loved being a student there, so of course I loved teaching there. It was where I had had my first academic success after years of being told I was the problem for not being able to conform to the system, instead of the other way around. The GCC instructors I loved were still there—with the exception of one beloved man who helped me more than I knew those first two years and died while I was in Brazil. My peers supported me, enthusiastically, and I carried that connection over to my students.

In addition to English and creative writing, I taught

courses for the Achieving a College Education (ACE) program, which was a program and scholarship for minority
high school students to take college courses. To qualify,
they had to meet two of the following criteria: first gen-
eration to attend college; live in a single-parent home;
be a member of an underrepresented group; experience
economic hardship; meet environmental factors such as
working ten to thirty hours per week while attending high
school; live in foster care or temporary housing; be a teen
parent. They were some of the best and most honest students I had. When I told them about that former middle
school teacher, they filled the room with nods and knowing
smiles.

The last ACE course I taught before quitting was online. We met for three hours each Saturday. After I told that
story, one of the girls raised her hand from her box on the
screen. She was my best student—spoke up even though
she was shy, worked hard, took every assignment and discussion to heart, and talked about the work she did with
the local Native American youth in Phoenix. She shared
with the class that she'd been punished in high school for
correcting her history teacher. Right before Thanksgiving,
he told the class that the Pilgrims suffered an unprovoked
Indian massacre. That was the real story of Thanksgiving.
He pointed at my student and asked, "Did you know your
people did that?"

"No. My 'people' didn't murder Pilgrims on the first

Thanksgiving. That's incorrect. My 'people' aren't even from the nation you mentioned."

"He sent me to the principal's office, Mr. Martinez," she said through her computer microphone. "I got in trouble."

"Good for you," I said. "For standing up like that. That was some bullshit from that teacher."

It was an amazing five years. But something bigger was going wrong. It had always been wrong, but it became more apparent as my former instructors began to retire, as I began to teach, and as Mike began to fall further and further into the system.

Like Mike, I knew I wasn't white and never had been, no matter how much we were taught we needed to be. I wasn't getting beat for being mixed like Mike was in prison, nothing remotely close to that. But broadly, higher education is a white institution, even though most of my students were not white. In 2020, of all GCC students, only 39 percent were white; 41 percent were Hispanic. The other 20 percent were a mix of American Indian, Asian/Pacific Islander, Black, or more than one race. Like at the Title I middle school and at my high school in Puerto Rico, the students I was teaching were, for the most part, like me. The full-time English faculty, however, was over 93 percent white. When I was a student there, of course I'd noticed that most of the instructors were white. When one wasn't, it was rare enough to attract attention. My experiences at other universities were similar. They taught me that the world between white and non-white was separated by a very real wall.

When I transferred from GCC to ASU as an undergrad, I took a Shakespeare class my first semester there. I was coming from the very different atmosphere of community college, not to mention my underwhelming educational experiences prior to that, and to make me even more unsure of myself, I was still on drugs, and ASU—while still more diverse than many schools—was whiter. I sat next to a white girl who started talking about how she'd gone to London over summer break and seen the Globe Theatre.

"Have you ever been to Europe?" she asked. I told her I hadn't. "Well have you ever been out of the country?" I told her I'd lived in Brazil for a while, and Puerto Rico, though Puerto Rico is a commonwealth of the US so it wasn't technically out of the country. I also shared that I had dual citizenship between the US and Brazil. She asked what classes I'd taken the previous semesters; I said I'd transferred from the community college. "That's so cool," she said with a smile.

The professor had us stand and introduce ourselves and list which Shakespearian plays we'd read. I'd read every single one during the period when I was trying to teach myself on the floor of my room after dropping out of high school, and I said so to the class.

"Wow," the girl said. "You're such a good representative of your people."

Growing up, I'd heard the statistics saying black and Latino and Native students didn't do well in school, or in life. Asian students were the best, and after them were the white students. But I'd never been taught what caused those patterns.

In Idaho, I had a second-grade teacher who came to class almost every day in sweatpants that were frayed and worn. She smelled funny and misspelled the words she wrote on the board. She also put me in a remedial reading class with the rest of the students with Hispanic last names: Hernandez, Garcia, Mendez, Martinez. It didn't matter that at home I read books upon books and was hungry for stories and words—I believed I wasn't at the same level as the rest of the class, wasn't smart enough to keep up. It didn't matter that a few months later, when I was tested, it was discovered I had a high school reading level. My abilities, when compared to my last name, meant nothing.

About thirty years after that second-grade class, Phoenix police officers found a brown man sleeping on the ground with his Native American girlfriend. They didn't like the look of him, so they woke them up and questioned him. He lied, of course, because he had skipped out on the halfway house he was supposed to be in, stopped staying in contact with his probation officer, and disappeared into the streets. The cops didn't believe him. When they searched him, they found an ID with the name Michael Neto Martinez. Then, Michael Neto Martinez was arrested for the last time and Michael Neto Martinez went to prison. And when COVID hit, Michael Neto Martinez was swallowed up in the tidal wave of prison mortality, disappeared with no comment on the autopsy report to indicate that the thirty-three-year-old man who had no drugs in his system when he died had been sick for a while before the sepsis had taken hold.

When we first went into COVID lockdown, I'd been working as a temporary full-time One Year Only (OYO) faculty member. That meant benefits and consistent pay and lots of work. I took over two extra classes, bringing my total load to seven, after another teacher was fired. I taught a creative nonfiction course that hadn't been offered since I was a student there a decade prior. I worked harder than I ever had in my life. My student evaluations were good, and I was preparing to apply for a permanent full-time faculty position when my transcripts didn't upload properly in the portal and my application was rejected on a technicality. Because of the shutdown, no one was hiring elsewhere, and once my OYO contract ended, I was forbidden by state law to go back to adjunct work for the community college for six months. And like that, I was unemployed for nine months because the end of the six-month period happened to end in the middle of a semester, when there wouldn't be any immediate openings.

The last time Mike was arrested, I knew before anyone else. I felt it like I always did, and when I looked him up online, my suspicions were confirmed. I did what I'd always done. I wrote him a letter. He was banned from making calls for failing some urine analysis tests, so I had to physically write letters until they were all given tablets.

"Dear Professor Dave," he wrote back. "What's up brother? How the hell are you man? I knew you'd be the first letter I'd get! Wow that made no sense. Anywho it's good to hear from you. Damn I miss you man." The letter went on to describe how he had to detox with methadone after getting picked up off the street, how during the first few weeks he was back behind bars, two cops were arrested for leaving a cell open for a group of inmates to beat another inmate so badly he was left brain dead. "I am now on one of the last remaining general population yards in the state. Most of the yards in this state are now integrated where they try and desegregate us. In fact all 3 yards and below are in fact integrated and honestly I hear those yards are awesome . . ." He ended the letter with, "Anyways brother you know I love you incredibly and you are and always will be my best friend and I hope you can write back soon . . . All my Love Big Bro, MIKE."

access to the system they were using. As I sat staring at
the desks and naming in my head who sat where, I began
mentally calling up the ghosts of my former students to
keep me company. I was traumatized in that ghost room,
in a traumatized time for a traumatized nation, everyone
quarantined, isolated, watching our old lives flash by on
Facebook memories, losing the ability to perceive time,
on the edge of a new emotional breakdown every day, multiple times a day. The kids I summoned to fill the classroom weren't dead, of course. Neither was I. But we were
also not the same people we were when we had shared
that space years ago, millennia ago. A strange calm came
over me from that tired place that emerges when a person
can no longer distinguish the positive from the negative.
I'd already fallen apart too many times that year to do
it again. The ghosts brought with them a melancholic joy
that rose in my stomach, a quiet aching void. I don't know
where most of the kids I taught went, but some of them
had added me on their social media accounts. One went
to juvie for a while, took selfies of himself holding guns,
showing off his ankle bracelet, posting prices of weed.
One had just had her first baby at sixteen. Others were
finishing up high school, posting pictures in scrubs working at dentists' offices, recording music, posting politically
intelligent comments. In the interim between teaching
them and sitting in that classroom, I'd finished a master's
degree, held my wife as she went through and recovered
from thyroid cancer surgery and treatment, and started

teaching at the community college where I had once been a student. We were all on the edge or in the middle of new, unprecedented historical events or unbelievably absurd news stories every few days. I looked at the empty chairs around me, no idea the worst was to come.

The worst wasn't when I caught COVID at the school, though my wife and I were both sick for a month, hardly able to move and losing our minds. We hallucinated for three days straight. I could see the half-closed bedroom closet I was staring at, but in my mind's eye, like a waking dream, I also saw a vast, endless plain with enormous, walking figures made of small, spherical, almost transparent pieces. I was on the smooth floor, where all the pieces of my life had fallen apart and had scattered around me. I knew I would never be able to pull myself together again, never be able to pretend to be more than a former figure now scattered on the ground. I wrote to Mike about it.

"Hey broham!!!!," he replied.

Hey yea i got your emails and ya dude thats ctaziness that it had you guys both trippin balls at the same time!! Did you have to guide your wife thru it at times?? Anyways ya its a good thing you are a pro at it, otherwise you might have been lost. . . . Whats been up with you lately though man. . . . Anyways brotha i miss you dude and i hope youre doing o.k.

I was still suffering from a little brain fog when I got back to online teaching as an adjunct in January. My lungs still hurt—at one point when I had COVID, I hadn't been able to finish a full sentence without pausing and pulling in air. Online teaching was different, but I was enjoying it, partially because it limited the meetings I had to attend and allowed me to focus on my students.

Mike told me he'd been sick, and I kept telling him to go to the medic. He didn't want to because then he'd have to be quarantined, which was essentially like solitary confinement—a punishment that even the prison system generally acknowledged was extreme and torturous—and he couldn't handle that.

On February 28, 2021, he wrote:

Ya ive Been having cold sweats, fevers, my vision is Getting fucked up, Heart palpitations, my blood pressure is at times super high. its all bad and sometimes my liver is hurting. idk but I love ya. and thank you . . .

I was expecting him to write to me again the next day. He didn't. He finally went to the medic, where he passed out mid-sentence as the doctor was examining him, his organs already infected and swollen as he went into septic shock, the result of a widespread infection that causes dangerously low blood pressure and organ failure. Hours later, on March 1, 2021, Michael Neto Martinez was dead.

When I got the call from the prison, I crumpled on the carpet in my living room and sobbed as quietly as I could. It was a strange storm, a soundless hurricane. I didn't want to wake Veronica. I texted in silence all the old friends whose numbers I still had—the broken and lost who had tethered themselves to Mike and me through needles and blood and broken bones. "He's gone," I told them.

Shortly after Mike died, I had my interview for the full-time faculty position. It was more than a year after my failed application. I knew many of the people on the virtual panel, though almost all my former instructors had left by that point. Eviction notices were sprouting on doors all over my apartment complex of mostly minority households, one of the Americas hidden from me in part of my childhood but where I lived my entire adult life. For over a year, most of my interactions had been with my Hispanic and black and Middle Eastern students. My brother had just died in the most segregated and racist institution in the country. The hiring committee appeared in boxes on my screen one by one. "They're all white," I thought. I knew it would be the case (there were maybe two people of color in the English department), but it was like stepping off the plane from Puerto Rico to Florida all over again. While my reality was mixed, was populated by people of

color, the institutions and government around me were
white. I knew it. I'd always known it, but I felt it so glaring
in that moment. A wall went up in my mind, and I couldn't
tear it down.

Those people didn't know me. I had worked with some
of them for years, but how many would be shocked at
where I lived? Would Mike's life have even registered as
real, much less relatable, to them? I knew they had done
well in school their entire lives and came from homes
where that was expected of them. The thoughts flooded
in, interrupted my speech, screamed at me. Maybe things
would change with the new hires—even if I wasn't one.
Were the people on this panel forced to go to remedial
reading because of their last names, or were they praised
for their abilities? Did they have teachers who lectured on
the dangers of their heritage? Did they come up in a family
in which the white side genuinely believed that the black
side were children of the first murderer? Did they know the
value of diverse educators in the lives of the students—if
not me then someone, anyone? They asked about teaching
methods. They asked about my ability to work with other
faculty. I thought about Mike. Nothing about the situation
added up. I waited for a question on diversity. I waited
for something actually important and fundamental to me
and my experience to be mentioned, to be asked. It wasn't.
The last question was something technical about assessments. I was being judged by a panel whose experiences
and life and educational journey were opposite of my own,

by people who couldn't see me. Doubt, as always, crept in. Was I being too sensitive? Was I blowing my experience out of proportion? I sat on those doubts, tried to let them percolate, make sense. I tried to reason them away. I sat in silence for a moment after disconnecting from the call, knowing I didn't get the job. I didn't present myself well. I didn't speak well. I'd fumbled. My heart wasn't in it. I was still in the thick of grief, the kind of grief that never really goes away, just changes us until we learn to house it better.

A few months later, the new hires were announced. Another middle-aged white man, and a middle-aged white woman. I thought I would be crushed again, but to my surprise, I'd quit caring about getting the position. Even though I loved the students, being in the classroom and teaching, I felt deflated by the academic atmosphere. That full-time position had gone from a dream to a conduit for insurance and steady pay to something I didn't even want anymore. I assumed the new instructors were both amazing, had impressive résumés. I'm sure they were more than qualified to teach English. I had nothing against either of them—I didn't know them—but I wanted to know *why* they were chosen. Why, in a school in which white is the minority, did the department continue to display so little concern about having their students' backgrounds represented in positions of power? How did they not perceive that wall, that gulf, between their faculty and student body? Why did it seem like I was the only one who cared?

Every semester we had an entire day of meetings called Assessment Day dedicated to bolstering student numbers and retention through analysis of test scores. The semester I quit, Assessment Day included presentations on "Culturally Responsive Teaching," and "Who Is in Our Classrooms?: Meeting the Needs of Our Students." After my disastrous job interview, I was paying very close attention. The whole show was a box to check off. There was a pie chart I'd seen a hundred times that showed student demographics: we were a majority Hispanic population. Meanwhile, the white woman giving the lecture informed us that Native Americans on average took longer to answer a question than white students. She had attended some diversity meeting and was parroting the content passed to her. It wasn't relevant to her. It wasn't relevant to anyone. No matter how hard I strained, I heard no human experience, no similar or relevant discussion of what it meant to be a person of color in the world of academia right now, either as a student or faculty or an employee. People and experiences were replaced with numbers and charts.

GCC had refugee students, but tallying them did not communicate that one of the best students I ever had was a Syrian refugee who was shot in the leg when he was thirteen in a civil war he was too young to understand. It didn't tell me about his heroic journey to overcome run-on sentences while being haunted, or that what haunted him most wasn't the horrors of the war he fought in as a teenager—it was covering the body of a girl he used to sit next to in a GCC class after she died of an overdose at the homeless shelter where he worked. Five percent of GCC's students were black, but that number didn't account for how many of my students were shocked to learn about Medgar Evers, a man they'd never learned of in school, as we went over a James Baldwin essay (another man never mentioned during their formal education). I knew the majority of my students were Hispanic. What that slice of the pie chart didn't tell me was that something as simple as mentioning *El Chavo del Ocho* in passing, the show many of my Latinx students watched as children, could light up a face, give a look that only those of us who have long felt invisible can recognize: being seen. The statistics didn't articulate the terror that came with Arizona's Senate Bill 1070, which stated cops could pull over and stop anyone to ask if they were a citizen and had the papers to prove it, or the devastation when DREAMers were forced to pay out-of-state tuition. Numbers don't tell the stories students have shared with me of being beaten by police when they were seventeen because they were with a cousin the cops thought looked like a drug trafficker, or those of the single mothers who pleaded for extensions on their essays because their kid got sick or work demanded they come in, or the guys who came in to class dirty from construction work, or the black and Hispanic and white

veterans who cried and shook in my office as they told me
how no one could understand them anymore after they'd
come home from war so they thanked me for doing nothing more than listening. The school wasn't keeping track
of the scores of students who sat individually with me to
work on essays, who failed my class but signed up to take
it again the next semester with the hope that the next time
around they would make it. The numbers meant nothing,
the assessments meant nothing, without the individuals
behind them. Numbers and assessments were statistics
and stereotypes. They were mandatory sentencing laws.
They were another brown man dead in prison, a tragedy
that could be traced, in part, back to the language of his
last name, a name the system replaced with an inmate
number.

In the aftermath of the hurricane of Mike's death, I sat
through the first faculty evaluation I'd had in years. By
that time, I knew I wouldn't be back. I was nervous, not of
failing but because of how angry I was. The woman who
conducted the evaluation had been an acquaintance, someone who'd been on the hiring committee. She appeared on
the screen from her backyard in suburbia, stressed, she
said, because her teenager had been throwing a tantrum.

It was the first time I'd done poorly, after a litany of
"Exceeds Expectations" in previous years. But this time,
I hadn't put together the online portion of the course with

the care expected. I didn't use the book assigned by the department. It was too much work for something I didn't feel was effective. My assessments were all but nonexistent. She told me that my main strength was that I connected to the students. It felt like a pity prize of consolation. I had a similar background to many of them (which plenty of research shows could likely improve their educational outcomes). She said I didn't come off as a disconnected elitist like some of the other instructors, and I made it look easy. I showed my humanity, but that wasn't enough to "exceed expectations." It wasn't enough to merit stability and fair pay. It wasn't enough to turn me into more than a weak gesture toward diversity without nurturing and compensating me for the special skills I brought to the role.

According to National Center for Education Statistics research reported by PEW in 2019, "In sharp contrast with the growing share of Hispanic students, the share of *faculty* who were Hispanic remained fairly flat, increasing from 3% in fall 1997 to 5% in fall 2017. Similarly, black faculty made up only 5% of the total in 1997 and 6% in 2017." Of course, those faculty are more likely to be found in the most precarious positions. "Overall, a larger share of assistant professors (junior faculty without tenure) were nonwhite in fall 2017, compared with fully tenured professors (27% vs. 19%)." The plight of the adjunct is heavily documented. In 2017, *The Guardian* reported on adjuncts moonlighting as sex workers and living in their cars to make ends meet. Reports of adjuncts making be-

tween $20,000 and $25,000 a year (which is about what
I made) are common. The teaching load is close to that
of a full-time instructor, the level of education is often
the same, but the schools don't have to pay for insurance
or into 401Ks or anything else needed to build a steady
life. It's the same across the country. It's how colleges and
universities save money. Every adjunct knows they're ex-
ploited, the same way every public school teacher does. I
don't know why we do it. I guess I did it for the dream, for
the love of it, until I couldn't anymore.

I didn't believe any of my colleagues were malicious,
but I was still uncomfortable bringing up racial issues in
department meetings. I don't believe any of my teachers
were particularly malicious either—even the middle school
teacher spoke with an earnest fear that evoked my sym-
pathy, even if it was mixed with my disgust. But the gulf
between their life experiences and mine was undeniable.
That divide loomed larger than ever in the wake of my
brother's death. It dominated every faculty meeting. I
sensed it every time I left my neighborhood and wandered
into a white side of town, part of me wondering who there
would fear me the way my middle school teacher did.
Trying to navigate that divide without falling into it was
exhausting.

And I still don't know how to identify. What I know
is that despite my European ancestry, I'm not white by
American standards; I'm Latino, cearense, Brazilian,
mixed indigenous-white-black, American. What I know is

that in situations like Mike's, being mixed in a white space is potentially fatal. What I know is that it's a topic I think of every day. What I know is that I am an other in a nation and world that demands categorization. What I know is that I feel confused. What I know is that I feel like I know nothing.

love

Mike didn't leave his daughter because he wanted to. He did it because he knew the risks he posed. He knew he wasn't stable. He at least knew something was wrong. He knew he would use, and he didn't want to bring that on her. When she was born, he had been living behind a Circle K dumpster in Florida. After seeing her for the first and last time in person a few hours after she entered the world, Mike was on a plane from Orlando to Phoenix on our grandparents' dime.

"She's the most beautiful baby girl," he told me when I picked him up and he showed me her picture, truly cute, tiny and wrinkled like all newborns.

"Look, man," I would say every time we would get to talking about his daughter. "You're going to stop with the shit and find a way to take care of her. Maybe go to school. I don't know. I know it sucks, but what are you going to do for her if you were there? You got this, brother. You got this."

There were other complications. His daughter's grand-mother, who had custody since the child's mother was also

on drugs and in and out of mental health institutions, refused to allow Mike's name on the birth certificate, and
Mike had no legal claim on his daughter. Part of his trying
to clean himself up was so he could fight that in court,
and while his relationship with the grandmother fluctu-
ated between amicability and enmity, he never did have
his name on that birth certificate until after he died.

But I didn't help. I don't know anyone with an addiction able to stop for anyone else. We all have loved ones,
and loved ones can provide *some* assistance, but no one
thing ever seems to be enough. I was married to a woman I
adored, but I was depressed anyway, manic anyway, being
crushed by a force I didn't understand but knew I needed
shit to make it okay. I can only imagine Mike's situation.
He loved his daughter more than anything, and in a way,
as fucked up as it sounds, his absence proved it. He knew
he would only bring chaos to her life, and he wanted to get
himself straight before going back, wanted to make sure
he could legally become a father. Problem was, he could
never get himself straight.

He called her though, when she was old enough to understand. And he sent her grandmother money for diapers
and food and daycare with what he earned selling dope—
though the grandmother never knew Mike was selling—
and he never faltered until he went to prison, and it was
his greatest pleasure and pride to send money.

The documents in the box I inherited from Mike contained mostly legal papers and receipts and police reports,

but there were a few pages of scattered writings as well. In
what I can only assume was a plea to the court or prison
for leniency, Mike wrote this:

> I am a drug addict. I need help. Prison is not the
> best place for that. I need rehab.
>
> I got out of prison last time and went to a half-
> way house and was doing okay there for a while.
> I got kicked out of there for being late more than
> once coming home. I became homeless. When I
> was in the halfway house I was talking to my 8 yr.
> old daughter every day who lives in Florida. Af-
> ter I got kicked out of the halfway house I became
> homeless and hadn't talked to my daughter for a
> couple weeks and I became depressed once more. I
> relapsed and ended up using drugs again and my
> daughter's grandma wouldn't let me talk to her
> anymore and things gradually got worse. I realized
> I was going back to my old ways so I decided to get
> some help and I went to a methadone clinic to be-
> gin treatment. I was still in the process of getting
> myself to a stable dose that would help me when I
> got arrested.
>
> The fact of the matter is, is I was getting the help
> I needed a little too late. I had already absconded
> from probation and I wasn't to the point yet where
> I was 100% clean of any drug use. I spent the next
> 2 to 3 months in jail until my parents bonded me

out in hope of getting me more help as well as some better legal counsel. I stayed with my parents for a week and I was going to my methadone clinic every day and seeing a doctor and a counselor for my problem. I saw a girl that I had met when I first got out of prison a Native girl that was in the middle of a rough time that was on the streets at the time. She smoked some weed but besides that didn't get high. I fell in love with her and despite knowing that I needed to help myself before anything else I didn't have the heart to leave her alone on the street and due to the fact that I didn't have the best track record with my parents and women, us staying with my parents was out of the question. I was homeless again but I was doing good with my recovery and I stayed sober besides my methadone. The only time I ever slipped up was when I missed 2 days at the clinic and I got high. I was going to my court dates until I missed one. I had the date wrong. I blew it again. I reveled in the time I had left with the women I loved. When the police found me I was asleep behind a closed building with my arms around this woman.

It's true that he didn't have a good track record, but when Mike loved, he loved with everything he had, everything he could.

Papo with Mike II

Superman and Batman. Post Falls, Idaho.

The last time I hung out with Mike, the first time he ended up in prison for the long term rather than jail for the short term, I was working on my master's degree in California. I was living in Salt Lake while completing the low-residency program. I hadn't seen Mike for a while, so I took an afternoon and night off from my lectures and workshops during my stay in California to drive the three hours from Palm Desert to Phoenix to see him. I'd had the growing impression that I needed to, that I wouldn't get to see him again for a long time, and I would regret not doing it when I had the chance. I pleaded the whole way there and back that it wouldn't be the last time I saw him. I flew through the desert, straight to his house, where we talked and smoked black tar with a little piece of tinfoil and a straw that we passed back and forth to each other, at that time of the day when the sun goes down and everything turns orange.

The next morning, before heading back to California, I stopped by Mike's place again, drove him to a couple of spots he needed to go, got high. He showed me his collection of drugs, grinning and proud: heroin, meth, coke, a small gram of weed, pills. It was to impress me, sure, tell me how much money he was making selling, but I think he was also trying to show how much he had to fight against that old sadness. We ended up at a gas station that morning right before I was to leave again. Mike was shifty and sad, and so was I. We sat, high, talking about getting sober, doing projects together, how great it was going to be, and passed a cigarette between us. We were always talking about how great it was going to be without ever defining what *it* was or how we'd get there. It was just important to talk, to have at least that. Mike seemed so dejected. I had my schooling, my wife, a job. Mike was looking at a dead end. Though I saw him a couple of more times, that was the last time we hung out, that we had time to talk, just the two of us. When I visited him in prison a year or two later, he told me that he'd wanted to get caught, that really he owed some bad people a lot of money, and he just wanted it all to end.

An hour later, after leaving Mike at the gas station, while I was driving back through the desert, he was arrested. It would be years before I would see him again. I spent the next few days high and sick after learning the news, pacing my room alone between workshops and lectures and panels. I hated myself for lying to my professors and friends about being off drugs, hated myself as I drove back to LA to eat with some family members who have always been great to me, hated myself the most when I got back to Salt Lake and looked at the wife I had been lying to. My sister was visiting as well, and I looked at her and her children and my sister-in-law and brother-in-law and niece and hated myself even more. I was hating myself but walking free, unlike my brother, who I had never been able to save, despite the connection we shared. I had never been able to do anything to save myself, to be what everyone around me needed me to be.

ME: I made a lot of really fucked-up mistakes.

MIKE: Yeah, but I mean, like, you know, it's like you corrected them. Corrected what you were doing wrong and—

ME: Sort of. I mean, really? Am I really all that correct?

MIKE: Yeah, dude. You are. You're, you're working on your master's degree right now. I mean, honestly, all that other bullshit is is is in my own opinion it's it's it's not *un*important because trust me it's

very important . . . but as for what Mom or Dad
or anyone in general thinks you should be doing,
you know. You're doing well. You're going to college.
You're married.

ME: Almost got divorced though—

MIKE: I feel like you put too much weight on your
shoulders.

ME: I realize that I am . . . I am—

MIKE: The best. Just kidding.

ME: I do put a lot of weight on my shoulders, but at
the same time, you know . . . I mean, I'm a fucking
heroin addict.

MIKE: Well, who isn't, right? Haha!

ME: I try really fucking hard to undo that shit I've done.

MIKE: Fuck. We had our problems because . . . of course.
But what are we going to do?

When Mike was maybe eight, a cop came to the door in his
blue uniform, holding a BB gun in his left hand, asking for
him. I was the one who answered and called to the basement, where my mom was watching TV.

"Mom! There's a cop at the door!"

"What?" she yelled from the bottom of the stairs.

"A cop, Mom. There's a cop at the door."

She came up into the living room with my second-
youngest brother on her hip and invited the officer in. Mike
had been playing with the BB gun in a public playground

with some of my friends while I was at home. A worried mother—the same one who had told me that toothpaste was good for burns—called the police.

"What?" my mom said to the cop. "I am so sorry. I had no idea." She yelled, "Michael!" but he didn't answer. "Michael!" She turned to me and said, "David, go get your brother."

He had been pretending to sleep in the room we shared, where less than a year later I would cut a hole in the wall behind a poster, and he would carve one into a textbook to hide our cigarettes and later weed. The carpet in the room was rainbow colored, and over his bed, in giant letters, stained into the paint with hairspray was "Mike." When my parents saw it, after who knows how long, Mike denied that he was responsible, saying one of his friends must have done it. He said the same thing about the dictionary of curse words he scrawled in pen on the wood under his bed. Mike was not a good liar, but that never stopped him. He lied about everything because the truth never helped him.

He was defiant to the cop at the door too, telling him yes, that was his BB gun, but he had no idea why it was in the park. The cop lectured him while my mother, embarrassed and exasperated, tended to the baby on her hip. I sat with them in the living room, knowing I was expected to be there, though not sure exactly why. Mike had been with my friends, so somehow I must share in the blame.

~

MIKE: I was super young when we started that shit.

ME: You know, that's one thing that I feel bad about. Because, I mean, I was three years older than you. I was eleven. I mean, I was doing shit no eleven-year-old should ever be doing. But you were fucking eight. And it was because you were hanging out with *my* friends.

MIKE: But you can't really put on anything like that, because, one, the fact is we were growing up in a little town. You know. I mean, everyone knew everyone. Two, it wasn't that strange of a thing—I don't think, anyways. The little tagalong kid that shouldn't even be there in the first place. And you weren't . . . the point that I'm trying to get across is that you weren't the one like, "Here, hit this. Smoke some weed." You were the one who all the time was like, "Don't give my brother that shit," you know? So, I mean, you know, I can't, I can't think about holding you accountable for anything. I mean, you were just a kid too.

~

The last time I saw Mike out of custody was outside a Walgreens next to the light rail on a one-hundred-twenty-degree desert afternoon. He looked like he had been starving, like he shouldn't have been able to walk. His face was picked at. He was wired, teeth rotted, and he smelled so bad it was hard for me to hug him even though I hadn't heard from him in months. He had been walking and sleeping on the streets after the system's failed attempts to provide housing and resources. Housing and resources, while necessary, are never enough for someone wounded so badly they're delusional about the extent and severity of their problems. I bought him some food and a bus pass. He told me as he was getting on the bus that I shouldn't worry about him. He said he had it all under control, like always.

"You're living on the street, Mike," I said.

"But I'm alive," he said.

"Alive doesn't mean you're okay."

"It does for people like us." He turned his back and walked away while I watched his ragged shirt disappear through the bus's open door.

One of our favorite stories to retell, the one about stealing cigarettes from the local grocery store in Rigby, was really about a door, how I figured it would be better if only one of us was caught while walking out. If they stopped me, at least Mike would be on the other side of the building and able to get away.

But we both escaped. We smoked our bounty at the park behind our church building, with one of my friends and his older sister who thought it was cool that Mike and I had stolen cigarettes. We were at the back of the park, past the playground, behind a brown roofed area lined with wooden picnic tables, when my parents pulled up in their red minivan. They saw my friend's sister with smoke billowing from her mouth as she ran to the ditch. I knew they could see us and knew running was only going to raise more suspicion, so I stayed behind to talk to them, watched the dust rise behind the car as they made their way over to us along the short dirt road. We'd been caught, and the tension when I got to the car was palpable. "Did I just see you smoking?" my dad said.

"No," I said, feeling weak, leaning back from the window so he couldn't smell me.

"Yes, you were," he said. "I saw you, guys. Someone was smoking."

"Um . . ." I crossed my arms.

"I can smell it," my dad said. Tears gathered in his eyes, and I was ashamed of them. He said he was scared that Mike and I were going to have drug problems, that we would leave church and fall away from god, and he couldn't bear to see it. With that, my parents took off to the library to return some books and told Mike and me to go home.

We had all the time we needed to get our story straight on the way to the house. We said we'd found the cigarettes outside by bikes that some older kids had left on the side of the store. We stole them because we wanted to be cool, which sounded better than saying I felt sick and sad and dirty all the time and hoped smoking would help in some way, because it might outwardly show the type of jadedness that I was building inside me.

When it was time to perform, Mike did well with the story. At first. The bike next to the cigarettes was red. Yeah, we knew the kids who'd left them there but not by name because they were a year or two older than me. We took them and went straight to the park to smoke. The truth was, we'd stolen them two days prior.

MIKE: Of course of course, but when it came down to it, you know, I . . . I tried to tell him the truth. But that . . . that didn't work so well. And he asked me, like, where did you guys get them from, and I was completely and one hundred percent honest with him. And he looks at me . . . and I don't know what it is about me, but people do this to me. I'll tell them the truth and then it's like . . . no, nope, you're lying. You are lying. And I was like, you know, yeah. Yeah. I felt immediate pride, and that's why immediately I agreed with what he said.

ME: Pride?

MIKE: Yeah, I mean it was like getting away with it. I mean, we didn't really get away with it, but we did, you know. Plus it seemed like maybe kind of better that we didn't steal them, you know?

ME: They wanted to believe my version.

MIKE: I know, right? What the fuck?

ME: It was obviously the lie, but it was, you know, less damning.

The summer before I went into eighth grade, and Mike was ten, a few friends, Mike, and I decided to skateboard and smoke on top of the middle school roof, but someone had caught us throwing little metal disks we'd found out onto the yard and called the cops. Mike was the first one to spot them. He wanted to get down there to skate the stairs and lip down below, and when he stuck his head over the side, we heard the crackle of a megaphone: "You kids ready to come down now?" There were three or four cop cars waiting for us.

Our parents were called but never showed up. My dad was at work, and my mom was without a car for the day. The father of one of the friends who had been with us was the school janitor. As the cops talked to us, he weaved his way through and started yelling. "What the hell were you kids thinking? What's the matter with you? We have a huge problem with vandalism at this school, and now every time something happens, they're going to think it's you. And by the way, any of you kids know who this damn Wu is keeps writing his name all over the school?"

We all stood straight and confused.

"You don't know him? Wu Tang? Probably some little Chinese kid."

I had to bite my cheek and close my eyes not to laugh in the poor angry man's face. Mike didn't have that much restraint.

The cops didn't bust us for smoking—another friend had cleared that up somehow—but one of the officers who had been there was assigned to the school, which was known for having a drug problem. He stopped me every day afterward to ask if I was keeping off the roof and staying out of trouble. A few boys from Rigby had recently murdered a woman in a gas station over a few cartons of cigarettes and fifty dollars, then sped off to LA to try to join the Bloods, and I think he wanted to make sure I wasn't that type. We moved to Puerto Rico a few months later. I don't remember any conversation with my parents about that event, but I'm sure they at least said something to address it at the time. Later, if talked about in my dad's presence, he'll get angry and say he barely remembers. He only thinks about pleasant things these days, he says, before he shuts down.

According to my parents, they put Mike in that drug abuse facility he told me about when I was a missionary because they couldn't control him. They said they'd found him in a corner of the living room one night high and cutting himself with a letter opener. "Yeah, no," Mike said later. "You know I've done some fucked-up shit, but I wasn't doing that, man. High? Yeah, of course. But cutting myself with a fucking letter opener? Nah." And though I've seen him do

some crazy shit—come into the house stumbling and pouring milk into spaghetti to eat it; mash the coke and weed
he was selling together with a spoon and flip out when I
took the spoon away to stop him from destroying his products; pee on a houseplant in the corner thinking he was
in the bathroom—I've never seen him cut himself, and I
always believed him over my parents.

Mike had gone to a friend's house, and my dad offered
to pick him up in that old minivan.

MIKE: He was, like, taking me home. But we weren't like
    going toward the house, and I was starting to freak
    out, you know? I kept asking, like "Where are we go-
    ing?" But Dad wouldn't say shit. And, you know, he
    took me to the fucking sheriff's office and these cops
    came and dragged me out of the car and shit and took
    me to that place. It was fucked, man. That place was
    ridiculous. It was to the point where we went outside
    once in a week, and outside was literally a cage. There
    were fences all around and up top was all caged in. I
    mean they literally had us in a cage. And so when
    I got out, I think it was Ricky or something hit me
    up and was like, you know, let's kick it or whatever.
    You know, I just remember Dad or Mom or whoever
    being like, being like, "No, you're not going out." I
    completely lost my mind. I flipped out. And I started
    yelling at him. And I said, "Look, man, I'm going out."
    And he hit me in the chest. He, like, punched me. And

I started, like, tearing up and then Dad started crying. And I completely just ran, went down the stairs, and I walked out the door. And Dad was like, "You better not go anywhere." But I just took off. I went to my buddy's house across the street in Remington Park, and I was smoking weed or whatever. And then all of a sudden, I seen Dad's car, I seen him going down the road, or whatever. And so he pulls up at my buddy's house, and I'm hiding, you know, but it was getting ridiculous. And then I don't know what had happened, but I kind of decided to go out and talk to him a little bit. And I said, "I love you, but you know, you just kind of put me in this place for a week, where, you know, you kind of trapped me in cage, and I'm not gonna go home right now. I'm sorry." And he literally got out of the car and started running after me. He chased me, you know, for a good mile, but I just had in my mind at that point that I was not going to allow him to control what I was doing. And I think that, that later on, when I reflected on it, you know, it just killed me. I still see that image. Like, when I think about it, it haunts me now just to see him like run after me like that. And he literally was, you know, and you could see in his face too, that he was he was beat, like he was done. You know, like there was no more for him. But at the same time, when he first started running, he was just like dedicated to get me, even though like I knew that he couldn't catch me. You know, his health. And it's like, you know, I just was hurt at the fact that he picked me up saying we're going home and then took me to the sheriff's office and had a cop take me out the car to take me to the place. And you know, it's just I didn't trust him. I couldn't.

When I was a missionary, there were nights I would lie wide-eyed in the solitary dark and stare into the tangible shadows as my mission companions dreamed in the beds next to mine. On some nights, I thought I could hear Mike talking to me through the stillness. It wasn't a telepathic conversation so much as enjoying one another's company, like a wordless conversation between two spirits just hanging out. I'd known he was as alone as I was. I'd known he was in trouble. I'd always known. He *was* in trouble, having knocked over a line of Bob's Barricades while driving our family's red minivan while under the influence. Years later, he would tell me that sometimes he would lie in bed at night when he was on acid and have conversations with me, and I wondered if they were on the same nights I was with him, alone in São Paulo.

Even if sometimes we were all the other had, we didn't do everything together, and yet our paths took the same course, until they didn't. Mike wasn't there the first time

I smoked weed from a dented Coke can my friend's tall, blond, cool older sister brought out. She was in high school, and I was twelve. Afterward, I skateboarded in the parking lot of the redbrick church my family attended in Rigby, Idaho. Mike wasn't there when I started snorting coke and crushed painkillers and muscle relaxers and whatever else I could in the back of my high school class-rooms in Puerto Rico when the teachers weren't looking. I wasn't around the first time Mike smoked weed, but he did it with my friends in that same church parking lot. I don't know where I was. I wasn't around when he started with the painkillers either, but like the skateboarding and the ever-changing cities we lived in and the *Mortal Kombat* we played on the couch with ties wrapped around our heads, our lives merged regardless.

In Idaho, when I was twelve and he was nine, we smoked in a car with my friend and his older brother—who died in an accident years later—parked on a steep hill on a reservation at dusk. In Puerto Rico, when I was in high school and Mike was in sixth grade, we would smoke and drink on the hill where the school bus left us, and once he laughed so hard he was unable to stop, and I looked at his bloodshot and swollen eyes and said, "Shit, Mike. You look high as fuck. You are going to get me in so much trouble," as I pulled out the Visine I always kept in my pocket, held his eyes open with my left hand, and poured the liquid with my right.

Of course, no one would ever notice. There was a fifty-fifty chance our mom was even home when we got back from school. Our house had a gate in place of a garage door, locked with a chain and padlock. It was the only entrance, and none of us ever had the keys. If our mom wasn't home, we'd have to send our little sister up to the second floor since she was the only one who could both fit in the window and climb up the side of the house, and she would pull the gate open wide enough for my five-year-old brother to get through while Mike and I sat in the driveway waiting for someone to show up. I was too big to fit through the gap and I was expected to be responsible, so I would sit and wait. Mike could fit through the gate, so sometimes he would, but he would often opt to stand sentinel with me anyway. By the time we were tying off in my room in Florida in our twenties, helping each other find the most usable veins, getting high together was a continuation of that solidarity. It thickened our brotherhood into a new kind of family relationship, one we didn't share with our parents or anyone else.

MIKE: I sometimes worry about, you know, how Mom and Dad handled this, how they handled that, and how we turned out the way we are. And I wish I could explain that . . .

ME: I don't know, man. I think it all revolves around

the same fucking thing. I mean, it's something that's
shaped us whether we want it to or not.

MIKE: You know, it's always been, you know, you and
   me.

ME: Yeah.

MIKE: Our whole lives.

ME: Our whole lives, right.

I am three, in Post Falls. I am on a sofa, holding Mike as
a baby, stiff, afraid to drop him. We are twelve and fifteen
in Puerto Rico, watching our friend Carlos tumble over
the wood box we built for skating, his arm bent and wrong
when he comes up, making our stomachs freeze in horror.
We're seven and ten in Rigby, Idaho, cleaning dog poop in
the backyard with a shovel and rake, calling out, "Pooper!"
when one of us finds a pile, and "Scooper," as the other
walks over to help. We're in our twenties in Florida, and
I ask Mike to hold the steering wheel as we drive in the
dark down a highway in the country so I can wrap my seat
belt around my left arm and plunge the inch-long syringe
filled with hydromorphone and coke. We're two and five in
Post Falls, watching *Pinocchio*, me in a Superman costume,
him as Batman, smiling a toddler grin. We're teenagers in
Florida, sitting in my room downstairs, listening to Jane's
Addiction when the rest of the world our age was in school,
or we're playing guitar with our friend Ricky, recording our
jam on our little 4-track. We're eleven and fourteen in Puerto

Rico, driving with my friend in his dad's stolen car, his dad
flying after us, and we're jumping out of the car as soon as
we pull over. We're driving in Florida, five in the morning,
bleary-eyed, to the seminary our parents make us go to at
the church. We're talking on the phone in our thirties, Mike
in prison in Tucson, me on the floor in my third-story Phoenix apartment, discussing Buddhism, meditation, and the
prices paid to get off drugs. Mike's dead, and I'm driving to
Tucson passing a billboard that reads, "Call Mike and Dave
to file your legal claim now!" on my way to pick up his single box of belongings. Our stories pile on, are infinite, and
our wounds cross one another, tie into knots, so that though
he's dead, he is alive, because we are bound in some places,
like twins conjoined across dimensions. We are bound by a
silence that should be broken, and we are bound by a quiet
sanctity that never will be.

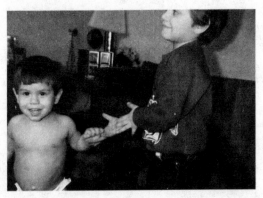

Mike trying to hold on to me so he doesn't fall. Post Falls, Idaho.

Bibliography

Baldwin, James. "A Talk to Teachers." *James Baldwin: Collected Essays*. New York: Library of America, 1998, p. 679.

Camus, Albert. "Appendix: Hope and the Absurd in the Work of Franz Kafka." *The Myth of Sisyphus*. New York: Vintage International, 2018.

Engel, Beverly. "Why Adult Victims of Childhood Sexual Abuse Don't Disclose." *Psychology Today*, March 6, 2019. https://www.psychology today.com/us/blog/the-compassion-chronicles/201903/why-adult -victims-childhood-sexual-abuse-dont-disclose.

Kimball, Spencer W. *The Miracle of Forgiveness*. Salt Lake City: Bookcraft Inc., 1969, p. 77.

McConkie, Bruce R. *Mormon Doctrine*. 2nd edition. Salt Lake City: Bookcraft Inc., 1979, p. 527.

University of North Carolina School of Medicine. "Abused Children More Likely to Suffer Unexplained Abdominal Pain, Nausea or Vomiting." *ScienceDaily*, March 9, 2010.

Young, Brigham. "Until the Redemption of Abel's Seed/Intermarriage." *The Teachings of Brigham Young: Vol 3, 1852–1854*. Salt Lake City: Collier's Publishing, 1987, pp. 48–49.

Acknowledgments

Thank you, Mike. Always thank you.

I have been working on this book for years, and there are so many people who have worked with me and supported me as I wrote it that it would be impossible to thank them all.

The biggest thank-you to my wife, Veronica, the first person to read most of what is written here, the first person to tell me if what was on the page worked or not. You lived through a lot of this and have stayed by my side anyway. Te amo mais do que há palavras para descrever.

A huge thank-you to Mariah Stovall, agent extraordinaire, whose writing is inspirational, who had an infectious enthusiasm for this book, who helped edit these pages through I-don't-know-how-many drafts, who helped find the title *Bones Worth Breaking*.

Thank you so much to everyone at MCD/FSG for believing in *Bones* and wanting to get this out into the world. Thank you to Sean McDonald and Ben Brooks for taking a chance on me. A special thanks to Ben Brooks for editing draft after draft of this book together with me and helping me delve deeper into myself to find what the pages needed. I couldn't have dreamed of a better editor!

I have an unending debt of gratitude for John Ventola, Laura White, David Nelson, and Johnny May, my first creative writing instructors at GCC. I am beyond lucky to have found you and to have been in your classes. While I loved reading and writing growing up, I never imagined it would be such an important part of my life until taking your classes at a time when I was so vulnerable. You helped me find what I needed.

David Miller: You gave me a job at GCC and taught and mentored me. I learned not only how to teach from you but also how to be confident. Your kindness and support have meant so much.

Tara Ison, thank you for all the reference letters and classes and support, my best creative writing teacher at ASU.

Elizabeth Crane, Rob Roberge, Anthony McCann, Mary Waters, John Schimmel, Deanne Stillman, and all my instructors at the UCR Low-Residency MFA program: You taught me that I can do this, and you taught me so much about writing. Betsy and Rob, you were both instrumental in helping me make the final steps that have helped me stay off drugs for as long as I have.

Tod Goldberg: If you hadn't called me and asked why I hadn't finished my MFA application, I probably would have given up on grad school. Your support and emails and calls and texts over the years have made me feel not only like I was doing the right thing but also that I was cared for.

Thank you so much to everyone who is in this book, to all my saudades. I love you all, and you are embedded in my soul.

A very extra special thank-you to Douglas Wood. You helped me edit the early drafts. You wrote my query letter for me. But most importantly, you have been a dear friend to me when I needed it, when I didn't know who else to talk to or where to turn.

Veronica Martinez gets an extra thank-you. Você é tudo.